Inca Land

*

"SOMETHING HIDDEN. GO AND FIND IT. GO AND LOOK BEHIND THE RANGES—
SOMETHING LOST BEHIND THE RANGES. LOST AND WAITING FOR YOU. GO!"
–RUDYARD KIPLING, "The Explorer."

Inca Land

*

Explorations in the Highlands of Peru

Hiram Bingham

with an introduction by Anthony Brandt

National Geographic
Adventure Classics

Washington, D.C.

Copyright ©2003 National Geographic Society.

Library of Congress Cataloging-in-Publication Data

Bingham, Hiram, 1875-1956.
    Inca land: explorations in the highlands of Peru/ by Hiram Bingham; with a new
introduction by Anthony Brandt.
        p. cm — (National Geographic adventure classics)
Originally published: Boston: Houghton Mifflin, 1922.
Includes bibliographical references.
ISBN 0-7922-6194-1
Peru—Description and travel. 2. Incas. 3. Peru—Antiquities. I. Title. II. Series.

F3423.B46 2003
918.504' 631—dc21

                                                                    2003046436

Illustration credits: (all images) Hiram Bingham, National Geographic Society.

One of the world's largest nonprofit scientific and educational organizations, the National Geographic Society was founded in 1888 "for the increase and diffusion of geographic knowledge." Fulfilling this mission, the Society educates and inspires millions every day through its magazines, books, television programs, videos, maps and atlases, research grants, the National Geographic Bee, teacher workshops, and innovative classroom materials. The Society is supported through membership dues, charitable gifts, and income from the sale of its educational products. This support is vital to National Geographic's mission to increase global understanding and promote conservation of our planet through exploration, research, and education.

For more information, please call 1-800-NGS LINE (647-5463) or write to the following address:
National Geographic Society
1145 17th Street N.W.
Washington, D.C. 20036-4688 U.S.A.

Visit the Society's Web site at www.nationalgeographic.com.

CONTENTS

*

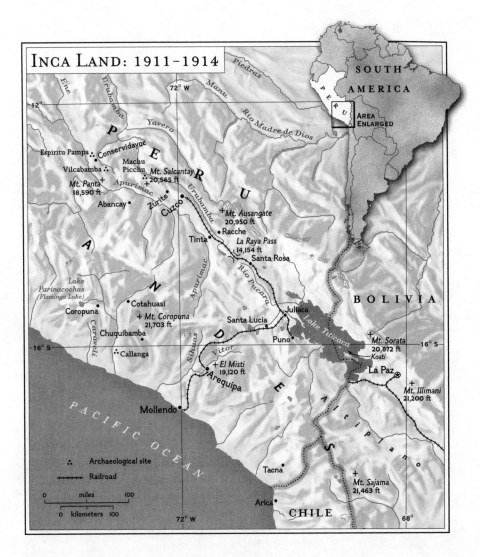

INCA LAND: 1911–1914

SOUTH AMERICA

PERU

AREA ENLARGED

72° W

72° W

68°

12°

16° S

16° S

Piedras

Manu

Rio Madre de Dios

Ene

Urubamba

Yavero

P E R U

Espiritu Pampa ∴ ∴Conservidayoc
Vilcabamba ∴   Machu
        ∴ Picchu + Mt. Salcantay
Mt. Panta +   20,565 ft
18,590 ft   *Apurimac*
  Abancay • Zurite•
              Cuzco•   *Urubamba*
                      +Mt. Ausangate
                        20,950 ft
                      • Racche
        Tinta •   La Raya Pass
                      14,154 ft
                       Santa Rosa•
                    Rio Pucara
  A
  N
  D
Lake
Parinacochas
(Flamingo Lake)
          • Cotahuasi   Juliaca•
  Coropuna • + Mt. Coropuna   B O L I V I A
              21,703 ft   Santa Lucia•   *Lake Titicaca*
  Chuquibamba •   Puno•   +Mt. Sorata
                                          20,872 ft
  ∴ Callanga   *Sihuas* *Vitor*   Koati
                    +El Misti   La Paz ⊗
                     19,120 ft   + Mt. Illimani
                   Arequipa•   21,200 ft
  Caraveli
              Mollendo•
                                      A
P A C I F I C   O C E A N   l
                                      t
                                      i
                                      p
                                      l   + Mt. Sajama
                                      a   21,463 ft
  ∴   Archaeological site   Tacna• n
  ┼┼┼┼ Railroad   o
                                  Arica• C H I L E
  0   miles   100
  0   kilometers   100

INTRODUCTION

✳

HIRAM BINGHAM III HAD a rich and varied, one might say restless, career in aviation, politics, and academia. He taught at Princeton briefly and then at Yale, becoming a full professor, teaching South American history, at a very young age. When World War I broke out he learned how to fly and went on to serve in France, running training schools for American pilots, rising rapidly in the Army Air Service. After that he became an early and prominent advocate of air travel. He knew personally two Presidents of the United States, Theodore Roosevelt and William Howard Taft, and was able to use his influence with them. He served as lieutenant governor of the state of Connecticut, then for one day as Governor, moving on immediately to fill an unexpired term in the U.S. senate when a Connecticut senator died. When that term came to an end he was re-elected to the senate. The Air Commerce Act of 1926 bore his name.

But he considered himself to be an explorer first and foremost and so listed himself in *Who's Who in America* even to the end of his life, long after his last expedition to South America, and he is remembered not for his political success or his teaching or his aviation career. He is remembered for one thing, and one thing only. He was the explorer who found the most famous ancient ruins in the Western Hemisphere: the lost Inca city of Machu Picchu.

That discovery forms the climax of *Inca Land*, this remarkable book, as if it were also the climax of the 1911 expedition through the Inca heartland of Peru it describes. But in fact the discovery of Machu Picchu happened early on in the expedition, it was almost inadvertent, and it took years for Bingham to realize what he had stumbled upon. Bingham was not a trained archaeologist. He did not know that much about the history of the Inca. His goal on this particular expedition, and its actual climax in terms of the expedition's time line, was climbing what he hoped was the highest mountain in South America, Mount Coropuna in southern Peru (the actual highest, by 2,000 feet, is Mount. Aconcagua in Argentina), and, although he never mentions it in the book, he was in a race to the top with an American schoolteacher in her early 60s named Annie Peck. Peck was a leader of the Joan of Arc Suffrage League and left the League's yellow flag on the mountain she did climb—she mistook another mountain for Mount Coropuna—inscribed with the words VOTES FOR WOMEN. When Bingham climbed the actual Mount Coropuna he left an American flag and the Yale flag on top.

(It's worth noting that he, too, missed the true summit. Mount Coropuna has two summits. He climbed the more southerly. The northern, alas, 2 miles distant, is 87 feet higher. Although we have no record of his views on the subject, Bingham was a conservative Republican and would probably have opposed votes for women.)

Alfred, one of Bingham's seven sons, wrote the only biography of the man, and he makes it plain that what his father was truly seeking was not a mountain-climbing first or Inca ruins, but fame. He came from a line that had achieved a certain local fame as missionaries. His grandfather, the first Hiram, had almost single-handedly converted the natives of Hawaii to Christianity and had written a well-known book about the islands. His own father, Hiram II, was also a missionary, but a failed one; his mission in the Gilbert Islands left few Christian converts behind, and they quickly reverted to their original tribal beliefs once he retired, his health broken, to Hawaii. The Hiram Binghams II were God-obsessed Puritans in the old-fashioned sense, and, although Hiram Bingham III, who was born in 1875 grew up in Hawaii, no one could argue that he had a happy childhood. He escaped to Yale, working his way through by tutoring the children of the wealthy. He was six feet four inches tall, thin, good-looking, charming, and smart, with a naturally ambitious man's eye for the main chance. Later in life he took full advantage of the connections he made at Yale to advance his career. Before he had a career he married extremely well, a woman named Alfreda Mitchell whose grandfather was Charles Tiffany, the founder of Tiffany & Company; Louis Comfort Tiffany was her uncle. Her parents provided her with an income on a grand scale when she married Bingham, and for the rest of his life he never lacked for money. When he was teaching at Yale the Mitchells built them a 30-room mansion, and furnished it. We cannot hold it against him. He did not want such a large house, but he was helpless to interfere; and he was no gold digger. He genuinely loved his wife, and his own accomplishments were far too substantial to accuse him of leeching off her fortune.

But there can be no doubt that he was something of an opportunist. His original interest in South American history lay in its colonial phase, and he collected a Ph.D. in the subject at Harvard. He took his first trip to South America, in 1906-7, to follow the path of the South American liberator Simon Bolívar across Venezuela and Colombia. He was planning a biography of Bolívar at the time; he traveled overland on mule trails through hazardous country, living off the land, and it was during this trip that he developed a taste for exploration. He was a natural-born wanderer, never happier than when he was going into unexplored territory; thereafter he would often be away from home for long periods of time. He wrote a book about this trip and then another about his next, in 1909, when he crossed South America from Montevideo in Uruguay to Mollendo, Valparaíso and Lima on the Pacific coast. It was on this trip that he saw his first Inca ruins. Two years later he went back as the leader of the Yale Peruvian Expedition, sponsored largely by Edward Harkness, a Yale graduate and acquaintance whom Bingham had reconnected with at a resort on one of Georgia's sea islands and had persuaded to help with the financing. Bingham organized the expedition around a number of different goals, all of them, in a sense, an excuse for him to go exploring. One of them was to climb Mount Coropuna. He also thought it might be a good idea to map the Peruvian interior along the 73rd meridian.

And there were Incan ruins to find. Archaeology was still a young discipline in the early 1900s and most of the public interest it generated centered on finds in Europe and the Middle East—the ruins of Homer's Troy, the Valley of the Kings in Egypt, Knossos in Crete, the ancient civilizations of Mesopotamia. But although the English historian Sir Clements Markham had recently written authoritatively on the history of the short-lived Inca empire, there had been almost no archaeological work done on Inca ruins, and the Peruvians who took an interest in them cared mostly for finding the legendary caches of gold the Incans had supposedly hidden somewhere in the mountains when they were fleeing Pizarro and Spanish domination in the early 1500s. Bingham could see clearly enough that Inca archaeology presented a vast opportunity. No one had ever found the Inca strongholds in the mountains that were known from old Spanish chronicles to exist. Much about Inca culture remained obscure.

Although he was no expert in the subject, Bingham was a quick study and he studied up on the Inca before he left for Peru. When he got there, he found the right people to talk to. In Lima he met a scholar named Carlos A. Romero who had investigated the early Spanish chronicles thoroughly and was able to tell Bingham in greater depth about the city known as Vilcabamba or Vilcapampa, the last stronghold of the Inca emperors. When he arrived in Cuzco on July 2, 1911, he met the rector of the University there, an American named Albert Giesecke, who told him about the rumored existence of ruins in the Urubamba Valley, which was not far from the city. In the meantime, just two days after his arrival, Bingham found some human bones 80 feet under the surface of the ground above in a road cut. The depth was such, and the state of the bones such, that he thought he had discovered remains 30,000 years old, thus moving the date of humankind's arrival in the Americas backward by some 20,000 years. This was exciting stuff and would have made him famous all by itself, if he had been right. It was far more exciting to him at the time than the ruins at Machu Picchu.

He found them about three weeks later. In the intervening time he had been organizing the expedition, sending its various members on mapping and exploring missions, hiring mules and the men to manage them to carry supplies. Then on July 17 he set off himself from Cuzco down the Urubamba Valley, stopping first at the well-known ruins of Ollantaytambo to photograph them, then, on July 23, leaving the cultivated portion of the valley and entering a more tropical environment. That night he and his two companions set up camp at a small sugar plantation run by a farmer named Melchor Arteaga. Arteaga said there were some ruins high above the narrow valley of the Urubamba, on top of a mountain called Huainapichu. The next day Bingham offered him a dollar to take him there. The last chapter of *Inca Land* explains in some detail what happened then.

What it does not explain is why Bingham, having found Machu Picchu, took so little interest in it. The ruins stand some 2,000 feet above the Urubamba River, it was a difficult climb to reach them, and it was hot. Bingham spent a single afternoon exploring them, and the notes he took then give no indication that he was excited by his find. When he returned to the area later in the expedition and camped once more at the foot of the mountain, he did not bother to revisit the site; he left the clearing of the ruins and the initial survey of them to his Yale undergraduate assistant. Part of the reason for his disinterest may be that he was not looking for Machu Picchu. The human mind is conditioned to find only what it hopes or expects to find. Christopher Columbus was never able to wrap his mind around the idea that he had not reached the eastern coasts of Asia, but an entirely new world. Hiram Bingham wanted to find Vilcabamba and Vitcos and the other lost Inca cities he had read about in the Spanish chronicles. The ruins at Machu Picchu did not match the descriptions of those other cities, and they weren't in the right place. They were partly overgrown with vegetation as well, so that it was hard to see their full extent and the glory of the stonework.

The discovery also raises interesting questions about what we mean by the word "discovery." Albert Giesecke had heard about the ruins. Melchor Arteaga knew they were there and had visited them. When he got to the site Bingham found a name—Augustin Lizarraga—scrawled in chalk on one of the walls and a date: 1902. The name was of another local person of Spanish origin who had found the ruins. And there were three local families living on the site. They had partly cleared the 500-year-old Inca terraces and were farming them. "Discovery" in this case is the act of publishing one's findings, not the act of finding itself; other people had already "found" Machu Picchu. And it was clear from his behavior that Bingham himself was not sure what, exactly, he had found. Ultimately he persuaded himself that Machu Picchu was in fact the city where the last Inca ruler, Tupac Amaru, had made his stand against the Spanish invaders—that it was, in short, Vilcabamba—even though he himself had found the actual ruins of Vilcabamba in dense jungle more or less precisely where the chronicles indicated it was supposed to be. Once he came to this conclusion he held it against growing evidence to the contrary the rest of his life.

To his credit, however, he acknowledged in 1922 that he had not himself "discovered" Machu Picchu and explained the difference between finding a site and publishing it, and he did begin over time to recognize the importance of the site he is famous for—well, for finding. In 1912 he came back to Machu Picchu, finished the job of clearing it of overgrowth, and began to dig. He found no gold, but he did find a good number of graves, mostly of women, and theorized from this that Machu Picchu had had religious significance as well—that the graves, in other words, were the graves of virgins dedicated to worship of the sun. But he was more of an explorer than an archaeologist and did not have the patience for detailed fieldwork. Even in 1912 Machu Picchu was not his main objective, and he spent only two weeks on the site, leaving expedition staff members to do the rest of the work.

He did, however, take meticulous photographs, and in 1913 the National Geographic Society became involved in his work, taking the unusual step of devoting an entire issue of the Society's magazine to his discoveries in Peru. In 1914-15 he organized a third expedition, this time with the dual backing of Yale and the National Geographic Society. Bingham was on his way to the fame he had been seeking. This final expedition ran into trouble politically in Peru, when anti-government politicians accused him of carting national treasures off to the United States. Almost all of the archaeological material Bingham took out of the country consisted of nothing but bones and pottery shards and small objects of no intrinsic value, but he was accused of taking large quantities of that gold treasure the Peruvians believed still lay in the ground. Heretofore he had been able to navigate the rapids of Peruvian national politics quite easily. He knew the national leaders; he was charming; he understood the ways of power. It no longer sufficed. He arrived in Peru in March 1915. He left under threat of arrest early in the fall. He would never again travel to Peru and never again lead an exploring expedition. But he had become the man who found Machu Picchu—and Vitcos, and the famous "White Rock" nearby, and various other Inca ruins, and the city of Vilcabamba, buried in the lowland jungle. He had become the Hiram Bingham who deserves an important place in the history of archaeology and exploration.

Bingham wrote *Inca Land* in 1922, seven years after his return from the last expedition. Because in telling his story he reversed the order of the 1911 expedition, the narrative line of the book is a little confusing, and he incorporated much of what he found on later expeditions into the book without bothering to explain. It is, nevertheless, an interesting and often delightful book. He tells his stories accurately and without the inflation of his later returns to the subject, when he made more of his own role than he deserved, and he wonderfully evokes a lost world, not just the world of the Inca but also a world of freewheeling exploration where an adventurous entrepreneurial spirit like Bingham's could take you a long way. Yale's Peabody Museum recently devoted an exhibition to Machu Picchu, displaying many of the objects that Bingham found there. Recent archaeological investigation of the site indicates that Machu Picchu was a winter retreat built by the Inca Pachacuti at the height of the empire's prosperity, somewhere between 1450 and 1470. For many years tourists believing Bingham's theory that it was partly a religious site inhabited by virgins worshiping the sun have been coming to Machu Picchu for its spiritual vibes, but that theory no longer has any adherents. No matter. Bingham was an explorer, not an archaeologist; it was not his destiny to understand Machu Picchu, only to find it. Whatever purpose it served when it was built, it remains a massive and magnificent achievement in worked stone, an architectural miracle. It's only fitting that the ancient Inca trail that leads up to it now bears Hiram Bingham's name.

CHAPTER I

CROSSING THE DESERT

✭

A KIND FRIEND IN BOLIVIA once placed in my hands a copy of a most interesting book by the late E. George Squier, entitled "Peru. Travel and Exploration in the Land of the Incas." In that volume is a marvelous picture of the Apurimac Valley. In the foreground is a delicate suspension bridge which commences at a tunnel in the face of a precipitous cliff and hangs in mid-air at great height above the swirling waters of the "great speaker." In the distance, towering above a mass of stupendous mountains, is a magnificent snow-capped peak. The desire to see the Apurimac and experience the thrill of crossing that bridge decided me in favor of an overland journey to Lima.

As a result I went to Cuzco, the ancient capital of the mighty empire of the Incas, and was there urged by the Peruvian authorities to visit some newly re-discovered Inca ruins. As readers of "Across South America" will remember, these ruins were at Choqquequirau, an interesting place on top of a jungle-covered ridge several thousand feet above the roaring rapids of the great Apurimac. There was some doubt as to who had originally lived here. The prefect insisted that the ruins represented the residence of the Inca Manco and his sons, who had sought refuge from Pizarro and the Spanish conquerors of Peru in the Andes between the Apurimac and Urubamba rivers.

While Mr. Clarence L. Hay and I were on the slopes of Choqquequirau the clouds would occasionally break away and give us tantalizing glimpses of snow-covered mountains. There seemed to be an unknown region, "behind the Ranges," which might contain great possibilities. Our guides could tell us nothing about it. Little was to be found in books. Perhaps Manco's capital was hidden there. For months afterwards the fascination of the unknown drew my thoughts to Choqquequirau and beyond. In the words of Kipling's "Explorer":

"...a voice, as bad as Conscience, rang interminable changes

On one everlasting Whisper day and night repeated—so: 'Something hidden. Go and find it. Go and look behind the Ranges—

Something lost behind the Ranges. Lost and waiting for you. Go!'"

To add to my unrest, during the following summer I read Bandelier's "Titicaca and Koati," which had just appeared. In one of the interesting footnotes was this startling remark: "It is much to be desired that the elevation of the most prominent peaks of the western or coast range of Peru be accurately determined. It is likely...that *Coropuna*, in the Peruvian coast range of the Department Arequipa, is the culminating point of the continent. It exceeds 23,000 feet in height, whereas Aconcagua [conceded to be the highest peak in the Western Hemisphere] is but 22,763 feet (6940 meters) above sea level." His estimate was based on a survey made by the civil engineers of the Southern Railways of Peru, using a section of the railroad as a base. My sensations when I read this are difficult to describe. Although I had been studying South American history and geography for more than ten years, I did not remember ever to have heard of Coropuna. On most maps it did not exist. Fortunately, on one of the sheets of Raimondi's large-scale map of Peru, I finally found "Coropuna—6,949 m."—9 *meters higher than Aconcagua!*—one hundred miles northwest of Arequipa, near the 73d meridian west of Greenwich.

Looking up and down the 73d meridian as it crossed Peru from the Amazon Valley to the Pacific Ocean, I saw that it passed very near Choqquequirau, and actually traversed those very lands "behind the Ranges" which had been beckoning to me. The coincidence was intriguing. The desire to go and find that "something hidden" was now reënforced by the temptation to go and see whether Coropuna really was the highest mountain in America. There followed the organization of an expedition whose object was a geographical reconnaissance of Peru along the 73d meridian, from the head of canoe navigation on the Urubamba to tidewater on the Pacific. We achieved more than we expected.

Our success was due in large part to our "unit-food-boxes," a device containing a balanced ration which Professor Harry W. Foote had coöperated with me in assembling. The object of our idea was to facilitate the provisioning of small field parties by packing in a single box everything that two men would need in the way of provisions for a given period. These boxes have given such general satisfaction, not only to the explorers themselves, but to the surgeons who had the responsibility of keeping them in good condition, that a few words in regard to this feature of our equipment may not be unwelcome.

The best unit-food-box provides a balanced ration for two men for eight days, breakfast and supper being hearty, cooked meals, and luncheon light and uncooked. It was not intended that the men should depend entirely on the food-boxes, but should vary their diet as much as possible with whatever the country afforded, which in southern Peru frequently means potatoes, corn, eggs, mutton, and bread. Nevertheless each box contained sliced bacon, tinned corned beef, roast beef, chicken, salmon, crushed oats, milk, cheese, coffee, sugar, rice, army bread, salt, sweet chocolates, assorted jams, pickles, and dried fruits and vegetables. By seeing that the jam, dried fruits, soups, and dried vegetables were well assorted, a sufficient variety was procured without destroying the balanced character of the ration. On account of the great difficulty of transportation in the southern Andes we had to eliminate foods that contained a large amount of water, like French peas, baked beans, and canned fruits, however delicious and desirable they might be. In addition to food, we found it desirable to include in each box a cake of laundry soap, two yards of dish toweling, and three empty cotton-cloth bags, to be used for carrying lunches and collecting specimens. The most highly appreciated article of food in our boxes was the rolled oats, a dish which on account of its being already partially cooked was easily prepared at high elevations, where rice cannot be properly boiled. It was difficult to satisfy the members of the Expedition by providing the right amount of sugar. At the beginning of the field season the allowance—one third of a pound per day per man—seemed excessive, and I was criticized for having overloaded the boxes. After a month in the field the allowance proved to be too small and had to be supplemented.

Many people seem to think that it is one of the duties of an explorer to "rough it," and to "trust to luck" for his food. I had found on my first two expeditions, in Venezuela and Colombia and across South America, that the result of being obliged to subsist on irregular and haphazard rations was most unsatisfactory. While "roughing it" is far more enticing to the inexperienced and indiscreet explorer, I learned in Peru that the humdrum expedient of carefully preparing, months in advance, a comprehensive bill of fare sufficiently varied, wholesome, and well-balanced, is "the better part of valor." The truth is that providing an abundance of appetizing food adds very greatly to the effectiveness of a party. To be sure, it may mean trouble and expense for one's transportation department, and some of the younger men may feel that their reputations as explorers are likely to be damaged if it is known that strawberry jam, sweet chocolate and pickles are frequently found on their menu! Nevertheless, experience has shown that the results of "trusting to luck" and "living as the natives do" means not only loss of efficiency in the day's work, but also lessened powers of observation and diminished enthusiasm for the drudgery of scientific exploration. Exciting things are always easy to do, no matter how you are living, but frequently they produce less important results than tasks which depend upon daily drudgery; and daily drudgery depends upon a regular supply of wholesome food.

We reached Arequipa, the proposed base for our campaign against Mt. Coropuna, in June, 1911. We learned that the Peruvian "winter" reaches its climax in July or August, and that it would be folly to try to climb Coropuna during the winter snowstorms. On the other hand, the "summer months," beginning with November, are cloudy and likely to add fog and mist to the difficulties of climbing a new mountain. Furthermore, June and July are the best months for exploration in the eastern slopes of the Andes in the upper Amazon Basin, the lands "behind the Ranges." Although the montaña, or jungle country, is rarely actually dry, there is less rain then than in the other months of the year; so we decided to go first to the Urubamba Valley. The story of our discoveries there, of identifying Uiticos, the capital of the last Incas, and of the finding of Machu Picchu will be found in later chapters. In September I returned to Arequipa and started the campaign against Coropuna by endeavoring to get adequate transportation facilities for crossing the desert.

Arequipa, as everybody knows, is the home of a station of the Harvard Observatory, but Arequipa is also famous for its large mules. Unfortunately, a "mule trust" had recently been formed—needless to say, by an American— and I found it difficult to make any satisfactory arrangements. After two weeks of skirmishing, the Tejada brothers appeared, two arrieros, or muleteers, who seemed willing to listen to our proposals. We offered them a thousand soles (five hundred dollars gold) if they would supply us with a pack train of eleven mules for two months and go with us wherever we chose, we agreeing not to travel on an average more than seven leagues[1] a day. It sounds simple enough but it took no end of argument and persuasion on the part of our friends in Arequipa to convince these worthy *arrieros* that they were not going to be everlastingly ruined by this bargain. The trouble was that they owned their mules, knew the great danger of crossing the deserts that lay between us and Mt. Coropuna, and feared to travel on unknown trails. Like most muleteers, they were afraid of unfamiliar country. They magnified the imaginary evils of the road to an inconceivable pitch. The argument that finally persuaded them to accept the proffered contract was my promise that after the first week the cargo would be so much less that at least two of the pack mules could always be free. The Tejadas, realizing only too well the propensity of pack animals to get sore backs and go lame, regarded my promise in the light of a factor of safety. Lame mules would not have to carry loads.

Everything was ready by the end of the month. Mr. H. L. Tucker, a member of Professor H. C. Parker's 1910 Mt. McKinley Expedition and thoroughly familiar with the details of snow-and-ice-climbing, whom I had asked to be responsible for securing the proper equipment, was now entrusted with planning and directing the actual ascent of Coropuna. Whatever success was achieved on the mountain was due primarily to Mr. Tucker's skill and foresight. We had no Swiss guides, and had originally intended to ask two other members of the Expedition to join us on the climb. However, the exigencies of making a geological and topographical cross section along the 73d meridian through a practically unknown region, and across one of the highest passes in the Andes (17,633 ft.), had delayed the surveying party to such an extent as to make it impossible for them to reach Coropuna before the first of November. On account of the approach of the cloudy season it did not seem wise to wait for their coöperation. Accordingly, I secured in Arequipa the services of Mr. Casimir Watkins, an English naturalist, and of Mr. F. Hinckley, of the Harvard Observatory. It was proposed that Mr. Hinckley, who had twice ascended El Misti (19,120 ft.), should accompany us to the top, while Mr. Watkins, who had only recently recovered from a severe illness, should take charge of the Base Camp.

The prefect of Arequipa obligingly offered us a military escort in the person of Corporal Gamarra, a full-blooded Indian of rather more than average height and considerably more than average courage, who knew the country. As a member of the mounted *gendarmerie*, Gamarra had been stationed at the provincial capital of Cotahuasi a few months previously. One day a mob of drunken, riotous revolutionists stormed the government buildings while he was on sentry duty. Gamarra stood his ground and, when they attempted to force their way past him, shot the leader of the crowd. The mob scattered. A grateful prefect made him a corporal and, realizing that his life was no longer safe in that particular vicinity, transferred him to Arequipa. Like nearly all of his race, however, he fell an easy prey to alcohol. There is no doubt that the chief of the mounted police in Arequipa, when ordered by the prefect to furnish us an escort for our journey across the desert, was glad enough to assign Gamarra to us. His courage could not be called in question even though his habits might lead him to become troublesome. It happened that Gamarra did not know we were planning to go to Cotahuasi. Had he known this, and also had he suspected the trials that were before him on Mt. Coropuna, he probably would have begged off—but I am anticipating.

On the 2d of October, Tucker, Hinckley, Corporal Gamarra and I left Arequipa; Watkins followed a week later. The first stage of the journey was by train from Arequipa to Vitor, a distance of thirty miles. The *arrieros* sent the cargo along too. In addition to the food-boxes we brought with us tents, ice axes, snowshoes, barometers, thermometers, transit, fiber cases, steel boxes, duffle bags, and a folding boat. Our pack train was supposed to have started from Arequipa the day before. We hoped it would reach Vitor about the same time that we did, but that was expecting too much of *arrieros* on the first day of their journey. So we had an all-day wait near the primitive little railway station.

We amused ourselves wandering off over the neighboring *pampa* and studying the *médanos*, crescent-shaped sand dunes which are common in the great coastal desert. One reads so much of the great tropical jungles of South America and of well-nigh impenetrable forests that it is difficult to realize that the West Coast from Ecuador, on the north, to the heart of Chile, on the south, is a great desert, broken at intervals by oases, or valleys whose rivers, coming from melting snows of the Andes, are here and there diverted for purposes of irrigation. Lima, the capital of Peru, is in one of the largest of these oases. Although frequently enveloped in a damp fog, the Peruvian coastal towns are almost never subjected to rain. The causes of this phenomenon are easy to understand. Winds coming from the east, laden with the moisture of the Atlantic Ocean and the steaming Amazon Basin, are rapidly cooled by the eastern slopes of the Andes and forced to deposit this moisture in the *montaña*. By the time the winds have crossed the mighty cordillera there is no rain left in them. Conversely, the winds that come from the warm Pacific Ocean strike a cold area over the frigid Humboldt Current, which sweeps up along the west coast of South America. This cold belt wrings the water out of the westerly winds, so that by the time they reach the warm land their relative humidity is low. To be sure, there are months in some years when so much moisture falls on the slopes of the coast range that the hillsides are clothed with flowers, but this verdure lasts but a short time and does not seriously affect the great stretches of desert *pampa* in the midst of which we now were. Like the other *pampas* of this region, the flat surface inclines toward the sea. Over it the sand is rolled along by the wind and finally built into crescent-shaped dunes. These *médanos* interested us greatly.

The prevailing wind on the desert at night is a relatively gentle breeze that comes down from the cool mountain slopes toward the ocean. It tends to blow the lighter particles of sand along in a regular dune, rolling it over and over downhill, leaving the heavier particles behind. This is reversed in the daytime. As the heat increases toward noon, the wind comes rushing up from the ocean to fill the vacuum caused by the rapidly ascending currents of hot air that rise from the overheated *pampas*. During the early afternoon this wind reaches a high velocity and swirls the sand along in clouds. It is now strong enough to move the heavier particles of sand, uphill. It sweeps the heaviest ones around the base of the dune and deposits them in pointed ridges on either side. The heavier material remains stationary at night while the lighter particles are rolled downhill, but the whole mass travels slowly uphill again during the gales of the following afternoon. The result is the beautiful crescent-shaped *médano*.

About five o'clock our mules, a fine-looking lot—far superior to any that we had been able to secure near Cuzco—trotted briskly into the dusty little plaza. It took some time to adjust the loads, and it was nearly seven o'clock before we started off in the moonlight for the oasis of Vitor. As we left the plateau and struck the dusty trail winding down into a dark canyon we caught a glimpse of something white shimmering faintly on the horizon far off to the northwest; Coropuna! Shortly before nine o'clock we reached a little corral, where the mules were unloaded. For ourselves we found a shed with a clean, stone-paved floor, where we set up our cots, only to be awakened many times during the night by passing caravans anxious to avoid the terrible heat of the desert by day.

Where the oases are only a few miles apart one often travels by day,

HIRAM BINGHAM (FAR LEFT) LEADS THE EXPEDITION PARTY
TO MT. COROPUNA, VISIBLE IN THE DISTANCE.

but when crossing the desert is a matter of eight or ten hours' steady jogging with no places to rest, no water, no shade, the pack animals suffer greatly.
Consequently, most caravans travel, so far as possible, by night. Our first
desert, the *pampa* of Sihuas, was reported to be narrow, so we preferred to
cross it by day and see what was to be seen. We got up about half-past four
and were off before seven. Then our troubles began. Either because he lived
in Arequipa or because they thought he looked like a good horseman, or
for reasons best known to themselves, the Tejadas had given Mr. Hinckley
a very spirited saddle-mule. The first thing I knew, her rider, carrying a heavy
camera, a package of plate-holders, and a large mercurial barometer, borrowed
from the Harvard Observatory, was pitched headlong into the sand.
Fortunately no damage was done, and after a lively chase the runaway
mule was brought back by Corporal Gamarra. After Mr. Hinckley was
remounted on his dangerous mule we rode on for a while in peace, between
cornfields and vineyards, over paths flanked by willows and fig trees. The
chief industry of Vitor is the making of wine from vines which date back
to colonial days. The wine is aged in huge jars, each over six feet high, buried
in the ground. We had a glimpse of seventeen of them standing in a line,
awaiting sale. It made one think of Ali Baba and the Forty Thieves, who
would have had no trouble at all hiding in these Cyclopean crocks.

The edge of the oasis of Vitor is the contour line along which the irrigating canal runs. There is no gradual petering out of foliage. The desert begins with a stunning crash. On one side is the bright, luxurious green of fig trees and vineyards; on the other side is the absolute stark nakedness of the sandy desert. Within the oasis there is an abundance of water. Much of it runs to waste. The wine growers receive more than they can use; in fact, more land could easily be put under cultivation. The chief difficulties are the scarcity of ports from which produce can be shipped to the outer world, the expense of the transportation system of pack trains over the deserts which intervene between the oases and the railroad, and the lack of capital. Otherwise the irrigation system might be extended over great stretches of rich, volcanic soil, now unoccupied.

A steady climb of three quarters of an hour took us to the northern rim of the valley. Here we again saw the snowy mass of Coropuna, glistening in the sunlight, seventy-five miles away to the northwest. Our view was a short one, for in less than three minutes we had to descend another canyon. We crossed this and climbed out on the *pampa* of Sihuas. There was little to interest us in our immediate surroundings, but in the distance was Coropuna, and I had just begun to study the problem of possible routes for climbing the highest peak when Mr. Hinckley's mule trotted briskly across the trail directly in front of me, kicked up her heels, and again sent him sprawling over the sand, barometer, camera, plates, and all. Unluckily, this time his foot caught in a stirrup and, still holding the bridle, he was dragged some distance before he got it loose. He struggled to his feet and tried to keep the mule from running away, when a violent kick released his hold and knocked him out. We immediately set up our little "Mummery" tent on the hot, sandy floor of the desert and rendered first-aid to the unlucky astronomer. We found that the sharp point of one of the vicious mule's new shoes had opened a large vein in Mr. Hinckley's leg. The cut was not dangerous, but too deep for successful mountain climbing. With Gamarra's aid, Mr. Hinckley was able to reach Arequipa that night, but his enforced departure not only shattered his own hopes of climbing Coropuna, but also made us wonder how we were going to have the necessary three-men-on-the-rope when we reached the glaciers. To be sure, there was the corporal—but would he go? Indians do not like snow mountains. Packing up the tent again, we resumed our course over the desert.

The oasis of Sihuas, another beautiful garden in the bottom of a huge canyon, was reached about four o'clock in the afternoon. We should have been compelled to camp in the open with the *arrieros* had not the parish priest invited us to rest in the cool shade of his vine-covered arbor. He graciously served us with cakes and sweet native wine, and asked us to stay as long as we liked. The desert of Majes, which now lay ahead of us, is perhaps the widest, hottest, and most barren in this region. Our *arrieros* were unwilling to cross it in the daytime. They said it was forty-five miles between water and water. The next day we enjoyed the hospitality of our kindly host until after supper.

So sure are the inhabitants of these oases that it is not going to rain that their houses are built merely as a shelter against the sun and wind. They are made of the canes that grow in the jungles of the larger river bottoms, or along the banks of irrigating ditches. On the roof the spaces between the canes are filled with adobe, sun-dried mud. It is not necessary to plaster the sides of the houses, for it is pleasant to let the air have free play, and it is amusing to look out through the cracks and see everything that is passing.

That evening we saddled in the moonlight. Slowly we climbed out of the valley, to spend the night jogging steadily, hour after hour, across the desert. As the moon was setting we entered a hilly region, and at sunrise found ourselves in the midst of a tumbled mass of enormous sand dunes— the result of hundreds of *médanos* blown across the *pampa* of Majes and deposited along the border of the valley. It took us three hours to wind slowly down from the level of the desert to a point where we could see the great canyon, a mile deep and two miles across. Its steep sides are of various colored rocks and sand. The bottom is a bright green oasis through which flows the rapid Majes River, too deep to be forded even in the dry season. A very large part of the flood plain of the unruly river is not cultivated, and consists of a wild jungle, difficult of access in the dry season and impossible when the river rises during the rainy months. The contrast between the gigantic hills of sand and the luxurious vegetation was very striking; but to us the most beautiful thing in the landscape was the long, glistening, white mass of Coropuna, now much larger and just visible above the opposite rim of the valley.

At eight o'clock in the morning, as we were wondering how long it would be before we could get down to the bottom of the valley and have some breakfast, we discovered, at a place called Pitas (or Cerro Colorado), a huge volcanic boulder covered with rude pictographs. Further search in the vicinity revealed about one hundred of these boulders, each with its quota of crude drawings. I did not notice any ruins of houses near the rocks.

Neither of the Tejada brothers, who had been past here many times, nor any of the natives of this region appeared to have any idea of the origin or meaning of this singular collection of pictographic rocks. The drawings represented jaguars, birds, men, and dachshund-like dogs. They deserved careful study. Yet not even the interest and excitement of investigating the "*rocas jeroglificos*," as they are called here, could make us forget that we had no food or sleep for a good many hours. So after taking a few pictures we hastened on and crossed the Majes River on a very shaky temporary bridge. It was built to last only during the dry season. To construct a bridge which would withstand floods is not feasible at present. We spent the day at Coriri, a pleasant little village where it was almost impossible to sleep, on account of the myriads of gnats.

The next day we had a short ride along the western side of the valley to the town of Aplao, the capital of the province of Castilla, called by its present inhabitants "Majes," although on Raimondi's map that name is applied only to the river and the neighboring desert. In 1865, at the time of his visit, it had a bad reputation for disease. Now it seems more healthy. The subprefect of Castilla had been informed by telegraph of our coming, and invited us to an excellent dinner.

The people of Majes are largely of mixed white and Indian ancestry. Many of them appeared to be unusually businesslike. The proprietor of one establishment was a great admirer of American shoes, the name of which he pronounced in a manner that puzzled us for a long time. "W" is unknown in Spanish and the letters "a," "l," and "k" are never found in juxtaposition. When he asked us what we thought of "Valluck-ofair'," accenting strongly the last syllable, we could not imagine what he meant. He was equally at a loss to understand how we could be so stupid as not to recognize immediately the well-advertised name of a widely known shoe.

At Majes we observed cotton, which is sent to the mills at Arequipa, alfalfa, highly prized as fodder for pack animals, sugar cane, from which *aguardiente*, or white rum, is made, and grapes. It is said that the Majes vineyards date back to the sixteenth century, and that some of the huge, buried, earthenware wine jars now in use were made as far back as the reign of Philip II. The presence of so much wine in the community does not seem to have a deleterious effect on the natives, who were not only hospitable but energetic—far more so, in fact, than the natives of towns in the high Andes, where the intense cold and the difficulty of making a living have reacted upon the Indians, often causing them to be morose, sullen, and without ambition.

The residences of the wine growers are sometimes very misleading. A typical country house of the better class is not much to look at. Its long, low, flat roof and rough, unwhitewashed, mud-colored walls give it an unattractive appearance; yet to one's intense surprise the inside may be clean and comfortable, with modern furniture, a piano, and a phonograph.

Our conscientious and hard-working *arrieros* rose at two o'clock the next morning, for they knew their mules had a long, hard climb ahead of them, from an elevation of 1000 feet above sea level to 10,000 feet. After an all-day journey we camped at a place where forage could be obtained. We had now left the region of tropical products and come back to potatoes and barley. The following day a short ride brought us past another pictographic rock, recently blasted open by an energetic "treasure seeker" of Chuquibamba. This town has 3000 inhabitants and is the capital of the province of Condesuyos. It was the place which we had selected several months before as the rendezvous for the attack on Coropuna. The climate here is delightful and the fruits and cereals of the temperate zone are easily raised. The town is surrounded by gardens, vineyards, alfalfa and grain fields; all showing evidence of intensive cultivation. It is at the head of one of the branches of the Majes Valley and is surrounded by high cliffs.

The people of Chuquibamba were friendly. We were kindly welcomed by Señor Benavides, the sub-prefect, who hospitably told us to set up our cots in the grand salon of his own house. Here we received calls from the local officials, including the provincial physician, Dr. Pastór, and the director of the Colegio Nacional, Professor Alejandro Coello. The last two were keen to go with us up Mt. Coropuna. They told us that there was a hill near by called the Calvario, whence the mountain could be seen, and offered to take us up there. We accepted, thinking at the same time that this would show who was best fitted to join in the climb, for we needed another man on the rope. Professor Coello easily distanced the rest of us and won the coveted place.

From the Calvario hill we had a splendid view of those white solitudes whither we were bound, now only twenty-five miles away. It seemed clear that the western or truncated peak, which gives its name to the mass (*koro* = "cut off at the top"; *puna* = "a cold, snowy height"), was the highest point of the range, and higher than all the eastern peaks. Yet behind the flat-topped dome we could just make out a northerly peak. Tucker wondered whether or not that might prove to be higher than the western peak which we decided to climb. No one knew anything about the mountain. There were no native guides to be had. The wildest opinions were expressed as to the best routes and methods of getting to the top. We finally engaged a man who said he knew how to get to the foot of the mountain, so we called him "guide" for want of a more appropriate title. The Peruvian spring was now well advanced and the days were fine and clear. It appeared, however, that there had been a heavy snowstorm on the mountain a few days before. If summer were coming unusually early it behooved us to waste no time, and we proceeded to arrange the mountain equipment as fast as possible.

Our instruments for determining altitude consisted of a special mountain-mercurial barometer made by Mr. Henry J. Green, of Brooklyn, capable of recording only such air pressures as one might expect to find above 12,000 feet; a hypsometer loaned us by the Department of Terrestrial Magnetism of the Carnegie Institution of Washington, with thermometers especially made for us by Green; a large mercurial barometer, borrowed from the Harvard Observatory, which, notwithstanding its rough treatment by Mr. Hinckley's mule, was still doing good service; and one of Green's sling psychrometers. Our most serious want was an aneroid, in case the fragile mercurials should get broken. Six months previously I had written to J. Hicks, the celebrated instrument maker of London, asking him to construct, with special care, two large "Watkins" aneroids capable of recording altitudes five thousand feet higher than Coropuna was supposed to be. His reply had never reached me, nor did any one in Arequipa know anything about the barometers. Apparently my letter had miscarried. It was not until we opened our specially ordered "mountain grub" boxes here in Chuquibamba that we found, alongside of the pemmican and self-heating tins of stew which had been packed for us in London by Grace Brothers, the two precious aneroids, each as large as a big alarm clock. With these two new aneroids, made with a wide margin of safety, we felt satisfied that, once at the summit, we should know whether there was a chance that Bandelier was right and this was indeed the top of America.

For exact measurements we depended on Topographer Hendriksen, who was due to triangulate Coropuna in the course of his survey along the 73d meridian. My chief excuse for going up the mountain was to erect a signal at or near the top which Hendriksen could use as a station in order to make his triangulation more exact. My real object, it must be confessed, was to enjoy the satisfaction, which all Alpinists feel, of conquering a "virgin peak."

---

[1] A league, usually about 3 ^{1}/3 miles, is really the distance an average mule can walk in an hour.

CHAPTER 2

CLIMBING COROPUNA

✳

THE DESERT PLATEAU above Chuquibamba is nearly 2500 feet higher than the town, and it was nine o'clock on the morning of October 10th before we got out of the valley. Thereafter Coropuna was always in sight, and as we slowly approached it we studied it with care. The plateau has an elevation of over 15,000 feet, yet the mountain stood out conspicuously above it. Coropuna is really a range about twenty miles long. Its gigantic massif was covered with snow fields from one end to the other. So deep did the fresh snow lie that it was generally impossible to see where snow fields ended and glaciers began. We could see that of the five well-defined peaks the middle one was probably the lowest. The two next highest are at the right, or eastern, end of the massif. The culminating truncated dome at the western end, with its smooth, uneroded sides, apparently belonged to a later volcanic period than the rest of the mountain. It seemed to be the highest peak of all. To reach it did not appear to be difficult. Rock-covered slopes ran directly up to the snow. Snow fields, without many rock-falls, appeared to culminate in a saddle at the base of the great snowy dome. The eastern slope of the dome itself offered an unbroken, if steep, path to the top. If we could once reach the snow line, it looked as though, with the aid of ice-creepers or snowshoes, we could climb the mountain without serious trouble.

Between us and the first snow-covered slopes, however, lay more than twenty miles of volcanic desert intersected by deep canyons, steep *quebradas*, and very rough *aa* lava. Directed by our "guide," we left the Cotahuasi road and struck across country, dodging the lava flows and slowly ascending the gentle slope of the plateau. As it became steeper our mules showed signs of suffering. While waiting for them to get their wind we went ahead on foot, climbed a short rise, and to our surprise and chagrin found ourselves on the rim of a steep-walled canyon, 1500 feet deep, which cut right across in front of the mountain and lay between us and its higher slopes. After the mules had rested, the guide now decided to turn to the left instead of going straight toward the mountain. A dispute ensued as to how much he knew, even about the foot of Coropuna. He denied that there were any huts whatever in the canyon. "*Abandonado; despoblado; desierto.*" "A waste; a solitude; a wilderness." So he described it. Had he been there? "No, Señor." Luckily we had been able to make out from the rim of the canyon two or three huts near a little stream. As there was no question that we ought to get to the snow line as soon as possible, we decided to dispense with the services of so well-informed a "guide," and make such way as we could alone. The altitude of the rim of the canyon was 16,000 feet; the mules showed signs of acute distress from mountain sickness. The *arrieros* began to complain loudly, but did what they could to relieve the mules by punching holes in their ears; the theory being that bloodletting is a good thing for *soroche*. As soon as the timid *arrieros* reached a point where they could see down into the canyon, they spotted some patches of green pasture, cheered up a bit, and even smiled over the dismal ignorance of the "guide." Soon we found a trail which led to the huts.

Near the huts was a taciturn Indian woman, who refused to furnish us with either fuel or forage, although we tried to pay in advance and offered her silver. Nevertheless, we proceeded to pitch our tents and took advantage of the sheltering stone wall of her corral for our camp fire. After peace had settled down and it became perfectly evident that we were harmless, the door of one of the huts opened and an Indian man appeared. Doubtless the cause of his disappearance before our arrival had been the easily discernible presence in our midst of the brass buttons of Corporal Gamarra. Possibly he who had selected this remote corner of the wilderness for his abode had a guilty conscience and at the sight of a *gendarme* decided that he had better hide at once. More probably, however, he feared the visit of a recruiting party, since it is quite likely that he had not served his legal term of military service. At all events, when his wife discovered that we were not looking for her man, she allowed his curiosity to overcome his fears. We found that the Indians kept a few llamas. They also made crude pottery,

PASS BETWEEN PANTICALLA AND HAVASPAMPA, PERU

firing it with straw and llama dung. They lived almost entirely on gruel made from *chuño*, frozen bitter potatoes. Little else than potatoes will grow at 14,000 feet above the sea. For neighbors the Indians had a solitary old man, who lived half a mile up nearer the glaciers, and a small family, a mile and a half down the valley.

Before dark the neighbors came to call, and we tried our best to persuade the men to accompany us up the mountain and help to carry the loads from the point where the mules would have to stop; but they declined absolutely and positively. I think one of the men might have gone, but as soon as his quiet, well-behaved wife saw him wavering she broke out in a torrent of violent denunciation, telling him the mountain would "eat him up" and that unless he wanted to go to heaven before his time he had better let well enough alone and stay where he was. Cieza de Leon, one of the most careful of the early chroniclers (1550), says that at Coropuna "the devil" talks "more freely" than usual. "For some secret reason known to God, it is said that devils walk visibly about in that place, and that the Indians see them and are much terrified. I have also heard that these devils have appeared to Christians in the form of Indians." Perhaps the voluble housewife was herself one of the famous Coropuna devils. She certainly talked "more freely" than usual. Or possibly she thought that the Coropuna "devils" were now appearing to Indians "in the form of" Christians! Anyhow the

Indians said that on top of Coropuna there was a delightful, warm paradise containing beautiful flowers, luscious fruits, parrots of brilliant plumage, macaws, and even monkeys, those faithful denizens of hot climates. The souls of the departed stop to rest and enjoy themselves in this charming spot on their upward flight. Like most primitive people who live near snow-capped mountains, they had an abject terror of the forbidding summits and the snowstorms that seem to come down from them. Probably the Indians hope to propitiate the demons who dwell on the mountain tops by invent-ing charming stories relating to their abode. It is interesting to learn that in the neighboring hamlet of Pampacolca, the great explorer Raimondi, in 1865, found the natives "exiled from the civilized world, still preserving their primitive customs...carrying idols to the slopes of the great snow moun-tain Coropuna, and there offering them as a sacrifice." Apparently the mountain still inspires fear in the hearts of all those who live near it.

The fact that we agreed to pay in advance unheard-of wages, ten times the usual amount earned by laborers in this vicinity, that we added offers of the precious *coca* leaves, the greatly-to-be-desired "fire-water," the rarely seen tobacco, and other good things usually coveted by Peruvian highlanders, had no effect in the face of the terrors of the mountain. They knew only too well that snow-blindness was one of the least of ills to be encountered; while the advantages of dark-colored glasses, warm clothes, kerosene stoves, and plenty of good food, which we freely offered, were far too remote from the realm of credible possibilities. Professor Coello understood all these mat-ters perfectly and, being able to speak Quichua, the language of our prospec-tive carriers, did his best in the way of argument, not only out of loyalty to the Expedition, but because Peruvian gentlemen always regard the carry-ing of a load as extremely undignified and improper. I have known one of the most energetic and efficient business men in Peru, a highly respected gentleman in a mountain city, so to dislike being obliged to carry a rolled and unmounted photograph, little larger than a lead pencil, that he sent for a *cargador*, an Indian porter, to bear it for him!

As a matter of fact, Professor Coello was perfectly willing to do his share and more; but neither he nor we were anxious to climb with heavy packs on our backs, in the rarefied air of elevations several thousand feet higher than Mont Blanc. The argument with the Indians was long and verbose and the offerings of money and goods were made more and more generous. All was in vain. We finally came to realize that whatever supplies and provi-sions were carried up Coropuna would have to be borne on our own shoulders. That evening the top of the truncated dome, which was just visible from the valley near our camp, was bathed in a roseate Alpine glow, unspeakably beautiful. The air, however, was very bitter and the neighboring brook froze solid. During the night the *gendarme's* mule became homesick and disappeared with Coello's horse. Gamarra was sent to look for the strays, with orders to follow us as soon as possible.

As no bearers or carriers were to be secured, it was essential to persuade the Tejadas to take their pack mules up as far as the snow, a feat they declined to do. The mules, Don Pablo said, had already gone as far as and farther than mules had any business to go. Soon after reaching camp Tucker had gone off on a reconnaissance. He reported that there was a path leading out of the canyon up to the llama pastures on the lower slopes of the mountains. The *arrieros* denied the accuracy of his observations. However, after a long argument, they agreed to go as far as there was a good path, and no farther. There was no question of our riding. It was simply a case of getting the loads as high up as possible before we had to begin to carry them ourselves. It may be imagined that the *arrieros* packed very slowly and grudgingly, although the loads were now considerably reduced. Finally, leaving behind our saddles, ordinary supplies, and everything not considered absolutely necessary for a two weeks' stay on the mountain, we set off.

We could easily walk faster than the loaded mules, and thought it best to avoid trouble by keeping far enough ahead so as not to hear the *arrieros'* constant complaints. After an hour of not very hard climbing over a fairly good llama trail, the Tejadas stopped at the edge of the pastures and shouted to us to come back. We replied equally vociferously, calling them to come ahead, which they did for half an hour more, slowly zigzagging up a slope of coarse, black volcanic sand. Then they not only stopped but commenced to unload the mules. It was necessary to rush back and commence a violent and acrimonious dispute as to whether the letter of contract had been fulfilled and the mules had gone "as far as they could reasonably be expected to go." The truth was, the Tejadas were terrified at approaching mysterious Coropuna. They were sure it would take revenge on them by destroying their mules, who would "certainly die the following day of *soroche*." We offered a bonus of thirty *soles*—fifteen dollars—if they would go on for another hour, and threatened them with all sorts of things if they would not. At last they readjusted the loads and started climbing again.

The altitude was now about 16,000 feet, but at the foot of a steep little rise the *arrieros* stopped again. This time they succeeded in unloading two mules before we could scramble down over the sand and boulders to stop them. Threats and prayers were now of no avail. The only thing that would satisfy was a legal document! They demanded an agreement "in writing" that in case any mule or mules died as a result of this foolish attempt to get up to the snow line, I should pay in gold two hundred *soles* for each and every mule that died. Further, I must agree to pay a bonus of fifty *soles* if they would keep climbing until noon or until stopped by snow. This document, having been duly drawn up by Professor Coello, seated on a lava rock amidst the clinkerlike cinders of the old volcano, was duly signed and sealed. In order that there might be no dispute as to the time, my best chronometer was handed over to Pablo Tejada to carry until noon. The mules were reloaded and again the ascent began. Presently the mules encountered some pretty bad going, on a steep slope covered with huge lava boulders and scoriaceous sand. We expected more trouble every minute. However, the *arrieros*, having made an advantageous bargain, did their best to carry it out. Fortunately the mules reached the snow line just fifteen minutes before twelve o'clock. The Tejadas lost no time in unloading, claimed their bonus, promised to return in ten days, and almost before we knew it had disappeared down the side of the mountain.

We spent the afternoon establishing our Base Camp. We had three tents, the "Mummery," a very light and diminutive wall tent about four feet high, made by Edgington of London; an ordinary wall tent, 7 by 7, of fairly heavy material, with floor sewed in; and an improved pyramidal tent, made by David Abercrombie, but designed by Mr. Tucker after one used on Mt. McKinley by Professor Parker. Tucker's tent had two openings—a small vent in the top of the pyramid, capable of being closed by an adjustable cap in case of storm, and an oval entrance through which one had to crawl. This opening could be closed to any desired extent with a pucker string. A fairly heavy, waterproof floor, measuring 7 by 7, was sewed to the base of the pyramid so that a single pole, without guy ropes, was all that was necessary to keep the tent upright after the floor had been securely pegged to the ground, or snow. Tucker's tent offered the advantages of being carried without difficulty, easily erected by one man, readily ventilated and yet giving shelter to four men in any weather. We proposed to leave the wall tent at the Base, but to take the pyramidal tent with us on the climb. We determined to carry the "Mummery" to the top of the mountain to use while taking observations.

The elevation of the Base Camp was 17,300 feet. We were surprised and pleased to find that at first we had good appetites and no *soroche*. Less than a hundred yards from the wall tent was a small diurnal stream, fed by melting snow. Whenever I went to get water for cooking or washing purposes I noticed a startling and rapid rise in pulse and increasing shortness of breath. My normal pulse is 70. After I walked slowly a hundred feet on a level at this altitude it rose to 120. After I had been seated awhile it dropped down to 100. Gradually our sense of well-being departed and was followed by a feeling of malaise and general disability. There was a splendid sunset, but we were too sick and cold to enjoy it. That night all slept badly and had some headache. A high wind swept around the mountain and threatened to carry away both of our tents. As we lay awake, wondering at what moment we should find ourselves deserted by the frail canvas shelters, we could not help thinking that Coropuna was giving us a fair warning of what might happen higher up.

For breakfast we had pemmican, hard-tack, pea soup and tea. We all wanted plenty of sugar in our tea and drank large quantities of it. Experience on Mt. McKinley had led Tucker to believe heartily in the advantages of pemmican, a food especially prepared for Arctic explorers. Neither Coello nor Gamarra nor I had ever tasted it before. We decided that it is not very palatable on first acquaintance. Although doubtless of great value when one has to spend long periods of time in the Arctic, where even seal's blubber is a delicacy "as good as cow's cream," I presume we could have done just as well without it.

It was decided to carry with us from the Base enough fuel and supplies to last through any possible misadventure, even of a week's duration. Accounts of climbs in the high Andes are full of failures due to the necessity of the explorers' being obliged to return to food, warmth, and shelter before having effected the conquest of a new peak. One remembers the frequent disappointments that came to such intrepid climbers as Whymper in Ecuador, Martin Conway in Bolivia and Fitzgerald in Chile and Argentina, due to high winds, the sudden advent of terrific snowstorms and the weakness caused by *soroche*. At the cost of carrying extra-heavy loads we determined to try to avoid being obliged to turn back. We could only hope that no unforeseen event would finally defeat our efforts.

Tucker decided to establish a cache of food and fuel as far up the mountain side as he and Coello could carry fifty pounds in a single day's climb. Leaving me to reset the demoralized tents and do other chores, they started off, packing loads of about twenty-five pounds each. To me their progress up the mountain side seemed extraordinarily slow. Were they never going to get anywhere? Their frequent stops seemed ludicrous. I was to learn later that it is as difficult at a high elevation for one who is not climbing to have any sympathy for those suffering from *soroche* as it is for a sailor to appreciate the sensations of one who is seasick.

During the morning I set up the barometers and took a series of observations. It was pleasant to note that the two new mountain aneroids registered exactly alike. All the different units of the cargo that was to be taken up the mountain then had to be weighed, so that they might be equitably distributed in our loads the following day. We had two small kerosene stoves with Primus burners. Our grub, ordered months before, specially for this climb, consisted of pemmican in 8 $\frac{1}{4}$-pound tins, Kola chocolate in half-pound tins, seeded raisins in 1-pound tins, cube sugar in 4-pound tins, hard-tack in 6$\frac{1}{2}$-pound tins, jam, sticks of dried pea soup, Plasmon biscuit, tea, and a few of Silver's self-heating "mess-tins" containing Irish stew, beef à la mode, *et al.* Corporal Gamarra appeared during the day, having found his mule, which had strayed twelve miles down the canyon. He did not relish the prospect of climbing Coropuna, but when he saw the warm clothes which we had provided for him and learned that he would get a bonus of five gold sovereigns on top of the mountain, he decided to accept his duties philosophically.

Tucker and Coello returned in the middle of the afternoon, reported that there seemed to be no serious difficulties in the first part of the climb and that a cache had been established about 2000 feet above the Base Camp, on a snow field. Tucker now assigned our packs for the morrow and skillfully prepared the tump-lines and harness with which we were to carry them.

Notwithstanding an unusual headache which lasted all day long, I still had some appetite. Our supper consisted of pemmican pudding with raisins, hard-tack and pea soup, which every one was able to eat, if not to enjoy. That night we slept better, one reason being that the wind did not blow as hard as it had the night before. The weather continued fine. Watkins was due to arrive from Arequipa in a day or two, but we decided not to wait for him or run any further risk of encountering an early summer snowstorm. The next morning, after adjusting our fifty-pound loads to our unaccustomed backs, we left camp about nine o'clock. We wore Appalachian Mountain Club snow-creepers, or *crampons*, heavy Scotch mittens, knit woolen helmets, dark blue snow-glasses, and very heavy clothing. It will be remembered by visitors to the Zermatt Museum that the Swiss guides who once climbed Huascaran, in the northern Peruvian Andes, had been maimed for life by their experiences in the deep snows of those great altitudes. We determined to take no chances, and in order to prevent the possibility of frost-bite each man was ordered to put on four pairs of heavy woolen socks and two or three pairs of heavy underdrawers.

Professor Coello and Corporal Gamarra wore large, heavy boots. I had woolen puttees and "Arctic" overshoes. Tucker improvised what he regarded as highly satisfactory sandals out of felt slippers and pieces of a rubber poncho. Since there seemed to be no rock-climbing ahead of us, we decided to depend on *crampons* rather than on the heavy hob-nailed climbing boots with which Alpinists are familiar.

The snow was very hard until about one o'clock. By three o'clock it was so soft as to make further progress impossible. We found that, loaded as we were, we could not climb a gentle rise faster than twenty steps at a time. On the more level snow fields we took twenty-five or thirty steps before stopping to rest. At the end of each stint it seemed as though they would be the last steps we should ever take. Panting violently, fatigued beyond belief, and overcome with mountain-sickness, we would stop and lean on our ice axes until able to take twenty-five steps more.

It did not take very long to recover one's wind. Finally we reached a glacier marked by a network of crevasses, none very wide, and nearly all covered with snow-bridges. We were roped together, and although there was an occasional fall no great strain was put on the rope. Then came great snow fields with not a single crevasse. For the most part our day was simply an unending succession of stints—twenty-five steps and a rest, repeated four or five times and followed by thirty-five steps and a longer rest, taken lying down in the snow. We pegged along until about half-past two, when the rapidly melting snow stopped all progress. At an altitude of about 18,450 feet, the Tucker tent was pitched on a fairly level snow field. We now noticed with dismay that the two big aneroids had begun to differ. As the sun declined the temperature fell rapidly. At half-past five the thermometer stood at 22° F. During the night the minimum thermometer registered 9° F. We noticed a considerable number of lightning flashes in the northeast. They were not accompanied by any thunder, but alarmed us considerably. We feared the expected November storms might be ahead of time. We closed the tent door on account of a biting wind. Owing to the ventilating device at the top of the tent, we managed to breathe fairly well.

Mountain climbers at high altitudes have occasionally observed that one of the symptoms of acute *soroche* is a very annoying, racking cough, as violent as whooping cough and frequently accompanied by nausea. We had not experienced this at 17,000 feet, but now it began to be painfully noticeable, and continued during the ensuing days and nights, particularly nights, until we got back to the Indians' huts again. We slept very poorly and continually awakened one another by coughing.

The next morning we had very little appetite, no ambition, and a miserable sense of malaise and great fatigue. There was nothing for it but to shoulder our packs, arrange our tump-lines, and proceed with the same steady drudgery—now a little harder than the day before. We broke camp at half-past seven and by noon had reached an altitude of about 20,000 feet, on a snow field within a mile of the saddle between the great truncated peak and the rest of the range. It looked possible to reach the summit in one more day's climb from here. The aneroids now differed by over five hundred feet. Leaving me to pitch the tent, the others went back to the cache to bring up some of the supplies. Due to the fact that we were carrying loads twice as heavy as those which Tucker and Coello had first brought up, we had not passed their cache until to-day. By the time my companions appeared again I was so completely rested that I marveled at the snail-like pace they made over the nearly level snow field. It seemed incredible that they should find it necessary to rest four times after they were within one hundred yards of the camp.

We were none of us hungry that evening. We craved sweet tea. Before turning in for the night we took the trouble to melt snow and make a potful of tea which could be warmed up the first thing in the morning. We passed another very bad night. The thermometer registered 7° F., but we did not suffer from the cold. In fact, when you stow away four men on the floor of a 7 by 7 tent they are obliged to sleep so close together as to keep warm. Furthermore, each man had an eiderdown sleeping-bag, blankets, and plenty of heavy clothes and sweaters. We did, however, suffer from *soroche*. Violent whooping cough assailed us at frequent intervals. None of us slept much. I amused myself by counting my pulse occasionally, only to find that it persistently refused to go below 120, and if I moved would jump up to 135. I don't know where it went on the actual climb. So far as I could determine, it did not go below 120 for four days and nights.

On the morning of October 15th we got up at three o'clock. Hot sweet tea was the one thing we all craved. The tea-pot was found to be frozen solid, although it had been hung up in the tent. It took an hour to thaw and the tea was just warm enough for practical purposes when I made an awkward move in the crowded tent and kicked over the tea-pot! Never did men keep their tempers better under more aggravating circumstances. Not a word of reproach or indignation greeted my clumsy accident, although poor Corporal Gamarra, who was lying on the down side of the tent, had to beat a hasty retreat into the colder (but somewhat drier) weather outside. My clumsiness necessitated a delay of nearly an hour in starting. While we were melting more frozen snow and re-making the tea, we warmed up some pea soup and Irish stew. Tucker and I managed to eat a little. Coello and Gamarra had no stomachs for anything but tea. We decided to leave the Tucker tent at the 20,000 foot level, together with most of our outfit and provisions. From here to the top we were to carry only such things as were absolutely necessary. They included the Mummery tent with pegs and poles, the mountain-mercurial barometer, the two Watkins aneroids, the hypsometer, a pair of Zeiss glasses, two 3A kodaks, six films, a sling psychrometer, a prismatic compass and clinometer, a Stanley pocket level, an eighty-foot red-strand mountain rope, three ice axes, a seven-foot flagpole, an American flag and a Yale flag. In order to avoid disaster in case of storm, we also carried four of Silver's self-heating cans of Irish stew and mock-turtle soup, a cake of chocolate, and eight hard-tack, besides raisins and cubes of sugar in our pockets. Our loads weighed about twenty pounds each.

To our great satisfaction and relief, the weather continued fine and there was very little wind. On the preceding afternoon the snow had been so soft one frequently went in over one's knees, but now everything was frozen hard. We left camp at five o'clock. It was still dark. The great dome of Coropuna loomed up on our left, cut off from direct attack by gigantic ice falls. To reach it we must first surmount the saddle on the main ridge. From there an apparently unbroken slope extended to the top. Our progress was distressingly slow, even with the light loads. When we reached the saddle there came a painful surprise. To the north of us loomed a great snowy cone, the peak which we had at first noticed from the Chuquibamba Calvario. Now it actually looked higher than the dome we were about to climb! From the Sihuas Desert, eighty miles away, the dome had certainly seemed to be the highest point. So we stuck to our task, although constantly facing the possibility that our painful labors might be in vain and that eventually, this north peak would prove to be higher. We began to doubt whether we should have strength enough for both. Loss of sleep, *soroche*, and lack of appetite were rapidly undermining our endurance.

The last slope had an inclination of thirty degrees. We should have had to cut steps with our ice axes all the way up had it not been for our snow-creepers, which worked splendidly. As it was, not more than a dozen or fifteen steps actually had to be cut even in the steepest part. Tucker was first on the rope, I was second, Coello third, and Gamarra brought up the rear. We were not a very gay party. The high altitude was sapping all our ambition. I found that an occasional lump of sugar acted as the best rapid restorative to sagging spirits. It was astonishing how quickly the carbon in the sugar was absorbed by the system and came to the relief of smoldering bodily fires. A single cube gave new strength and vigor for several minutes. Of course, one could not eat sugar without limit, but it did help to tide over difficult places.

We zigzagged slowly up, hour after hour, alternately resting and climbing, until we were about to reach what seemed to be the top, obviously, alas, not as high as our enemy to the north. Just then Tucker gave a great shout. The rest of us were too much out of breath to ask him why he was wasting his strength shouting. When at last we painfully came to the edge of what looked like the summit we saw the cause of his joy. There, immediately ahead of us, lay another slope three hundred feet higher than where we were standing. It may seem strange that in our weakened condition we should have been glad to find that we had three hundred feet more to climb. Remember, however, that all the morning we had been gazing with dread at that aggravating north peak. Whenever we had had a moment to give to the consideration of anything but the immediate difficulties of our climb our hearts had sunk within us at the thought that possibly, after all, we might find the north peak higher. The fact that there lay before us another three hundred feet, which would undoubtedly take us above the highest point of that aggravating north peak, was so very much the less of two possible evils that we understood Tucker's shout. Yet none of us was lusty enough to echo it.

With faint smiles and renewed courage we pegged along, resting on our ice axes, as usual, every twenty-five steps until at last, at half-past eleven, after six hours and a half of climbing from the 20,000-foot camp, we reached the culminating point of Coropuna. As we approached it, Tucker, although naturally much elated at having successfully engineered the first ascent of this great mountain, stopped and with extraordinary courtesy and

ALEJANDRO COELL, CORPORAL GAMARRA, AND HIRAM BINGHAM
(LEFT TO RIGHT) STAND ATOP MT. COROPUNA

self-abnegation smilingly motioned me to go ahead in order that the director of the Expedition might be actually the first person to reach the culminating point. In order to appreciate how great a sacrifice he was willing to make, it should be stated that his willingness to come on the Expedition was due chiefly to a fondness for mountain climbing and his desire to add Coropuna to his sheaf of victories. Greatly as I appreciated his kindness in making way for me, I could only acquiesce in so far as to continue the climb by his side. We reached the top together, and sank down to rest and look about.

The truncated summit is an oval-shaped snow field, almost flat, having an area of nearly half an acre, about 100 feet north and south and 175 feet east and west. If it once were, as we suppose, a volcanic crater, the pit had long since been filled up with snow and ice. There were no rocks to be seen on the rim—only the hard crust of the glistening white surface. The view from the top was desolate in the extreme. We were in the midst of a great volcanic desert dotted with isolated peaks covered with snow and occasional glaciers. Not an atom of green was to be seen anywhere. Apparently we stood on top of a dead world. Mountain climbers in the Andes have frequently spoken of seeing condors at great altitudes. We saw none. Northwest, twenty miles away across the Pampa Colorada, a reddish desert, rose snow-capped Solimana. In the other direction we looked along the range of Coropuna itself; several of the lesser peaks being only a few hundred feet below our elevation. Far to the southwest we imagined we could see the faint blue of the Pacific Ocean, but it was very dim.

My father was an ardent mountain climber, glorying not only in the difficulties of the ascent, but particularly in the satisfaction coming from the magnificent view to be obtained at the top. His zeal had led him once, in winter, to ascend the highest peak in the Pacific, Mauna Kea on Hawaii. He taught me as a boy to be fond of climbing the mountains of Oahu and Maui and to be appreciative of the views which could be obtained by such expenditure of effort. Yet now I could not take the least interest or pleasure in the view from the top of Coropuna, nor could my companions. No sense of satisfaction in having attained a difficult objective cheered us up. We all felt greatly depressed and said little, although Gamarra asked for his bonus and regarded the gold coins with grim complacency.

After we had rested awhile we began to take observations. Unslinging the aneroid which I had been carrying, I found to my surprise and dismay that the needle showed a height of only 21,525 feet above sea level. Tucker's aneroid read more than a thousand feet higher, 22,550 feet, but even this fell short of Raimondi's estimate of 22,775 feet, and considerably below Bandelier's "23,000 feet." This was a keen disappointment, for we had hoped that the aneroids would at least show a margin over the altitude of Mt. Aconcagua, 22,763 feet. This discovery served to dampen our spirits still further. We took what comfort we could from the fact that the aneroids, which had checked each other perfectly up to 17,000 feet, were now so obviously untrustworthy. We could only hope that both might prove to be inaccurate, as actually happened, and that both might now be reading too low. Anyhow, the north peak did look lower than we were. To satisfy any doubts on this subject, Tucker took the wooden box in which we had brought the hypsometer, laid it on the snow, leveled it up carefully with the Stanley pocket level, and took a squint over it toward the north peak. He smiled and said nothing. So each of us in turn lay down in the snow and took a squint. It was all right. We were at least 250 feet higher than that aggravating peak.

We were also 450 feet higher than the east peak of Coropuna, and a thousand feet higher than any other mountain in sight. At any rate, we should not have to call upon our fast-ebbing strength for any more hard climbs in the immediate future. After arriving at this satisfactory conclusion we pitched the little Mummery tent, set up the tripod for the mercurial barometer, arranged the boiling point thermometer with its apparatus, and with the aid of kodaks and notebooks proceeded to take as many observations as possible in the next four hours. At two o'clock we read the mercurial, knowing that at the same hour readings were being made by Watkins at the Base Camp and by the Harvard astronomers in the Observatory at Arequipa. The barometer was suspended from a tripod set up in the shade of the tent. The mercury, which at sea level often stands at 31 inches, now stood at 13.838 inches. The temperature of the thermometer on the barometer was exactly +32° F. At the same time, inside the tent we got the water to boiling and took a reading with the hypsometer. Water boils at sea level at a temperature of 212° F. Here it boiled at 174° F. After taking the reading we greedily drank the water which had been heated for the hypsometer. We were thirsty enough to have drunk five times as much. We were not hungry, and made no use of our provisions except a few raisins, some sugar, and chocolate.

After completing our observations, we fastened the little tent as securely as possible, banking the snow around it, and left it on top, first having placed in it one of the Appalachian Mountain Club's brass record cylinders, in which we had sealed the Yale flag, a contemporary map of Peru, and two brief statements regarding the ascent. The American flag was left flying from a nine-foot pole, which we planted at the northwest rim of the dome, where it could be seen from the road to Cotahuasi. Here Mr. Casimir Watkins saw it a week later and Dr. Isaiah Bowman two weeks later. When Chief Topographer Hendriksen arrived three weeks later to make his survey, it had disappeared. Probably a severe storm had blown it over and buried it in the snow.

We left the summit at three o'clock and arrived at the 20,000 foot camp two hours and fifteen minutes later. The first part of the way down to the saddle we attempted a glissade. Then the slope grew steeper and we got up too much speed for comfort, so we finally had to be content with a slower method of locomotion. That night there was very little wind. Mountain climbers have more to fear from excessively high winds than almost any other cause. We were very lucky. Nothing occurred to interfere with the best progress we were physically capable of making. It turned out that we did not need to have brought so many supplies with us. In fact, it is an open question whether our acute mountain-sickness would have permitted us to outlast a long storm, or left us enough appetite to use the provisions. Although one does get accustomed to high altitudes, we felt very doubtful. No one in the Western Hemisphere had ever made night camps at 20,000 feet or pitched a tent as high as the summit of Coropuna. The severity of mountain-sickness differs greatly in different localities, apparently not depending entirely on the altitude. I do not know how long we could have stood it. It is difficult to believe that with strength enough to achieve the climb we should have felt as weak and ill as we did.

That night, although we were very weary, none of us slept much. The violent whooping cough continued and all of us were nauseated again in the morning. We felt so badly and were able to take so little nourishment that it was determined to get to a lower altitude as fast as possible. To lighten our loads we left behind some of our supplies. We broke camp at 9:20. Eighteen minutes later, without having to rest, the cache was reached and the few remnants were picked up. Although many things had been abandoned, our loads seemed heavier than ever. We had some difficulty in negotiating the crevasses, but Gamarra was the only one actually to fall in, and he was easily pulled out again. About noon we heard a faint halloo, and finally made out two animated specks far down the mountain side. The effect of again seeing somebody from the outside world was rather curious. I had a choking sensation. Tucker, who led the way, told me long afterward that he could not keep the tears from running down his cheeks, although we did not see it at the time. The "specks" turned out to be Watkins and an Indian boy, who came up as high as was safe without ropes or *crampons*, and relieved us of some weight. The Base Camp was reached at half-past twelve. One of the first things Tucker did on returning was to weigh all the packs. To my surprise and disgust I learned that on the way down Tucker, afraid that some of us would collapse, had carried sixty-one pounds, and Gamarra sixty-four, while he had given me only thirty-one pounds, and the same to Coello. This, of course, does not include the weight of our ice-creepers, axes, or rope.

The next day all of us felt very tired and drowsy. In fact, I was almost overcome with inertia. It was a fearful task even to lift one's hand. The sun had burned our faces terribly. Our lips were painfully swollen. We coughed and whooped. It seemed best to make every effort to get back to a still lower altitude for the mules. So we broke camp, got the loads ready without waiting, put our sleeping-bags and blankets on our backs, and went rapidly down to the Indians' huts. Immediately our malaise left us. We felt physically stronger. We took deep breaths as though we had gotten back to sea level. There was no sensation of oppression on the chest. Yet we were still actually higher than the top of Pike's Peak. We could move rapidly about without getting out of breath; the aggravating "whooping cough" left us; and our appetites returned. To be sure, we still suffered from the effects of snow and sun. On the ascent I had been very thirsty and foolishly had allowed myself to eat a considerable amount of snow. As a result my tongue was now so extremely sensitive that pieces of soda biscuit tasted like broken glass. Corporal Gamarra, who had been unwilling to keep his snowglasses always in place and thought to relieve his eyes by frequently dispensing with them, now suffered from partial snow-blindness. The rest of us were spared any inflammation of the eyes. There followed two days of resting and waiting. Then the smiling *arrieros*, surprised and delighted at seeing us alive again after our adventure with Coropuna, arrived with our mules. The Tejadas gave us hearty embraces and promptly went off up to the snow line to get the loads. The next day we returned to Chuquibamba.

In November Chief Topographer Hendriksen completed his survey and found the latitude of Coropuna to be 15° 31' South, and the longitude to be 72° 42' 40" West of Greenwich. He computed its altitude to be 21,703 feet above sea level. The result of comparing the readings of our mercurial barometer, taken at the summit, with the simultaneous readings taken at Arequipa gave practically the same figures. There was less than sixty feet difference between the two. Although Coropuna proves to be thirteen hundred feet lower than Bandelier's estimate, and a thousand feet lower than the highest mountain in South America, still it is a thousand feet higher than the highest mountain in North America. While we were glad we were the first to reach the top, we all agreed we would never do it again!

CHAPTER 3
To Parinacochas

✱

AFTER A FEW DAYS in the delightful climate of Chuquibamba we set out for Parinacochas, the "Flamingo Lake" of the Incas. The late Sir Clements Markham, literary and historical successor of the author of "The Conquest of Peru," had called attention to this unexplored lake in one of the publications of the Royal Geographical Society, and had named a bathymetric survey of Parinacochas as one of the principal desiderata for future exploration in Peru. So far as one could judge from the published maps Parinacochas, although much smaller than Titicaca, was the largest body of water entirely in Peru. A thorough search of geographical literature failed to reveal anything regarding its depth. The only thing that seemed to be known about it was that it had no outlet. General William Miller, once British consul general in Honolulu, who had as a young man assisted General San Martin in the Wars for the Independence of Chile and Peru, published his memoirs in London in 1828. During the campaigns against the Spanish forces in Peru he had had occasion to see many out-of-the-way places in the interior. On one of his rough sketch maps he indicates the location of Lake Parinacochas and notes the fact that the water is "brackish." This statement of General Miller's and the suggestion of Sir Clements Markham that a bathymetric survey of the lake would be an important contribution to geographical knowledge was all that we were able to learn. Our *arrieros*, the Tejadas, had never been to Parinacochas, but knew in a general way its location and were not afraid to try to get there. Some of their friends had been there and come back alive!

First, however, it was necessary for us to go to Cotahuasi, the capital of the Province of Antabamba, and meet Dr. Bowman and Mr. Hendriksen, who had slowly been working their way across the Andes from the Urubamba Valley, and who would need a new supply of food-boxes if they were to complete the geographical reconnaissance of the 73d meridian. Our route led us out of the Chuquibamba Valley by a long, hard climb up the steep cliffs at its head and then over the gently sloping, semi-arid desert in a northerly direction, around the west flanks of Coropuna. When we stopped to make camp that night on the Pampa of Chumpillo, our *arrieros* used dried moss and dung for fuel for the camp fire. There was some bunch-grass, and there were llamas pasturing on the plains. Near our tent were some Inca ruins, probably the dwelling of a shepherd chief, or possibly the remains of a temple described by Cieza de Leon (1519–1560), whose remarkable accounts of what he saw and learned in Peru during the time of the Pizarros are very highly regarded. He says that among the five most important temples in the Land of the Incas was one "much venerated and frequented by them, named Coropuna." "It is on a very lofty mountain which is covered with snow both in summer and winter. The kings of Peru visited this temple making presents and offerings.... It is held for certain [by treasure hunters!] that among the gifts offered to this temple there were many loads of silver, gold, and precious stones buried in places which are now unknown. The Indians concealed another great sum which was for the service of the idol, and of the priests and virgins who attended upon it. But as there are great masses of snow, people do not ascend to the summit, nor is it known where these are hidden. This temple possessed many flocks, farms, and service of Indians." No one lives here now, but there are many flocks and llamas, and not far away we saw ancient storehouses and burial places. That night we suffered from intense cold and were kept awake by the bitter wind which swept down from the snow fields of Coropuna and shook the walls of our tent violently.

The next day we crossed two small oases, little gulches watered from the melting snow of Coropuna. Here there was an abundance of peat and some small gnarled trees from which Chuquibamba derives part of its fuel supply. We climbed slowly around the lower spurs of Coropuna into a bleak desert wilderness of lava blocks and scoriaceous sand, the Red Desert, or Pampa Colorada. It is for the most part between 15,000 and 16,000 feet above sea level, and is bounded on the northwest by the canyon of the Rio Arma, 2000 feet deep, where we made our camp and passed a more agreeable night. The following morning we climbed out again on the farther side of the canyon and skirted the eastern slopes of Mt. Solimana. Soon the trail turned abruptly to the left, away from our old friend Coropuna.

We wondered how long ago our mountain was an active volcano. Today, less than two hundred miles south of here are live peaks, like El Misti and Ubinas, which still smolder occasionally and have been known in the memory of man to give forth great showers of cinders covering a wide area. Possibly not so very long ago the great truncated peak of Coropuna was formed by a last flickering of the ancient fires. Dr. Bowman says that the greater part of the vast accumulation of lavas and volcanic cinders in this vicinity goes far back to a period preceding the last glacial epoch. The enormous amount of erosion that has taken place in the adjacent canyons and the great numbers of strata, composed of lava flows, laid bare by the mighty streams of the glacial period all point to this conclusion.

My saddle mule was one of those cantankerous beasts that are gentle enough as long as they are allowed to have their own way. In her case this meant that she was happy only when going along close to her friends in the caravan. If reined in, while I took some notes, she became very restive, finally whirling around, plunging and kicking. Contrariwise, no amount of spurring or lashing with a stout quirt availed to make her go ahead of her comrades. This morning I was particularly anxious to get a picture of our pack train jogging steadily along over the desert, directly away from Coropuna. Since my mule would not gallop ahead, I had to dismount, *run* a couple of hundred yards ahead of the rapidly advancing animals and take the picture before they reached me. We were now at an elevation of 16,000 feet above sea level. Yet to my surprise and delight I found that it was relatively as easy to run here as anywhere, so accustomed had my lungs and heart become to very rarefied air. Had I attempted such a strenuous feat at a similar altitude before climbing Coropuna it would have been physically impossible. Any one who has tried to run two hundred yards at three miles above sea level will understand.

We were still in a very arid region; mostly coarse black sand and pebbles, with typical desert shrubs and occasional bunches of tough grass. The slopes of Mt. Solimana on our left were fairly well covered with sparse vegetation. Among the bushes we saw a number of vicuñas, the smallest wild camels of the New World. We tried in vain to get near enough for a photograph. They were extremely timid and scampered away before we were within three hundred yards.

Seven or eight miles more of very gradual downward slope brought us suddenly and unexpectedly to the brink of a magnificent canyon, the densely populated valley of Cotahuasi. The walls of the canyon were covered with innumerable terraces—thousands of them. It seemed at first glance as though every available spot in the canyon had been either terraced or allotted to some compact little village. One could count more than a score of towns, including Cotahuasi itself, its long main street outlined by whitewashed houses. As we zigzagged down into the canyon our road led us past hundreds of the artificial terraces and through little villages of thatched huts huddled together on spurs rescued from the all-embracing agriculture. After spending several weeks in a desert region, where only the narrow valley bottoms showed any signs of cultivation, it seemed marvelous to observe the extent to which terracing had been carried on the side of the Cotahuasi Valley. Although we were now in the zone of light annual rains, it was evident from the extraordinary irrigation system that agriculture here depends very largely on ability to bring water down from the great mountains in the interior. Most of the terraces and irrigation canals were built centuries ago, long before the discovery of America.

No part of the ancient civilization of Peru has been more admired than the development of agriculture. Mr. Cook says that there is no part of the world in which more pains have been taken to raise crops where nature made it hard for them to be planted. In other countries, to be sure, we find reclamation projects, where irrigation canals serve to bring water long distances to be used on arid but fruitful soil. We also find great fertilizer factories turning out, according to proper chemical formula, the needed constituents to furnish impoverished soils with the necessary materials for plant growth. We find man overcoming many obstacles in the way of transportation, in order to reach great regions where nature has provided fertile fields and made it easy to raise life-giving crops. Nowhere outside of Peru, either in historic or prehistoric times, does one find farmers spending incredible amounts of labor in actually creating arable fields, *besides* bringing the water to irrigate them and the guano to fertilize them; yet that is what was done by the ancient highlanders of Peru. As they spread over a country in which the arable flat land was usually at so great an elevation as to be suitable for only the hardiest of root crops, like the white potato and the *oca*, they were driven to use narrow valley bottoms and steep, though fertile, slopes in order to raise the precious maize and many of the other temperate and tropical plants which they domesticated for food and medicinal purposes. They were constantly confronted by an extraordinary scarcity of soil. In the valley bottoms torrential rivers, meandering from side to side, were engaged in an endless endeavor to tear away the arable land and bear it off to the sea. The slopes of the valleys were frequently so very steep as to discourage the most ardent modern agriculturalist. The farmer might wake up any morning to find that a heavy rain during the night had washed away a large part of his carefully planted fields. Consequently there was developed, through the centuries, a series of stone-faced *andenes*, terraces or platforms.

Examination of the ancient *andenes* discloses the fact that they were not made by simply hoeing in the earth from the hillside back of a carefully constructed stone wall. The space back of the walls was first filled in with coarse rocks, clay, and rubble; then followed smaller rocks, pebbles, and gravel, which would serve to drain the subsoil. Finally, on top of all this, and to a depth of eighteen inches or so, was laid the finest soil they could procure. The result was the best possible field for intensive cultivation. It seems absolutely unbelievable that such an immense amount of pains should have been taken for such relatively small results. The need must have been very great. In many cases the terraces are only a few feet wide, although hundreds of yards in length. Usually they follow the natural contours of the valley. Sometimes they are two hundred yards wide and a quarter of a mile long. To-day corn, barley, and alfalfa are grown on the terraces.

Cotahuasi itself lies in the bottom of the valley, a pleasant place where one can purchase the most fragrant and highly prized of all Peruvian wines. The climate is agreeable, and has attracted many landlords, whose estates lie chiefly on the bleak plateaus of the surrounding highlands, where shepherds tend flocks of llamas, sheep, and alpacas.

We were cordially welcomed by Señor Viscarra, the sub-prefect, and invited to stay at his house. He was a stranger to the locality, and, as the visible representative of a powerful and far-away central government, was none too popular with some of the people of his province. Very few residents of a provincial capital like Cotahuasi have ever been to Lima;—probably not a single member of the Lima government had ever been to Cotahuasi. Consequently one could not expect to find much sympathy between the two. The difficulties of traveling in Peru are so great as to discourage pleasure trips. With our letters of introduction and the telegrams that had preceded us from the prefect at Arequipa, we were known to be friends of the government and so were doubly welcome to the sub-prefect. By nature a kind and generous man, of more than usual education and intelligence, Señor Viscarra showed himself most courteous and hospitable to us in every particular. In our honor he called together his friends. They brought pictures of Theodore Roosevelt and Elihu Root, and made a large American flag; a courtesy we deeply appreciated, even if the flag did have only thirty-six stars. Finally, they gave us a splendid banquet as a tribute of friendship for America.

One day the sub-prefect offered to have his personal barber attend us. It was some time since Mr. Tucker and I had seen a barber-shop. The chances were that we should find none at Parinacochas. Consequently we accepted with pleasure. When the barber arrived, closely guarded by a *gendarme* armed with a loaded rifle, we learned that he was a convict from the local jail! I did not like to ask the nature of his crime, but he looked like a murderer. When he unwrapped an ancient pair of clippers from an unspeakably soiled and oily rag, I wished I was in a position to decline to place myself under his ministrations. The sub-prefect, however, had been so kind and was so apologetic as to the inconveniences of the "barber-shop" that there was nothing for it but to go bravely forward. Although it was unpleasant to have one's hair trimmed by an uncertain pair of rusty clippers, I could not help experiencing a feeling of relief that the convict did not have a pair of shears. He was working too near my jugular vein. Finally the period of torture came to an end, and the prisoner accepted his fees with a profound salutation. We breathed sighs of relief, not unmixed with sympathy, as we saw him marched safely away by the *gendarme*.

We had arrived in Cotahuasi almost simultaneously with Dr. Bowman and Topographer Hendriksen. They had encountered extraordinary difficulties in carrying out the reconnaissance of the 73d meridian, but were now past the worst of it. Their supplies were exhausted, so those which we had brought from Arequipa were doubly welcome. Mr. Watkins was assigned to assist Mr. Hendriksen and a few days later Dr. Bowman started south to study the geology and geography of the desert. He took with him as escort Corporal Gamarra, who was only too glad to escape from the machinations of his enemies. It will be remembered that it was Gamarra who had successfully defended the Cotahuasi barracks and jail at the time of a revolutionary riot which occurred some months previous to our visit. The sub-prefect accompanied Dr. Bowman out of town. For Gamarra's sake they left the house at three o'clock in the morning and our generous host agreed to ride with them until daybreak. In his important monograph, "The Andes of Southern Peru," Dr. Bowman writes: "At four o'clock our whispered arrangements were made. We opened the gates noiselessly and our small cavalcade hurried through the pitch-black streets of the town. The soldier rode ahead, his rifle across his saddle, and directly behind him rode the sub-prefect and myself. The pack mules were in the rear. We had almost reached the end of the street when a door opened suddenly and a shower of sparks flew out ahead of us. Instantly the soldier struck spurs into his mule and turned into a side street. The sub-prefect drew his horse back savagely, and when the next shower of sparks flew out pushed me against the wall and whispered, 'For God's sake, who is it?' Then suddenly he shouted, 'Stop blowing! Stop blowing!'"

The cause of all the disturbance was a shabby, hard-working tailor who had gotten up at this unearthly hour to start his day's work by pressing clothes for some insistent customer. He had in his hand an ancient smoothing-iron filled with live coals, on which he had been vigorously blowing. Hence the sparks! That a penitent tailor and his ancient goose should have been able to cause such terrific excitement at that hour in the morning would have interested our own Oliver Wendell Holmes, who was fond of referring to this picturesque apparatus and who might have written an appropriate essay on The Goose that Startled the Soldier of Cotahuasi; with Particular Reference to His Being a Possible Namesake of the Geese that Aroused the Soldiers of Ancient Rome.

The most unusual industry of Cotahuasi is the weaving of rugs and carpets on vertical hand looms. The local carpet weavers make the warp and woof of woolen yarn in which loops of alpaca wool, black, gray, or white, are inserted to form the desired pattern. The loops are cut so as to form a deep pile. The result is a delightfully thick, warm, gray rug. Ordinarily the native Peruvian rug has no pile. Probably the industry was brought from Europe by some Spaniard centuries ago. It seems to be restricted to this remote region. The rug makers are a small group of Indians who live outside the town but who carry their hand looms from house to house, as required. It is the custom for the person who desires a rug to buy the wool, supply the pattern, furnish the weaver with board, lodging, *coca*, tobacco and wine, and watch the rug grow from day to day under the shelter of his own roof. The rug weavers are very clever in copying new patterns. Through the courtesy of Señor Viscarra we eventually received several small rugs, woven especially for us from monogram designs drawn by Mr. Hendriksen.

THE SUB-PREFECT OF COTAHUASI, HIS MILITARY AIDE, AND MESSRS.
TUCKER, HENDRIKSEN, BOWMAN, AND BINGHAM INSPECTING
THE LOCAL RUG-WEAVING INDUSTRY

Early one morning in November we said good-bye to our friendly host, and, directed by a picturesque old guide who said he knew the road to Parinacochas, we left Cotahuasi. The highway crossed the neighboring stream on a treacherous-looking bridge, the central pier of which was built of the crudest kind of masonry piled on top of a gigantic boulder in mid-stream. The main arch of the bridge consisted of two long logs across which had been thrown a quantity of brush held down by earth and stones. There was no rail on either side, but our mules had crossed bridges of this type before and made little trouble. On the northern side of the valley we rode through a compact little town called Mungi and began to climb out of the canyon, passing hundreds of very fine artificial terraces, at present used for crops of maize and barley. In one place our road led us by a little waterfall, an altogether surprising and unexpected phenomenon in this arid region. Investigation, however, proved that it was artificial, as well as the fields. Its presence may be due to a temporary connection between the upper and lower levels of ancient irrigation canals.

Hour after hour our pack train painfully climbed the narrow, rocky zigzag trail. The climate is favorable for agriculture. Wherever the sides of the canyon were not absolutely precipitous, stone-faced terraces and irrigation had transformed them long ago into arable fields. Four thousand feet above the valley floor we came to a very fine series of beautiful terraces. On a shelf near the top of the canyon we pitched our tent near some rough stone corrals used by shepherds whose flocks grazed on the lofty plateau beyond, and near a tiny brook, which was partly frozen over the next morning. Our camp was at an elevation of 14,500 feet above the sea. Near by were turreted rocks, curious results of wind-and-sand erosion.

The next day we entered a region of mountain pastures. We passed occasional swamps and little pools of snow water. From one of these we turned and looked back across the great Cotahuasi Canyon, to the glaciers of Solimana and snow-clad Coropuna, now growing fainter and fainter as we went toward Parinacochas. At an altitude of 16,500 feet we struck across a great barren plateau covered with rocks and sand—hardly a living thing in sight. In the midst of it we came to a beautiful lake, but it was not Parinacochas. On the plateau it was intensely cold. Occasionally I dismounted and jogged along beside my mule in order to keep warm. Again I noticed that as the result of my experiences on Coropuna I suffered no discomfort, nor any symptoms of mountain-sickness, even after trotting steadily for four or five hundred yards. In the afternoon we began to descend from the plateau toward Lampa and found ourselves in the pasture lands of Ajochiucha, where *ichu* grass and other little foliage plants, watered by rain and snow, furnish forage for large flocks of sheep, llamas, and alpacas. Their owners live in the cultivated valleys, but the Indian herdsmen must face the storms and piercing winds of the high pastures.

Alpacas are usually timid. On this occasion, however, possibly because they were thirsty and were seeking water holes in the upper courses of a little swale, they stopped and allowed me to observe them closely. The fleece of the alpaca is one of the softest in the world. However, due to the fact that shrewd tradesmen, finding that the fabric manufactured from alpaca wool was highly desired, many years ago gave the name to a far cheaper fabric, the "alpaca" of commerce, a material used for coat linings, umbrellas, and thin, warm-weather coats, is a fabric of cotton and wool, with a hard surface, and generally dyed black. It usually contains no real alpaca wool at all, and is fairly cheap. The real alpaca wool which comes into the market today is not so called. Long and silky, straighter than the sheep's wool, it is strong, small of fiber, very soft, pliable and elastic. It is capable of being woven into fabrics of great beauty and comfort. Many of the silky, fluffy, knitted garments that command the highest prices for winter wear, and which are called by various names, such as "vicuña," "camel's hair," etc., are really made of alpaca.

The alpaca, like its cousin, the llama, was probably domesticated by the early Peruvians from the wild guanaco, largest of the camels of the New World. The guanaco still exists in a wild state and is always of uniform coloration. Llamas and alpacas are extremely variegated. The llama has so coarse a hair that it is seldom woven into cloth for wearing apparel, although heavy blankets made from it are in use by the natives. Bred to be a beast of burden, the llama is accustomed to the presence of strangers and is not any more timid of them than our horses and cows. The alpaca, however, requiring better and scarcer forage—short, tender grass and plenty of water—frequents the most remote and lofty of the mountain pastures, is handled only when the fleece is removed, seldom sees any one except the peaceful shepherds, and is extremely shy of strangers, although not nearly as timid as its distant cousin the vicuña. I shall never forget the first time I ever saw some alpacas. They looked for all the world like the "woolly-dogs" of our toys shops—woolly along the neck right up to the eyes and woolly along the legs right down to the invisible wheels! There was something inexpressibly comic about these long-legged animals. They look like toys on wheels, but actually they can gallop like cows.

The llama, with far less hair on head, neck, and legs, is also amusing, but in a different way. His expression is haughty and supercilious in the extreme. He usually looks as though his presence near one is due to circumstances over which he really had no control. Pride of race and excessive haughtiness lead him to carry his head so high and his neck so stiffly erect that he can be corralled, with others of his kind, by a single rope passed around the necks of the entire group. Yet he can be bought for ten dollars.

On the pasture lands of Ajochiucha there were many ewes and lambs, both of llamas and alpacas. Even the shepherds were mostly children, more timid than their charges. They crouched inconspicuously behind rocks and shrubs, endeavoring to escape our notice. About five o'clock in the afternoon, on a dry *pampa*, we found the ruins of one of the largest known Inca storehouses, Chichipampa, an interesting reminder of the days when benevolent despots ruled the Andes and, like the Pharaohs of old, provided against possible famine. The locality is not occupied, yet near by are populous valleys.

As soon as we left our camp the next morning, we came abruptly to the edge of the Lampa Valley. This was another of the mile-deep canyons so characteristic of this region. Our pack mules grunted and groaned as they picked their way down the corkscrew trail. It overhangs the mud-colored Indian town of Colta, a rather scattered collection of a hundred or more huts. Here again, as in the Cotahuasi Valley, are hundreds of ancient terraces, extending for thousands of feet up the sides of the canyon. Many of them were badly out of repair, but those near Colta were still being used for raising crops of corn, potatoes, and barley. The uncultivated spots were covered with cacti, thorn bushes, and the gnarled, stunted trees of a semi-arid region. In the town itself were half a dozen specimens of the Australian eucalyptus, that agreeable and extraordinarily successful colonist which one encounters not only in the heart of Peru, but in the Andes of Colombia and the new forest preserves of California and the Hawaiian Islands.

Colta has a few two-storied houses, with tiled roofs. Some of them have open verandas on the second floor—a sure indication that the climate is at times comfortable. Their walls are built of sun-dried adobe, and so are the walls of the little grass-thatched huts of the majority. Judging by the rather irregular plan of the streets and the great number of terraces in and around town, one may conclude that Colta goes far back of the sixteenth century and the days of the Spanish Conquest, as indeed do most Peruvian towns. The cities of Lima and Arequipa are noteworthy exceptions. Leaving Colta, we wound around the base of the projecting ridge, on the sides of which were many evidences of ancient culture, and came into the valley of Huancahuanca, a large arid canyon. The guide said that we were nearing Parinacochas. Not many miles away, across two canyons, was a snow-capped peak, Sarasara.

Lampa, the chief town in the Huancahuanca Canyon, lies on a great natural terrace of gravel and alluvium more than a thousand feet above the river. Part of the terrace seemed to be irrigated and under cultivation. It was proposed by the energetic farmers at the time of our visit to enlarge the system of irrigation so as to enable them to cultivate a larger part of the *pampa* on which they lived. In fact, the new irrigation scheme was actually in process of being carried out and has probably long since been completed. Our reception in Lampa was not cordial. It will be remembered that our military escort, Corporal Gamarra, had gone back to Arequipa with Dr. Bowman. Our two excellent *arrieros*, the Tejada brothers, declared they preferred to travel without any "brass buttons," so we had not asked the sub-prefect of Cotahuasi to send one of his small handful of *gendarmes* along with us. Probably this was a mistake. Unless one is traveling in Peru on some easily understood matter, such as prospecting for mines or representing one of the great importing and commission houses, or actually peddling goods, one cannot help arousing the natural suspicions of a people to whom traveling on muleback for pleasure is unthinkable, and scientific exploration for its own sake is incomprehensible. Of course, if the explorers arrive accompanied by a *gendarme* it is perfectly evident that the enterprise has the approval and probably the financial backing of the government. It is surmised that the explorers are well paid, and what would be otherwise inconceivable becomes merely one of the ordinary experiences of life. South American governments almost without exception are paternalistic, and their citizens are led to expect that all measures connected with research, whether it be scientific, economic, or social, are to be conducted by the government and paid for out of the national treasury. Individual enterprise is not encouraged. During all my preceding exploration in Peru I had had such an easy time that I not only forgot, but failed to realize, how often an ever-present *gendarme*, provided through the courtesy of President Leguia's government, had quieted suspicions and assured us a cordial welcome.

Now, however, when without a *gendarme* we entered the smart little town of Lampa, we found ourselves immediately and unquestionably the objects of extreme suspicion and distrust. Yet we could not help admiring the well-swept streets, freshly whitewashed houses, and general air of prosperity and enterprise. The *gobernador* of the town lived on the main street in a red-tiled house, whose courtyard and colonnade were probably two hundred years old. He had heard nothing of our undertaking from the government. His friends urged him to take some hostile action. Fortunately, our *arrieros*, respectable men of high grade, although strangers in Lampa, were able to allay his suspicions temporarily. We were not placed under arrest, although I am sure his action was not approved by the very suspicious town councilors, who found it far easier to suggest reasons for our being fugitives from justice than to understand the real object of our journey.

The very fact that we were bound for Lake Parinacochas, a place well known in Lampa, added to their suspicion. It seems that Lampa is famous for its weavers, who utilize the wool of the countless herds of sheep, alpacas, and vicuñas in this vicinity to make ponchos and blankets of high grade, much desired not only in this locality but even in Arequipa. These are marketed, as so often happens in the outlying parts of the world, at a great annual fair, attended by traders who come hundreds of miles, bringing the manufactured articles of the outer world and seeking the highly desired products of these secluded towns. The great fair for this vicinity has been held, for untold generations, on the shores of Lake Parinacochas. Every one is anxious to attend the fair, which is an occasion for seeing one's friends, an opportunity for jollification, carousing, and general enjoyment—like a large county fair at home. Except for this annual fair week, the basin of Parinacochas is as bleak and desolate as our own fair-grounds, with scarcely a house to be seen except those that are used for the purposes of the fair. Had we been bound for Parinacochas at the proper season nothing could have been more reasonable and praiseworthy. Why anybody should want to go to Parinacochas during one of the other fifty-one weeks in the year was utterly beyond the comprehension or understanding of these village worthies. So, to our "selectmen," are the idiosyncrasies of itinerant gypsies who wish to camp in our deserted fair-grounds.

The Tejadas were not anxious to spend the night in town—probably because, according to our contract, the cost of feeding the mules devolved entirely upon them and fodder is always far more expensive in town than in the country. It was just as well for us that this was so, for I am sure that before morning the village gossips would have persuaded the *gobernador* to arrest us. As it was, however, he was pleasant and hospitable, and considerably amused at the embarrassment of an Indian woman who was weaving at a hand loom in his courtyard and whom we desired to photograph. She could not easily escape, for she was sitting on the ground with one end of the loom fastened around her waist, the other end tied to a eucalyptus tree. So she covered her eyes and mouth with her hands, and almost wept with mortification at our strange procedure. Peruvian Indian women are invariably extremely shy, rarely like to be photographed, and are anxious only to escape observation and notice. The ladies of the *gobernador's* own family, however, of mixed Spanish and Indian ancestry, not only had no objection to being photographed, but were moved to unseemly and unsympathetic laughter at the predicament of their unfortunate sister.

After leaving Lampa we found ourselves on the best road that we had seen in a long time. Its excellence was undoubtedly due to the enterprise and energy of the people of this pleasant town. One might expect that citizens who kept their town so clean and neat and were engaged in the unusual act of constructing new irrigation works would have a comfortable road in the direction toward which they usually would wish to go, namely, toward the coast.

As we climbed out of the Huancahuanca Valley we noticed no evidences of ancient agricultural terraces, either on the sides of the valley or on the alluvial plain which has given rise to the town of Lampa and whose products have made its people well fed and energetic. The town itself seems to be of modern origin. One wonders why there are so few, if any, evidences of the ancient régime when there are so many a short distance away in Colta and the valley around it. One cannot believe that the Incas would have overlooked such a fine agricultural opportunity as an extensive alluvial terrace in a region where there is so little arable land. Possibly the very excellence of the land and its relative flatness rendered artificial terracing unnecessary in the minds of the ancient people who lived here. On the other hand, it may have been occupied until late Inca times by one of the coast tribes. Whatever the cause, certainly the deep canyon of Huancahuanca divides two very different regions. To come in a few hours, from thickly terraced Colta to unterraced Lampa was so striking as to give us cause for thought and speculation. It is well known that in the early days before the Inca conquest of Peru, not so very long before the Spanish Conquest, there were marked differences between the tribes who inhabited the high plateau and those who lived along the shore of the Pacific. Their pottery is as different as possible in design and ornamentation; the architecture of their cities and temples is absolutely distinct. Relative abundance of flat lands never led them to develop terracing to the same extent that the mountain people had done. Perhaps on this alluvial terrace there lived a remnant of the coastal peoples. Excavation would show.

Scarcely had we climbed out of the valley of Huancahuanca and surmounted the ridge when we came in sight of more artificial terraces. Beyond a broad, deep valley rose the extinct volcanic cone of Mt. Sarasara, now relatively close at hand, its lower slopes separated from us by another canyon. Snow lay in the gulches and ravines near the top of the mountain. Our road ran near the towns of Pararca and Colcabamba, the latter much like Colta, a straggling village of thatched huts surrounded by hundreds of terraces. The vegetation on the valley slopes indicated occasional rains. Near Pararca we passed fields of barley and wheat growing on old stone-faced terraces. On every hand were signs of a fairly large population engaged in agriculture, utilizing fields which had been carefully prepared for them by their ancestors. They were not using all, however. We noticed hundreds of terraces that did not appear to have been under cultivation recently. They may have been lying fallow temporarily.

Our *arrieros* avoided the little towns, and selected a camp site on the roadside near the *Finca Rodadero*. After all, when one has a comfortable tent, good food, and skillful *arrieros* it is far pleasanter to spend the night in the clean, open country, even at an elevation of 12,000 or 13,000 feet, than to be surrounded by the smells and noises of an Indian town.

The next morning we went through some wheat fields, past the town of Puyusca, another large Indian village of thatched adobe houses placed high on the shoulder of a rocky hill so as to leave the best arable land available for agriculture. It is in a shallow, well-watered valley, full of springs. The appearance of the country had changed entirely since we left Cotahuasi. The desert and its steep-walled canyons seemed to be far behind us. Here was a region of gently sloping hills, covered with terraces, where the cereals of the temperate zone appeared to be easily grown. Finally, leaving the grain fields, we climbed up to a shallow depression in the low range at the head of the valley and found ourselves on the rim of a great upland basin more than twenty miles across. In the center of the basin was a large, oval lake. Its borders were pink. The water in most of the lake was dark blue, but near the shore the water was pink, a light salmon-pink. What could give it such a curious color? Nothing but flamingoes, countless thousands of flamingoes—Parinacochas at last!

CHAPTER 4

FLAMINGO LAKE

★

THE PARINACOCHAS BASIN is at an elevation of between 11,500 and 12,000 feet above sea level. It is about 150 miles northwest of Arequipa and 170 miles southwest of Cuzco, and enjoys a fair amount of rainfall. The lake is fed by springs and small streams. In past geological times the lake, then very much larger, had an outlet not far from the town of Puyusca. At present Parinacochas has no visible outlet. It is possible that the large springs which we noticed as we came up the valley by Puyusca may be fed from the lake. On the other hand, we found numerous small springs on the very borders of the lake, generally occurring in swampy hillocks—built up perhaps by mineral deposits—three or four feet higher than the surrounding plain. There are very old beach marks well above the shore. The natives told us that in the wet season the lake was considerably higher than at present, although we could find no recent evidence to indicate that it had been much more than a foot above its present level. Nevertheless a rise of a foot would enlarge the area of the lake considerably.

When making preparations in New Haven for the "bathymetric survey of Lake Parinacochas," suggested by Sir Clements Markham, we found it impossible to discover any indication in geographical literature as to whether the depth of the lake might be ten feet or ten thousand feet. We decided to take a chance on its not being more than ten hundred feet. With the kind assistance of Mr. George Bassett, I secured a thousand feet of stout fish line, known to anglers as "24 thread," wound on a large wooden reel for convenience in handling. While we were at Chuquibamba Mr.

Watkins had spent many weary hours inserting one hundred and sixty-six white and red cloth markers at six-foot intervals in the strands of this heavy line, so that we might be able more rapidly to determine the result in fathoms.

Arrived at a low peninsula on the north shore of the lake, Tucker and I pitched our camp, sent our mules back to Puyusca for fodder, and set up the Acme folding boat, which we had brought so many miles on muleback, for the sounding operations. The "Acme" proved easy to assemble, although this was our first experience with it. Its lightness enabled it to be floated at the edge of the lake even in very shallow water, and its rigidity was much appreciated in the late afternoon when the high winds raised a vicious little "sea." Rowing out on waters which we were told by the natives had never before been navigated by craft of any kind, I began to take soundings. Lake Titicaca is over nine hundred feet deep. It would be aggravating if Lake Parinacochas should prove to be over a thousand, for I had brought no extra line. Even nine hundred feet would make sounding slow work, and the lake covered an area of over seventy square miles.

It was with mixed feelings of trepidation and expectation that I rowed out five miles from shore and made a sounding. Holding the large reel firmly in both hands, I cast the lead overboard. The reel gave a turn or two and stopped. Something was wrong. The line did not run out. Was the reel stuck? No, the apparatus was in perfect running order. Then what *was* the matter? The bottom was too near! Alas for all the pains that Mr. Bassett had taken to put a thousand feet of the best strong 24-thread line on one reel! Alas for Mr. Watkins and his patient insertion of one hundred and sixty-six "fathom-markers"! The bottom of the lake was only four feet away from the bottom of my boat! After three or four days of strenuous rowing up and down the eighteen miles of the lake's length, and back and forth across the seventeen miles of its width, I never succeeded in wetting Watkins's first marker! Several hundred soundings failed to show more than five feet of water anywhere. Possibly if we had come in the rainy season we might at least have wet one marker, but at the time of our visit (November, 1911), the lake had a maximum depth of $4^{1}/_{2}$ feet. The satisfaction of making this slight contribution to geographic knowledge was, I fear, lost in the chagrin of not finding a really noteworthy body of water.

Who would have thought that so long a lake could be so shallow? However, my feelings were soothed by remembering the story of the captain of a man-of-war who was once told that the salt lake near one of the red hills between Honolulu and Pearl Harbor was reported by the natives to be "bottomless." He ordered one of the ship's heavy boats to be carried from the shore several miles inland to the salt lake, at great expenditure of strength and labor. The story told me in my boyhood does not say how much sounding line was brought. Anyhow, they found this "fathomless" body of water to be not more than fifteen feet deep.

Notwithstanding my disappointment at the depth of Parinacochas, I was very glad that we had brought the little folding boat, for it enabled me to float gently about among the myriads of birds which use the shallow waters of the lake as a favorite feeding ground; pink flamingoes, white gulls, small "divers," large black ducks, sandpipers, black ibis, teal ducks, and large geese. On the banks were ground owls and woodpeckers. It is not surprising that the natives should have named this body of water "Parinacochas" (*Parina* = "flamingo," *cochas* = "lake"). The flamingoes are here in incredible multitudes; they far outnumber all other birds, and as I have said, actually make the shallow waters of the lake look pink. Fortunately they had not been hunted for their plumage and were not timid. After two days of familiarity with the boat they were willing to let me approach within twenty yards before finally taking wing. The coloring, in this land of drab grays and browns, was a delight to the eye. The head is white, the beak black, the neck white shading into salmon-pink; the body pinkish white on the back, the breast white, and the tail salmon-pink. The wings are salmon-pink in front, but the tips and the under-parts are black. As they stand or wade in the water their general appearance is chiefly pink-and-white. When they rise from the water, however, the black under-parts of the wings become strikingly conspicuous and cause a flock of flying flamingoes to be a wonderful contrast in black-and-white. When flying, the flamingo seems to keep his head moving steadily forward at an even pace, although the rope-like neck undulates with the slow beating of the wings. I could not be sure that it was not an optical delusion. Nevertheless, I thought the heavy body was propelled irregularly, while the head moved forward at uniform speed, the difference being caught up in the undulations of the neck.

The flamingo is an amusing bird to watch. With its haughty Roman nose and long, ropelike neck, which it coils and twists in a most incredible manner, it seems specially intended to distract one's mind from bathymetric disappointments. Its hoarse croaking, "What is it," "What is it," seemed to express deep-throated sympathy with the sounding operations. On one bright moonlight night the flamingoes were very noisy, keeping up a continual clatter of very hoarse "What-is-it's." Apparently they failed to find out the answer in time to go to bed at the proper time, for next morning we found them all sound asleep, standing in quiet bays with their heads tucked under their wings. During the course of the forenoon, when the water was quiet, they waded far out into the lake. In the afternoon, as winds and waves arose, they came in nearer the shores, but seldom left the water. The great extent of shallow water in Parinacochas offers them a splendid, wide feeding ground. We wondered where they all came from. Apparently they do not breed here. Although there were thousands and thousands of birds, we could find no flamingo nests, either old or new, search as we would. It offers a most interesting problem for some enterprising biological explorer. Probably Mr. Frank Chapman will some day solve it.

Next in number to the flamingoes were the beautiful white gulls (or terns?), looking strangely out of place in this Andean lake 11,500 feet above the sea. They usually kept together in flocks of several hundred. There were quantities of small black divers in the deeper parts of the lake where the flamingoes did not go. The divers were very quick and keen, true individualists operating alone and showing astonishing ability in swimming long distances under water. The large black ducks were much more fearless than the flamingoes and were willing to swim very near the canoe. When frightened, they raced over the water at a tremendous pace, using both wings and feet in their efforts to escape. These ducks kept in large flocks and were about as common as the small divers. Here and there in the lake were a few tiny little islands, each containing a single deserted nest, possibly belonging to an ibis or a duck. In the banks of a low stream near our first camp were holes made by woodpeckers, who in this country look in vain for trees and telegraph poles.

Occasionally, a mile or so from shore, my boat would startle a great amphibious ox standing in the water up to his middle, calmly eating the succulent water grass. To secure it he had to plunge his head and neck well under the surface.

While I was raising blisters and frightening oxen and flamingoes, Mr. Tucker triangulated the Parinacochas Basin, making the first accurate map of this vicinity. As he carried his theodolite from point to point he often stirred up little ground owls, who gazed at him with solemn, reproachful looks. And they were not the only individuals to regard his activities with suspicion and dislike. Part of my work was to construct signal stations by piling rocks at conspicuous points on the well-rounded hills so as to enable the triangulation to proceed as rapidly as possible. During the night some of these signal stations would disappear, torn down by the superstitious shepherds who lived in scattered clusters of huts and declined to have strange gods set up in their vicinity. Perhaps they thought their pastures were being preëmpted. We saw hundreds of their sheep and cattle feeding on flat lands formerly the bed of the lake. The hills of the Parinacochas Basin are bare of trees, and offer some pasturage. In some places they are covered with broken rock. The grass was kept closely cropped by the degenerate descendants of sheep brought into the country during Spanish colonial days. They were small in size and mostly white in color, although there were many black ones. We were told that the sheep were worth about fifty cents apiece here.

On our first arrival at Parinacochas we were left severely alone by the shepherds; but two days later curiosity slowly overcame their shyness, and a group of young shepherds and shepherdesses gradually brought their grazing flocks nearer and nearer the camp, in order to gaze stealthily on these strange visitors, who lived in a cloth house, actually moved over the forbidding waters of the lake, and busied themselves from day to day with strange magic, raising and lowering a glittering glass eye on a tripod. The women wore dresses of heavy material, the skirts reaching halfway from knee to ankle. In lieu of hats they had small variegated shawls, made on hand looms, folded so as to make a pointed bonnet over the head and protect the neck and shoulders from sun and wind. Each woman was busily spinning with a hand spindle, but carried her baby and its gear and blankets in a hammock or sling attached to a tump-line that went over her head. These sling carry-alls were neatly woven of soft wool and decorated with attractive patterns. Both women and boys were barefooted. The boys wore old felt hats of native manufacture, and coats and long trousers much too large for them.

At one end of the upland basin rises the graceful cone of Mt. Sarasara. The view of its snow-capped peak reflected in the glassy waters of the lake in the early morning was one long to be remembered. Sarasara must once have been much higher than it is at present. Its volcanic cone has been sharply eroded by snow and ice. In the days of its greater altitude, and consequently wider snow fields, the melting snows probably served to make Parinacochas a very much larger body of water. Although we were here at the beginning of summer, the wind that came down from the mountain at night was very cold. Our minimum thermometer registered 22° F. near the

banks of the lake at night. Nevertheless, there was only a very thin film of
ice on the borders of the lake in the morning, and except in the most shallow bays there was no ice visible far from the bank. The temperature of the
water at 10:00 A.M. near the shore, and ten inches below the surface, was
61° F., while farther out it was three or four degrees warmer. By noon the
temperature of the water half a mile from shore was 67.5° F. Shortly after
noon a strong wind came up from the coast, stirring up the shallow water
and cooling it. Soon afterwards the temperature of the water began to fall,
and, although the hot sun was shining brightly almost directly overhead,
it went down to 65° by 2:30 P.M.

The water of the lake is brackish, yet we were able to make our camps
on the banks of small streams of sweet water, although in each case near
the shore of the lake. A specimen of the water, taken near the shore, was
brought back to New Haven and analyzed by Dr. George S. Jamieson of the
Sheffield Scientific School. He found that it contained small quantities of
silica, iron phosphate, magnesium carbonate, calcium carbonate, calcium
sulphate, potassium nitrate, potassium sulphate, sodium borate, sodium sulphate, and a considerable quantity of sodium chloride. Parinacochas water
contains more carbonate and potassium than that of the Atlantic Ocean or
the Great Salt Lake. As compared with the salinity of typical "salt" waters,
that of Lake Parinacochas occupies an intermediate position, containing
more than Lake Koko-Nor, less than that of the Atlantic, and only one twentieth the salinity of the Great Salt Lake.

When we moved to our second camp the Tejada brothers preferred to
let their mules rest in the Puyusca Valley, where there was excellent alfalfa
forage. The *arrieros* engaged at their own expense a pack train which consisted chiefly of Parinacochas burros. It is the custom hereabouts to enclose
the packs in large-meshed nets made of rawhide which are then fastened
to the pack animal by a surcingle. The Indians who came with the burro
train were pleasant-faced, sturdy fellows, dressed in "store clothes" and
straw hats. Their burros were as cantankerous as donkeys can be, never frac-
tious or flighty, but stubbornly resisting, step by step, every effort to haul
them near the loads.

Our second camp was near the village of Incahuasi, "the house of the
Inca," at the northwestern corner of the basin. Raimondi visited it in 1863.
The representative of the owner of Parinacochas occupies one of the houses.
The other buildings are used only during the third week in August, at the
time of the annual fair. In the now deserted plaza were many low stone

rectangles partly covered with adobe and ready to be converted into booths. The plaza was surrounded by long, thatched buildings of adobe and stone, mostly of rough ashlars. A few ashlars showed signs of having been carefully dressed by ancient stonemasons. Some loose ashlars weighed half a ton and had baffled the attempts of modern builders.

In constructing the large church, advantage was taken of a beautifully laid wall of close-fitting ashlars. Incahuasi was well named; there had been at one time an Inca house here, possibly a temple—lakes were once objects of worship—or rest-house, constructed in order to enable the chiefs and tax-gatherers to travel comfortably over the vast domains of the Incas. We found the slopes of the hills of the Parinacochas Basin to be well covered with remains of ancient terraces. Probably potatoes and other root crops were once raised here in fairly large quantities. Perhaps deforestation and subsequent increased aridity might account for the desertion of these once-cultivated lands. The hills west of the lake are intersected by a few dry gulches in which are caves that have been used as burial places. The caves had at one time been walled in with rocks laid in adobe, but these walls had been partly broken down so as to permit the sepulchers to be rifled of whatever objects of value they might have contained. We found nine or ten skulls lying loose in the rubble of the caves. One of the skulls seemed to have been trepanned.

On top of the ridge are the remains of an ancient road, fifty feet wide, a broad grassy way through fields of loose stones. No effort had been made at grading or paving this road, and there was no evidence of its having been used in recent times. It runs from the lake across the ridge in a westerly direction toward a broad valley, where there are many terraces and cultivated fields; it is not far from Nasca. Probably the stones were picked up and piled on each side to save time in driving caravans of llamas across the stony ridges. The llama dislikes to step over any obstacle, even a very low wall. The grassy roadway would certainly encourage the supercilious beasts to proceed in the desired direction.

In many places on the hills were to be seen outlines of large and small rock circles and shelters erected by herdsmen for temporary protection against the sudden storms of snow and hail which come up with unexpected fierceness at this elevation (12,000 feet). The shelters were in a very ruinous state. They were made of rough, scoriaceous lava rocks. The circular enclosures varied from 8 to 25 feet in diameter. Most of them showed no evidences whatever of recent occupation. The smaller walls may have been the foundation of small circular huts. The larger walls were probably intended as corrals, to keep alpacas and llamas from straying at night and to guard against wolves or coyotes. I confess to being quite mystified as to the age of these remains. It is possible that they represent a settlement of shepherds within historic times, although, from the shape and size of the walls, I am inclined to doubt this. The shelters may have been built by the herdsmen of the Incas. Anyhow, those on the hills west of Parinacochas had not been used for a long time. Nasca, which is not very far away to the northwest, was the center of one of the most artistic pre-Inca cultures in Peru. It is famous for its very delicate pottery.

Our third camp was on the south side of the lake. Near us the traces of the ancient road led to the ruins of two large, circular corrals, substantiating my belief that this curious roadway was intended to keep the llamas from straying at will over the pasture lands. On the south shores of the lake there were more signs of occupation than on the north, although there is nothing so clearly belonging to the time of the Incas as the ashlars and finely built wall at Incahuasi. On top of one of the rocky promontories we found the rough stone foundations of the walls of a little village. The slopes of the promontory were nearly precipitous on three sides. Forty or fifty very primitive dwellings had been at one time huddled together here in a position which could easily be defended. We found among the ruins a few crude potsherds and some bits of obsidian. There was nothing about the ruins of the little hill village to give any indication of Inca origin. Probably it goes back to pre-Inca days. No one could tell us anything about it. If there were traditions concerning it they were well concealed by the silent, superstitious shepherds of the vicinity. Possibly it was regarded as an unlucky spot, cursed by the gods.

The neighboring slopes showed faint evidences of having been roughly terraced and cultivated. The *tutu* potato would grow here, a hardy variety not edible in the fresh state, but considered highly desirable for making potato flour after having been repeatedly frozen and its bitter juices all extracted. So would other highland root crops of the Peruvians, such as the *oca*, a relative of our sheep sorrel, the *añu*, a kind of nasturtium, and the *ullucu* (*ullucus tuberosus*).

On the flats near the shore were large corrals still kept in good repair. New walls were being built by the Indians at the time of our visit. Near the southeast corner of the lake were a few modern huts built of stone and adobe, with thatched roofs, inhabited by drovers and shepherds. We saw more cattle at the east end of the lake than elsewhere, but they seemed to prefer the sweet water grasses of the lake to the tough bunch-grass on the slopes of Sarasara.

Viscachas were common amongst the gray lichen-covered rocks. They are hunted for their beautiful pearly gray fur, the "chinchilla" of commerce; they are also very good eating, so they have disappeared from the more accessible parts of Peru. One rarely sees them, although they may be found on bleak uplands in the mountains of Uilcapampa, a region rarely visited by any one on account of treacherous bogs and deep tarns. Writers sometimes call *viscachas* "rabbit-squirrels." They have large, rounded ears, long hind legs, a long, bushy tail, and do look like a cross between a rabbit and a gray squirrel.

Surmounting one of the higher ridges one day, I came suddenly upon an unusually large herd of wild vicuñas. It included more than one hundred individuals. Their relative fearlessness also testified to the remoteness of Parinacochas and the small amount of hunting that is done here. Vicuñas have never been domesticated, but are often hunted for their skins. Their silky fleece is even finer than alpaca. The more fleecy portions of their skins are sewed together to make quilts, as soft as eider down and of a golden brown color.

After Mr. Tucker finished his triangulation of the lake I told the *arrieros* to find the shortest road home. They smiled, murmured "Arequipa," and started south. We soon came to the rim of the Maraicasa Valley where, peeping up over one of the hills far to the south, we got a little glimpse of Coropuna. The Maraicasa Valley is well inhabited and there were many grain fields in sight, although few seemed to be terraced. The surrounding hills were smooth and well rounded and the valley bottom contained much alluvial land. We passed through it and, after dark, reached Sondor, a tiny hamlet inhabited by extremely suspicious and inhospitable drovers. In the darkness Don Pablo pleaded with the owners of a well-thatched hut, and told them how "important" we were. They were unwilling to give us any shelter, so we were forced to pitch our tent in the very rocky and dirty corral immediately in front of one of the huts, where pigs, dogs, and cattle annoyed us all night. If we had arrived before dark we might have received a different welcome. As a matter of fact, the herdsmen only showed the customary hostility of mountaineers and wilderness folk to those who do not arrive in the daytime, when they can be plainly seen and fully discussed.

The next morning we passed some fairly recent lava flows and noted also many curious rock forms caused by wind and sand erosion. We had now left the belt of grazing lands and once more come into the desert. At length we reached the rim of the mile-deep Caraveli Canyon and our eyes were gladdened at sight of the rich green oasis, a striking contrast to the barren walls of the canyon. As we descended the long, winding road we passed many fine specimens of tree cactus. At the foot of the steep descent we found ourselves separated from the nearest settlement by a very wide river, which it was necessary to ford. Neither of the Tejadas had ever been here before and its depth and dangers were unknown. Fortunately Pablo found a forlorn individual living in a tiny hut on the bank, who indicated which way lay safety. After an exciting two hours we finally got across to the desired shore. Animals and men were glad enough to leave the high, arid desert and enter the oasis of Caraveli with its luscious, green fields of alfalfa, its shady fig trees and tall eucalyptus. The air, pungent with the smell of rich vegetation, seemed cooler and more invigorating.

We found at Caraveli a modern British enterprise, the gold mine of "La Victoria." Mr. Prain, the Manager, and his associates at the camp gave us a cordial welcome, and a wonderful dinner which I shall long remember. After two months in the coastal desert it seemed like home. During the evening we learned of the difficulties Mr. Prain had had in bringing his machinery across the plateau from the nearest port. Our own troubles seemed as nothing. The cost of transporting on muleback each of the larger pieces of the quartz stamping-mill was equivalent to the price of a first-class pack mule. As a matter of fact, although it is only a two days' journey, pack animals' backs are not built to survive the strain of carrying pieces of machinery weighing *five hundred pounds* over a desert plateau up to an altitude of 4000 feet. Mules brought the machinery from the coast to the brink of the canyon, but no mule could possibly have carried it down the steep trail into Caraveli. Accordingly, a windlass had been constructed on the edge of the precipice and the machinery had been lowered, piece by piece, by block and tackle. Such was one of the obstacles with which these undaunted engineers had had to contend. Had the man who designed the machinery ever traveled with a pack train, climbing up and down over these rocky stairways called mountain trails, I am sure that he would have made his castings much smaller.

It is astonishing how often people who ship goods to the interior of South America fail to realize that no single piece should be any heavier than a pack animal can carry comfortably on *one side*. One hundred and fifty pounds ought to be the extreme limit of a unit. Even a large, strong mule will last only a few days on such trails as are shown in the accompanying illustration if the total weight of his cargo is over three hundred pounds. When a single piece weighs more than two hundred pounds it has to be balanced on the back of the animal. Then the load rocks, and chafes the unfortunate mule, besides causing great inconvenience and constant worry to the muleteers. As a matter of expediency it is better to have the individual units weigh about seventy-five pounds. Such a weight is easier for the *arrieros* to handle in the loading, unloading, and reloading that goes on all day long, particularly if the trail is up-and-down, as usually happens in the Andes. Furthermore, one seventy-five-pound unit makes a fair load for a man or a llama, two are right for a burro, and three for an average mule. Four can be loaded, if necessary, on a stout mule.

The hospitable mining engineers urged us to prolong our stay at "La Victoria," but we had to hasten on. Leaving the pleasant shade trees of Caraveli, we climbed the barren, desolate hills of coarse gravel and lava rock and left the canyon. We were surprised to find near the top of the rise the scattered foundations of fifty little circular or oval huts averaging eight feet in diameter. There was no water near here. Hardly a green thing of any sort was to be seen in the vicinity, yet here had once been a village. It seemed to belong to the same period as that found on the southern slopes of the Parinacochas Basin. The road was one of the worst we encountered any-where, being at times merely a rough, rocky trail over and among huge piles of lava blocks. Several of the larger boulders were covered with pictographs. They represented a serpent and a sun, besides men and animals.

Shortly afterwards we descended to the Rio Grande Valley at Callanga, where we pitched our camps among the most extensive ruins that I have seen in the coastal desert. They covered an area of one hundred acres, the houses being crowded closely together. It gave one a strange sensation to find such a very large metropolis in what is now a desolate region. The gen-eral appearance of Callanga was strikingly reminiscent of some of the large groups of ruins in our own Southwest. Nothing about it indicated Inca origin. There were no terraces in the vicinity. It is difficult to imagine what such a large population could have done here, or how they lived. The walls were of compact cobblestones, rough-laid and stuccoed with adobe and sand. Most of the stucco had come off. Some of the houses had seats, or small sleeping-platforms, built up at one end. Others contained two or three small cells, possibly storerooms, with neither doors nor windows. We

Indian girl at railroad station near Juliaca, Peru

found a number of burial cists—some square, others rounded—lined with small cobblestones. In one house, at the foot of "cellar stairs" we found a subterranean room, or tomb. The entrance to it was covered with a single stone lintel. In examining this tomb Mr. Tucker had a narrow escape from being bitten by a *boba*, a venomous snake, nearly three feet in length, with vicious mouth, long fangs like a rattlesnake, and a strikingly mottled skin. At one place there was a low pyramid less than ten feet in height. To its top led a flight of rude stone steps.

Among the ruins we found a number of broken stone dishes, rudely carved out of soft, highly porous, scoriaceous lava. The dishes must have been hard to keep clean! We also found a small stone mortar, probably used for grinding paint; a broken stone war club; and a broken compact stone mortar and pestle possibly used for grinding corn. Two stones, a foot and a half long, roughly rounded, with a shallow groove across the middle of the flatter sides, resembled sinkers used by fishermen to hold down large nets, although ten times larger than any I had ever seen used. Perhaps they were to tie down roofs in a gale. There were a few potsherds lying on the surface of the ground, so weathered as to have lost whatever decoration they once had. We did no excavating. Callanga offers an interesting field for archeological investigation. Unfortunately, we had heard nothing of it previously, came upon it unexpectedly, and had but little time to give it. After the first night camp in the midst of the dead city we made the discovery that although it seemed to be entirely deserted, it was, as a matter of fact, well populated! I was reminded of Professor T. D. Seymour's story of his studies in the ruins of ancient Greece. We wondered what the fleas live on ordinarily.

Our next stopping-place was the small town of Andaray, whose thatched houses are built chiefly of stone plastered with mud. Near it we encountered two men with a mule, which they said they were taking into town to sell and were willing to dispose of cheaply. The Tejadas could not resist the temptation to buy a good animal at a bargain, although the circumstances were suspicious. Drawing on us for six gold sovereigns, they smilingly added the new mule to the pack train; only to discover on reaching Chuquibamba that they had purchased it from thieves. We were able to clear our *arrieros* of any complicity in the theft. Nevertheless, the owner of the stolen mule was unwilling to pay anything for its return. So they lost their bargain and their gold. We spent one night in Chuquibamba, with our friend Señor Benavides, the sub-prefect, and once more took up the well-traveled route to Arequipa. We left the Majes Valley in the afternoon and, as before, spent the night crossing the desert.

About three o'clock in the morning—after we had been jogging steadily along for about twelve hours in the dark and quiet of the night, the only sound the shuffle of the mules' feet in the sand, the only sight an occasional crescent-shaped dune, dimly visible in the starlight—the eastern horizon began to be faintly illumined. The moon had long since set. Could this be the approach of dawn? Sunrise was not due for at least two hours. In the tropics there is little twilight preceding the day; "the dawn comes up like thunder." Surely the moon could not be going to rise again! What could be the meaning of the rapidly brightening eastern sky? While we watched and marveled, the pure white light grew brighter and brighter, until we cried out in ecstasy as a dazzling luminary rose majestically above the horizon. A splendor, neither of the sun nor of the moon, shone upon us. It was the morning star. For sheer beauty, "divine, enchanting ravishment," Venus that day surpassed anything I have ever seen. In the words of the great Eastern poet, who had often seen such a sight in the deserts of Asia, "the morning stars sang together and all the sons of God shouted for joy."

CHAPTER 5
TITICACA

*

AREQUIPA IS ONE of the pleasantest places in the world: mountain air, bright sunshine, warm days, cool nights, and a sparkling atmosphere dear to the hearts of star-gazers. The city lies on a plateau, surrounded by mighty snow-capped volcanoes, Chachani (20,000 ft.), El Misti (19,000 ft.), and Pichu Pichu (18,000 ft.). Arequipa has only one nightmare—earthquakes. About twice in a century the spirits of the sleeping volcanoes stir, roll over, and go to sleep again. But they shake the bed! And Arequipa rests on their bed. The possibility of a "*terremoto*" is always present in the subconscious mind of the Arequipeño.

One evening I happened to be dining with a friend at the hospitable Arequipa Club. Suddenly the windows rattled violently and we heard a loud explosion; at least that is what it sounded like to me. To the members of the club, however, it meant only one thing—an earthquake. Everybody rushed out; the streets were already crowded with hysterical people, crying, shouting, and running toward the great open plaza in front of the beautiful cathedral. Here some dropped on their knees in gratitude at having escaped from falling walls, others prayed to the god of earthquakes to spare their city. Yet no walls had fallen! In the business district a great column of black smoke was rising. Gradually it became known to the panic-stricken throngs that the noise and the trembling had not been due to an earthquake, but to an explosion in a large warehouse which had contained gasoline, kerosene, dynamite *and* giant powder!

In this city of 35,000 people, the second largest of Peru, fires are so very rare, not even annual, scarcely biennial, that there were no fire engines. A bucket brigade was formed and tried to quench the roaring furnace by dipping water from one of the *azequias*, or canals, that run through the streets. The fire continued to belch forth dense masses of smoke and flame. In any American city such a blaze would certainly become a great conflagration.

While the fire was at its height I went into the adjoining building to see whether any help could be rendered. To my utter amazement the surface of the well next to the fiery furnace was not even warm. Such is the result of building houses with massive walls of stone. Furthermore, the roofs in Arequipa are of tiles; consequently no harm was done by sparks. So, without a fire department, this really terrible fire was limited to one warehouse! The next day the newspapers talked about the "dire necessity" of securing fire engines. It was difficult for me to see what good a fire engine could have done. Nothing could have saved the warehouse itself once the fire got under way; and surely the houses next door would have suffered more had they been deluged with streams of water. The facts are almost incredible to an American. We take it as a matter of course that cities should have fires and explosions. In Arequipa everybody thought it was an earthquake!

A day's run by an excellent railroad takes one to Puno, the chief port of Lake Titicaca, elevation 12,500 feet. Puno boasts a soldier's monument and a new theater, really a "movie palace." There is a good harbor, although dredging is necessary to provide for steamers like the *Inca*. Repairs to the lake boats are made on a marine—or, rather, a *lacustrine*—railway. The bay of Puno grows quantities of *totoras*, giant bulrushes sometimes twelve feet long. Ages ago the lake dwellers learned to dry the *totoras*, tie them securely in long bundles, fasten the bundles together, turn up the ends, fix smaller bundles along the sides as a free-board, and so construct a fishing-boat, or *balsa*. Of course the *balsas* eventually become water-logged and spend a large part of their existence on the shore, drying in the sun. Even so, they are not very buoyant. I can testify that it is difficult to use them without getting one's shoes wet. As a matter of fact one should go barefooted, or wear sandals, as the natives do.

The *balsas* are clumsy, and difficult to paddle. The favorite method of locomotion is to pole or, when the wind favors, sail. The mast is an A-shaped contraption, twelve feet high, made of two light poles tied together and fastened, one to each side of the craft, slightly forward of amidships.

Poles are extremely scarce in this region—lumber has to be brought from Puget Sound, 6000 miles away—so nearly all the masts I saw were made of small pieces of wood spliced two or three times. To the apex of the "A" is attached a forked stick, over which run the halyards. The rectangular "sail" is nothing more nor less than a large mat made of rushes. A short forestay fastened to the sides of the "A" about four feet above the hull prevents the mast from falling when the sail is hoisted. The main halyards take the place of a backstay. The *balsas* cannot beat to windward, but behave very well in shallow water with a favoring breeze. When the wind is contrary the boatmen must pole. They are extremely careful not to fall overboard, for the water in the lake is cold, 55° F., and none of them know how to swim. Lake Titicaca itself never freezes over, although during the winter ice forms at night on the shallow bays and near the shore.

When the Indians wish to go in the shallowest waters they use a very small *balsa* not over eight feet long, barely capable of supporting the weight of one man. On the other hand, large *balsas* constructed for use in crossing the rough waters of the deeper portions of the lake are capable of carrying a dozen people and their luggage. Once I saw a ploughman and his team of oxen being ferried across the lake on a bulrush raft. To give greater security two *balsas* are sometimes fastened together in the fashion of a double canoe.

One of the more highly speculative of the Bolivian writers, Señor Posnansky, of La Paz, believes that gigantic *balsas* were used in bringing ten-ton monoliths across the lake to Tiahuanaco. This theory is based on the assumption that Titicaca was once very much higher than it is now, a hypothesis which has not commended itself to modern geologists or geographers. Dr. Isaiah Bowman and Professor Herbert Gregory, who have studied its geology and physiography, have not been able to find any direct evidence of former high levels for Lake Titicaca, or of its having been connected with the ocean.

Nevertheless, Señor Posnansky believes that Lake Titicaca was once a salt sea which became separated from the ocean as the Andes rose. The fact that the lake fishes are fresh-water, rather than marine, forms does not bother him. Señor Posnansky pins his faith to a small dried seahorse once given him by a Titicaca fisherman. He seems to forget that dried specimens of marine life, including starfish, are frequently offered for sale in the Andes by the dealers in primitive medicines who may be found in almost every market-place. Probably Señor Posnansky's seahorse was brought from the ocean by some particularly enterprising trader. Although starfish are common enough in the Andes and a seahorse has actually found its resting-place in La Paz, this does not alter the fact that scientific investigators have never found any strictly marine fauna in Lake Titicaca. On the other hand, it has two or three kinds of edible fresh-water fish. One of them belongs to a species found in the Rimac River near Lima. It seems to me entirely possible that the Incas, with their scorn of the difficulties of carrying heavy burdens over seemingly impossible trails, might have deliberately transplanted the desirable fresh-water fishes of the Rimac River to Lake Titicaca.

Polo de Ondegardo, who lived in Cuzco in 1560, says that the Incas used to bring fresh fish from the sea by special runners, and that "they have records in their *quipus* of the fish having been brought from Tumbez, a distance of more than three hundred leagues." The actual transference of water jars containing the fish would have offered no serious obstacle whatever to the Incas, provided the idea happened to appeal to them as desirable. Yet I may be as far wrong as Señor Posnansky! At any rate, the romantic stories of a gigantic inland sea, vastly more extensive than the present lake and actually surrounding the ancient city of Tiahuanaco, must be treated with respectful skepticism.

Tiahuanaco, at the southern end of Lake Titicaca, in Bolivia, is famous for the remains of a pre-Inca civilization. Unique among prehistoric remains in the highlands of Peru or Bolivia are its carved monolithic images. Although they have suffered from weathering and from vandalism, enough remains to show that they represent clothed human figures. The richly decorated girdles and long tunics are carved in low relief with an intricate pattern. While some of the designs are undoubtedly symbolic of the rank, achievements, or attributes of the divinities or chiefs here portrayed, there is nothing hieroglyphic. The images are stiff and show no appreciation of the beauty of the human form. Probably the ancient artists never had an opportunity to study the human body. In Andean villages, even little children do not go naked as they do among primitive peoples who live in warm climates. The Highlanders of Peru and Bolivia are always heavily clothed, day and night. Forced by their climate to seek comfort in the amount and thickness of their apparel, they have developed an excessive modesty in regard to bodily exposure which is in striking contrast to people who live on the warm sands of the South Seas. Inca sculptors and potters rarely employed the human body as a *motif*. Tiahuanaco is pre-Inca, yet even here the images are clothed. They were not represented as clothed in order to make easier the work of the sculptor. His carving shows he had great skill, was observant, and had true artistic feeling. Apparently the taboo against "nakedness" was too much for him.

Among the thirty-six islands in Lake Titicaca, some belong to Peru, others to Bolivia. Two of the latter, Titicaca and Koati, were peculiarly venerated in Inca days. They are covered with artificial terraces, most of which are still used by the Indian farmers of to-day. On both islands there are ruins of important Inca structures. On Titicaca Island I was shown two caves, out of which, say the Indians, came the sun and moon at their creation. These caves are not large enough for a man to stand upright, but to a people who do not appreciate the size of the heavenly bodies it requires no stretch of the imagination to believe that those bright disks came forth from caves eight feet wide. The myth probably originated with dwellers on the western shore of the lake who would often see the sun or moon rise over this island. On an ancient road that runs across the island my native guide pointed out the "footprints of the sun and moon"—two curious effects of erosion which bear a distant resemblance to the footprints of giants twenty or thirty feet tall.

The present-day Indians, known as Aymaras, seem to be hardworking and fairly cheerful. The impression which Bandelier gives, in his "Islands of Titicaca and Koati," of the degradation and surly character of these Indians was not apparent at the time of my short visit in 1915. It is quite possible, however, that if I had to live among the Indians, as he did for several months, digging up their ancient places of worship, disturbing their superstitious prejudices, and possibly upsetting, in their minds, the proper balance between wet weather and dry, I might have brought upon myself uncivil looks and rough, churlish treatment such as he experienced. In judging the attitude of mind of the natives of Titicaca one should remember that they live under most trying conditions of climate and environment. During several months of the year everything is dried up and parched. The brilliant sun of the tropics, burning mercilessly through the rarefied air, causes the scant vegetation to wither. Then come torrential rains. I shall never forget my first experience on Lake Titicaca, when the steamer encountered a rain squall. The resulting deluge actually came through the decks. Needless to say, such downpours tend to wash away the soil which the farmers have painfully gathered for field or garden. The sun in the daytime is extremely hot, yet the difference in temperature between sun and shade is excessive. Furthermore, the winds at night are very damp; the cold is intensely penetrating. Fuel is exceedingly scarce, there is barely enough for cooking purposes, and none for artificial heat.

Food is hard to get. Few crops can be grown at 12,500 feet. Some barley is raised, but the soil is lacking in nitrogen. The principal crop is the bitter white potato, which, after being frozen and dried, becomes the insipid *chuño*, chief reliance of the poorer families. The Inca system of bringing guano from the islands of the Pacific coast has long since been abandoned. There is no money to pay for modern fertilizers. Consequently, crops are poor. On Titicaca Island I saw native women, who had just harvested their maize, engaged in shucking and drying ears of corn which varied in length from one to three *inches*. To be sure this miniature corn has the advantage of maturing in sixty days, but good soil and fertilizers would double its size and productiveness.

Naturally these Indians always feel themselves at the mercy of the elements. Either a long rainy season or a drought may cause acute hunger and extreme suffering. Consequently, one must not blame the Bolivian or Peruvian Highlander if he frequently appears to be sullen and morose. On the other hand, one ought not to praise Samoans for being happy, hospitable, and light-hearted. Those fortunate Polynesians are surrounded by warm waters in which they can always enjoy a swim, trees from which delicious food can always be obtained, and cocoanuts from which cooling drinks are secured without cost. Who could not develop cheerfulness under such conditions?

On the small island, Koati, some of the Inca stonework is remarkably good, and has several unusual features, such as the elaboration of the large, re-entrant, ceremonial niches formed by step-topped arches, one within the other. Small ornamental niches are used to break the space between these recesses and the upper corners of the whole rectangle containing them. Also unusual are the niches between the doorways, made in the form of an elaborate quadrate cross. It might seem at first glance as though this feature showed Spanish influence, since a Papal cross is created by the shadow cast in the intervening recessed courses within their design. As a matter of fact, the cross nowy quadrant is a natural outcome of using for ornamental purposes the step-shaped design, both erect and inverted. All over the land of the Incas one finds flights of steps or terraces used repeatedly for ornamental or ceremonial purposes. Some stairs are large enough to be used by man; others are in miniature. Frequently the steps were cut into the sacred boulders consecrated to ancestor worship. It was easy for an Inca architect, accustomed to the stairway *motif*, to have conceived these curious doorways on Koati and also the cross-like niches between them, even if he had never seen any representation of a Papal cross, or a cross nowy quadrant. My friend, Mr. Bancel La Farge, has also suggested a striking resemblance which the sedilia-like niches bear to Arabic or Moorish architecture, as shown, for instance, in the Court of the Lions in the Alhambra. The step-topped arch is distinctly Oriental in form, yet flights of steps or terraces are also thoroughly Incaic.

The principal structure on Koati was built around three sides of a small plaza, constructed on an artificial terrace in a slight depression on the eastern side of the island. The fourth side is open and affords a magnificent view of the lake and the wonderful snow-covered Cordillera Real, 200 miles long and nowhere less than 17,000 feet high. This range of lofty snow-peaks of surpassing beauty culminates in Mt. Sorata, 21,520 feet high. To the worshipers of the sun and moon, who came to the sacred islands for some of their most elaborate religious ceremonies, the sight of those heavenly luminaries, rising over the majestic snow mountains, their glories reflected in the shining waters of the lake, must have been a sublime spectacle. On such occasions the little plaza would indeed have been worth seeing. We may imagine the gayly caparisoned Incas, their faces lit up by the colors of "rosy-fingered dawn, daughter of the morning," their ceremonial formation sharply outlined against the high, decorated walls of the buildings behind them. Perhaps the rulers and high priests had special stations in front of the large, step-topped niches. One may be sure that a people who were fond of bright colors, who were able to manufacture exquisite textiles, and who loved to decorate their garments with spangles and disks of beaten gold, would have lost no opportunity for making the ancient ceremonies truly resplendent.

On the peninsula of Copacabana, opposite the sacred islands, a great annual pageant is still staged every August. Although at present connected with a pious pilgrimage to the shrine of the miraculous image of the "Virgin of Copacabana," this vivid spectacle, the most celebrated fair in all South America, has its origin in the dim past. It comes after the maize is harvested and corresponds to our Thanksgiving festival. The scene is laid in the plaza in front of a large, bizarre church. During the first ten days in August there are gathered here thousands of the mountain folk from far and near. Everything dear to the heart of the Aymara Indian is offered for sale, including quantities of his favorite beverages. Traders, usually women, sit in long rows on blankets laid on the cobblestone pavement. Some of them are protected from the sun by primitive umbrellas, consisting of a square cotton sheet stretched over a bamboo frame. In one row are those traders who sell parched and popped corn; in another those who deal in sandals and shoes, the simple gear of the humblest wayfarer and the elaborately decorated high-laced boots affected by the wealthy Chola women of La Paz. In another row are the dealers in Indian blankets; still another is devoted to such trinkets as one might expect to find in a "needle-and-thread" shop at home. There are stolid Aymara peddlers with scores of bamboo flutes varying in size from a piccolo to a bassoon; the hat merchants, with piles of freshly made native felts, warranted to last for at least a year; and vendors of aniline dyes. The fabrics which have come to us from Inca times are colored with beautifully soft vegetable dyes. Among Inca ruins one may find small stone mortars, in which the primitive pigments were ground and mixed with infinite care. Although the modern Indian still prefers the product of hand looms, he has been quick to adopt the harsh aniline dyes, which are not only easier to secure, but produce more striking results.

As a citizen of Connecticut it gave me quite a start to see, carelessly exposed to the weather on the rough cobblestones of the plaza, bright new hardware from New Haven and New Britain—locks, keys, spring scales, bolts, screw eyes, hooks, and other "wooden nutmegs."

At the tables of the "money-changers," just outside of the sacred enclosure, are the real money-makers, who give nothing for something. Thimble-riggers and three-card-monte-men do a brisk business and stand ready to fleece the guileless native or the unsuspecting foreigner. The operators may wear ragged ponchos and appear to be incapable of deep designs, but they know all the tricks of the trade! The most striking feature of the fair is the presence of various Aymara secret societies, whose members, wearing repulsive masks, are clad in the most extraordinary costumes which can be invented by primitive imaginations. Each society has its own uniform, made up of tinsels and figured satins, tin-foil, gold and silver leaf, gaudy textiles, magnificent epaulets bearing large golden stars on a background of silver decorated with glittering gems of colored glass; tinted "ostrich" plumes of many colors sticking straight up eighteen inches above the heads of their wearers, gaudy ribbons, beruffled bodices, puffed sleeves, and slashed trunks. Some of these strange costumes are actually reminiscent of the sixteenth century. The wearers are provided with flutes, whistles, cymbals, flageolets, snare drums, and rattles, or other noise-makers. The result is an indescribable hubbub; a garish human kaleidoscope, accompanied by fiendish clamor and unmusical noises which fairly outstrip a dozen jazz bands. It is bedlam let loose, a scene of wild uproar and confusion.

The members of one group were dressed to represent female angels, their heads tightly turbaned so as to bear the maximum number of tall, waving, variegated plumes. On their backs were gaudy wings resembling the butterflies of children's pantomimes. Many wore colored goggles. They marched solemnly around the plaza, playing on bamboo flageolets, their plaintive tunes drowned in the din of big bass drums and blatant trumpets. In an eddy in the seething crowd was a placid-faced Aymara, bedecked in the most tawdry manner with gewgaws from Birmingham or Manchester, sedately playing a melancholy tune on a rustic syrinx or Pan's pipe, charmingly made from little tubes of bamboo from eastern Bolivia.

At the close of the festival, on a Sunday afternoon, the costumes disappear and there occurs a bull-baiting. Strong temporary barriers are erected at the corners of the plaza; householders bar their doors. A riotous crowd, composed of hundreds of pleasure-seekers, well fortified with Dutch courage, gathers for the fray. All are ready to run helter-skelter in every direction should the bull take it into his head to charge toward them. It is not a bull-fight. There are no *picadors*, armed with lances to prick the bull to madness; no *banderilleros*, with barbed darts; no heroic *matador*, ready with shining blade to give a mad and weary bull the *coup de grace*. Here all is fun and frolic. To be sure, the bull is duly annoyed by boastful boys or drunken Aymaras, who prod him with sticks and shake bright ponchos in his face until he dashes after his tormentors and causes a mighty scattering of some spectators, amid shrieks of delight from everybody else. When one animal gets tired, another is brought on. There is no chance of a bull being wounded or seriously hurt. At the time of our visit the only animal who seemed at all anxious to do real damage was let alone. He showed no disposition to charge at random into the crowds. The spectators surrounded the plaza so thickly that he could not distinguish any one particular enemy on whom to vent his rage. He galloped madly after any individual who crossed the plaza. Five or six bulls were let loose during the excitement, but no harm was done, and every one had an uproariously good time.

Such is the spectacle of Copacabana, a mixture of business and pleasure, pagan and Christian, Spain and Titicaca. Bedlam is not pleasant to one's ears; yet to see the staid mountain herdsmen, attired in plumes, petticoats, epaulets, and goggles, blowing mightily with puffed-out lips on bamboo flageolets, is worth a long journey.

CHAPTER 6

The Vilcanota Country and the Peruvian Highlanders

✳

IN THE NORTHERNMOST part of the Titicaca Basin are the grassy foothills of the Cordillera Vilcanota, where large herds of alpacas thrive on the sweet, tender pasturage. Santa Rosa is the principal town. Here wool-buyers come to bid for the clip. The high prices which alpaca fleece commands have brought prosperity. Excellent blankets, renowned in southern Peru for their weight and texture, are made here on hand looms. Notwithstanding the altitude—nearly as great as the top of Pike's Peak—the stocky inhabitants of Santa Rosa are hardy, vigorous, and energetic. Ricardo Charaja, the best Quichua assistant we ever had, came from Santa Rosa. Nearly all the citizens are of pure Indian stock.

They own many fine llamas. There is abundant pasturage and the llamas are well cared for by the Indians, who become personally attached to their flocks and are loath to part with any of the individuals. Once I attempted through a Cuzco acquaintance to secure the skin and skeleton of a fine llama for the Yale Museum. My friend was favorably known and spoke the Quichua language fluently. He offered a good price and obtained from various llama owners promises to bring the hide and bones of one of their "camels" for shipment; but they never did. Apparently they regarded it as unlucky to kill a llama, and none happened to die at the right time. The llamas never show affection for their masters, as horses often do. On the other hand I have never seen a llama kick or bite at his owner.

The llama was the only beast of burden known in either North or South America before Columbus. It was found by the Spaniards in all parts of Inca

Land. Its small two-toed feet, with their rough pads, enable it to walk easily on slopes too rough or steep for even a nimble-footed, mountain-bred mule. It has the reputation of being an unpleasant pet, due to its ability to sneeze or spit for a considerable distance a small quantity of acrid saliva. When I was in college Barnum's Circus came to town. The menagerie included a dozen llamas, whose supercilious expression, inoffensive looks, and small size—they are only three feet high at the shoulder—tempted some little urchins to tease them. When the llamas felt that the time had come for reprisals, their aim was straight and the result a precipitate retreat. Their tormentors, howling and rubbing their eyes, had to run home and wash their faces. Curiously enough, in the two years which I have spent in the Peruvian highlands I have never seen a llama so attack a single human being. On the other hand, when I was in Santa Rosa in 1915 some one had a tame vicuña which was perfectly willing to sneeze straight at any stranger who came within twenty feet of it, even if one's motive was nothing more annoying than scientific curiosity. The vicuña is the smallest American "camel," yet its long, slender neck, small head, long legs, and small body, from which hangs long, feathery fleece, make it look more like an ostrich than a camel.

In the churchyard of Santa Rosa are two or three gnarled trees which have been carefully preserved for centuries as objects of respect and veneration. Some travelers have thought that 14,000 feet is above the tree line, but the presence of these trees at Santa Rosa would seem to show that the use of the words "tree line" is a misnomer in the Andes. Mr. Cook believes that the Peruvian plateau, with the exception of the coastal deserts, was once well covered with forests. When man first came into the Andes, everything except rocky ledges, snow fields, and glaciers was covered with forest growth. Although many districts are now entirely treeless, Mr. Cook found that the conditions of light, heat, and moisture, even at the highest elevations, are sufficient to support the growth of trees; also that there is ample fertility of soil. His theories are well substantiated by several isolated tracts of forests which I found growing alongside of glaciers at very high elevations. One forest in particular, on the slopes of Mt. Soiroccocha, has been accurately determined by Mr. Bumstead to be over 15,000 feet above sea level. It is cut off from the inhabited valley by rock falls and precipices, so it has not been available for fuel. Virgin forests are not known to exist in the Peruvian highlands on any lands which could have been cultivated. A certain amount of natural reforestation with native trees is taking place on

ALPACA NEAR SANTA ROSA, PERU

abandoned agricultural terraces in some of the high valleys. Although these trees belong to many different species and families, Mr. Cook found that they all have this striking peculiarity—when cut down they sprout readily from the stumps and are able to survive repeated pollarding; remarkable evidence of the fact that the primeval forests of Peru were long ago cut down for fuel or burned over for agriculture.

Near the Santa Rosa trees is a tall bell-tower. The sight of a picturesque belfry with four or five bells of different sizes hanging each in its respective window makes a strong appeal. It is quite otherwise on Sunday mornings when these same bells, "out of tune with themselves," or actually cracked, are all rung at the same time. The resulting clangor and din is unforgettable. I presume the Chinese would say it was intended to drive away the devils—and surely such noise must be "thoroughly uncongenial even to the most irreclaimable devil," as Lord Frederick Hamilton said of the Canton practices. Church bells in the United States and England are usually sweet-toned and intended to invite the hearer to come to service, or else they ring out in joyous peals to announce some festive occasion. There is nothing inviting or joyous about the bells in southern Peru. Once in a while one may hear a bell of deep, sweet tone, like that of the great bell in Cuzco, which is tolled when the last sacrament is being administered to a dying

Christian; but the general idea of bell-ringers in this part of the world seems to be to make the greatest possible amount of racket and clamor. On popular saints' days this is accompanied by firecrackers, aerial bombs, and other noise-making devices which again remind one of Chinese folkways. Perhaps it is merely that fundamental fondness for making a noise which is found in all healthy children.

On Sunday afternoon the plaza of Santa Rosa was well filled with Quichua holiday-makers, many of whom had been imbibing freely of *chicha*, a mild native brew usually made from ripe corn. The crowd was remarkably good-natured and given to an unusual amount of laughter and gayety. For them Sunday is truly a day of rest, recreation, and sociability. On week days, most of them, even the smaller boys, are off on the mountain pastures, watching the herds whose wool brings prosperity to Santa Rosa. One sometimes finds the mountain Indians on Sunday afternoon sodden, thoroughly soaked with *chicha*, and inclined to resent the presence of inquisitive strangers; not so these good folk of Santa Rosa.

To be sure, the female vendors of eggs, potatoes, peppers, and sundry native vegetables, squatting in two long rows on the plaza, did not enjoy being photographed, but the men and boys crowded eagerly forward, very much interested in my endeavors. Some of the Indian *alcaldes*, local magistrates elected yearly to serve as the responsible officials for villages or tribal precincts, were very helpful and, armed with their large, silver-mounted staffs of office, tried to bring the shy, retiring women of the market-place to stand in a frightened, disgruntled, barefooted group before the camera. The women were dressed in the customary tight bodices, heavy woolen skirts, and voluminous petticoats of the plateau. Over their shoulders were pinned heavy woolen shawls, woven on hand looms. On their heads were reversible "pancake" hats made of straw, covered on the wet-weather side with coarse woolen stuff and on the fair-weather side with tinsel and velveteen. In accordance with local custom, tassels and fringes hung down on both sides. It is said that the first Inca ordered the dresses of each village to be different, so that his officials might know to which tribe an Indian belonged. It was only with great difficulty and by the combined efforts of a good-natured priest, the *gobernador* or mayor, and the *alcaldes* that a dozen very reluctant females were finally persuaded to face the camera. The expression of their faces was very eloquent. Some were highly indignant, others looked foolish or supercilious, two or three were thoroughly frightened, not knowing what evil might befall them next. Not one gave any evidence of enjoying it or taking the matter as a good joke, although that was the attitude assumed by all their male acquaintances. In fact, some of the men were so anxious to have their pictures taken that they followed us about and posed on the edge of every group.

Men and boys all wore knitted woolen caps, with ear flaps, which they seldom remove either day or night. On top of these were large felt hats, turned up in front so as to give a bold aspect to their husky wearers. Over their shoulders were heavy woolen ponchos, decorated with bright stripes. Their trousers end abruptly halfway between knee and ankle, a convenient style for herdsmen who have to walk in the long, dewy grasses of the plateau. These "high-water" pantaloons do not look badly when worn with sandals, as is the usual custom; but since this was Sunday all the well-to-do men had put on European boots, which did not come up to the bottom of their trousers and produced a singular effect, hardly likely to become fashionable.

The prosperity of the town was also shown by corrugated iron roofs. Far less picturesque than thatch or tile, they require less attention and give greater satisfaction during the rainy season. They can also be securely bolted to the rafters. On this wind-swept plateau we frequently noticed that a thatched roof was held in place by ropes passed over the house and weights resting on the roof. Sometimes to the peak of a gable are fastened crosses, tiny flags, or the skulls of animals—probably to avert the Evil Eye or bring good luck. Horseshoes do not seem to be in demand. Horses' skulls, however, are deemed very efficacious.

On the rim of the Titicaca Basin is La Raya. The watershed is so level that it is almost impossible to say whether any particular raindrop will eventually find itself in Lake Titicaca or in the Atlantic Ocean. The water from a spring near the railroad station of Araranca flows definitely to the north. This spring may be said to be one of the sources of the Urubamba River, an important affluent of the Ucayali and also of the Amazon, but I never have heard it referred to as "the source of the Amazon" except by an adventurous lecturer, Captain Blank, whose moving picture entertainment bore the alluring title, "From the Source to the Mouth of the Amazon." As most of his pictures of wild animals "in the jungle" looked as though they were taken in the zoölogical gardens at Para, and the exciting tragedies of his canoe trip were actually staged near a friendly *hacienda* at Santa Ana, less than a week's journey from Cuzco, it is perhaps unnecessary to censure him for giving this particular little spring such a pretentious title.

The Urubamba River is known by various names to the people who live on its banks. The upper portion is sometimes spoken of as the Vilcanota, a term which applies to a lake as well as to the snow-covered peaks of the cordillera in this vicinity. The lower portion was called by the Incas the Uilca or Uilcamayu.

Near the water-parting of La Raya I noticed the remains of an interesting wall which may have served centuries ago to divide the Incas of Cuzco from the Collas or warlike tribes of the Titicaca Basin. In places the wall has been kept in repair by the owners of grazing lands, but most of it can be but dimly traced across the valley and up the neighboring slopes to the cliffs of the Cordillera Vilcanota. It was built of rough stones. Near the historic wall are the ruins of ancient houses, possibly once occupied by an Inca garrison. I observed no ashlars among the ruins nor any evidence of careful masonry. It seems to me likely that it was a hastily thrown-up fortification serving for a single military campaign, rather than any permanent affair like the Roman wall of North Britain or the Great Wall of China. We know from tradition that war was frequently waged between the peoples of the Titicaca Basin and those of the Urubamba and Cuzco valleys. It is possible that this is a relic of one of those wars.

On the other hand, it may be much older than the Incas. Montesinos,[1] one of the best early historians, tells us of Titu Yupanqui, Pachacuti VI, sixty-second of the Peruvian Amautas, rulers who long preceded the Incas. Against Pachacuti VI there came (about 800 A.D.) large hordes of fierce soldiers from the south and east, laying waste fields and capturing cities and towns; evidently barbarian migrations which appear to have continued for some time. During these wars the ancient civilization, which had been built up with so much care and difficulty during the preceding twenty centuries, was seriously threatened. Pachacuti VI, more religious than warlike, ruler of a people whose great achievements had been agricultural rather than military, was frightened by his soothsayers and priests; they told him of many bad omens. Instead of inducing him to follow a policy of military preparedness, he was urged to make sacrifices to the deities. Nevertheless he ordered his captains to fortify the strategic points and make preparations for defense. The invaders may have come from Argentina. It is possible that they were spurred on by hunger and famine caused by the gradual exhaustion of forested areas and the subsequent spread of untillable grasslands on the great *pampas*. Montesinos indicates that many of the people who came up into the highlands at that time were seeking arable lands for their crops and were "fleeing from a race of giants"—possibly Patagonians or Araucanians—who had expelled them from their own lands. On their journey they had passed over plains, swamps, and jungles. It is obvious that a great readjustment of the aborigines was in progress. The governors of the districts through which these hordes passed were not able to summon enough strength to resist them. Pachacuti VI assembled the larger part of his army near the pass of La Raya and awaited the approach of the enemy. If the accounts given in Montesinos are true, this wall near La Raya may have been built about 1100 years ago, by the chiefs who were told to "fortify the strategic points."

Certainly the pass of La Raya, long the gateway from the Titicaca Basin to the important cities and towns of the Urubamba Basin, was the key to the situation. It is probable that Pachacuti VI drew up his army behind this wall. His men were undoubtedly armed with slings, the weapon most familiar to the highland shepherds. The invaders, however, carried bows and arrows, more effective arms, swifter, more difficult to see, less easy to dodge. As Pachacuti VI was carried over the field of battle on a golden stretcher, encouraging his men, he was killed by an arrow. His army was routed. Montesinos states that only five hundred escaped. Leaving behind their wounded, they fled to "Tampu-tocco," a healthy place where there was a cave, in which they hid the precious body of their ruler. Most writers believe this to be at Paccaritampu where there are caves under an interesting carved rock. There is no place in Peru to-day which still bears the name of Tampu-tocco. To try and identify it with some of the ruins which do exist, and whose modern names are not found in the early Spanish writers, has been one of the principal objects of my expeditions to Peru, as will be described in subsequent chapters.

Near the watershed of La Raya we saw great flocks of sheep and alpacas, numerous corrals, and the thatched-roofed huts of herdsmen. The Quichua women are never idle. One often sees them engaged in the manufacture of textiles—shawls, girdles, ponchos, and blankets—on hand looms fastened to stakes driven into the ground. When tending flocks or walking along the road they are always winding or spinning yarn. Even the men and older children are sometimes thus engaged. The younger children, used as shepherds as soon as they reach the age of six or seven, are rarely expected to do much except watch their charges. Some of them were accompanied by long-haired *suncca* shepherd dogs, as large as Airedales, but very cowardly, given to barking and slinking away. It is claimed that the *sunccas*, as well as

URUBAMBA VALLEY, PERU

two other varieties, were domesticated by the Incas. None of them showed any desire to make the acquaintance of "Checkers," my faithful Airedale. Their masters, however, were always interested to see that "Checkers" could understand English. They had never seen a dog that could understand anything but Quichua!

On the hillside near La Raya, Mr. Cook, Mr. Gilbert, and I visited a healthy potato field at an elevation of 14,500 feet, a record altitude for potatoes. When commencing to plough or spade a potato field on the high slopes near here, it is the custom of the Indians to mark it off into squares, by "furrows" about fifteen feet apart. The Quichuas commence their task soon after daybreak. Due to the absence of artificial lighting and the discomfort of rising in the bitter cold before dawn, their wives do not prepare breakfast before ten o'clock, at which time it is either brought from home in covered earthenware vessels or cooked in the open fields near where the men are working.

We came across one energetic landowner supervising a score or more of Indians who were engaged in "ploughing" a potato field. Although he was dressed in European garb and was evidently a man of means and intelligence, and near the railroad, there were no modern implements in sight. We found that it is difficult to get Indians to use any except the implements of their ancestors. The process of "ploughing" this field was undoubtedly one that had been used for centuries, probably long before the Spanish Conquest. The men, working in unison and in a long row, each armed with a primitive spade or "foot plough," to the handle of which footholds were lashed, would, at a signal, leap forward with a shout and plunge their spades into the turf. Facing each pair of men was a girl or woman whose duty it was to turn the clods over by hand. The men had taken off their ponchos, so as to secure greater freedom of action, but the women were fully clothed as usual, modesty seeming to require them even to keep heavy shawls over their shoulders. Although the work was hard and painful, the toil was lightened by the joyous contact of community activity. Every one worked with a will. There appeared to be a keen desire among the workers to keep up with the procession. Those who fell behind were subjected to good-natured teasing. Community work is sometimes pleasant, even though it appears to require a strong directing hand. The "boss" was right there. Such practices would never suit those who love independence.

In the centuries of Inca domination there was little opportunity for individual effort. Private property was not understood. Everything belonged to the government. The crops were taken by the priests, the Incas and the nobles. The people were not as unhappy as we should be. One seldom had to labor alone. Everything was done in common. When it was time to cultivate the fields or to harvest the crops, the laborers were ordered by the Incas to go forth in huge family parties. They lessened the hardships of farm labor by village gossip and choral singing, interspersed at regular intervals with rest periods, in which quantities of *chicha* quenched the thirst and cheered the mind.

Habits of community work are still shown in the Andes. One often sees a score or more of Indians carrying huge bundles of sheaves of wheat or barley. I have found a dozen yoke of oxen, each a few yards from the other in a parallel line, engaged in ploughing synchronously small portions of a large field. Although the landlords frequently visit Lima and sometimes go to Paris and New York, where they purchase for their own use the products of modern invention, the fields are still cultivated in the fashion introduced three centuries ago by the *conquistadores*, who brought the first draft animals and the primitive pointed plough of the ancient Mediterranean.

Crops at La Raya are not confined to potatoes. Another food plant, almost unknown to Europeans, even those who live in Lima, is *cañihua*, a kind of pigweed. It was being harvested at the time of our visit in April. The threshing floor for *cañihua* is a large blanket laid on the ground. On top of this the stalks are placed and the flail applied, the blanket serving to prevent the small grayish seeds from escaping. The entire process uses nothing of European origin and has probably not changed for centuries.

We noticed also *quinoa* and even barley growing at an elevation of 14,000 feet. *Quinoa* is another species of pigweed. It often attains a height of three to four feet. There are several varieties. The white-seeded variety, after being boiled, may be fairly compared with oatmeal. Mr. Cook actually preferred it to the Scotch article, both for taste and texture. The seeds retain their form after being cooked and "do not appear so slimy as oatmeal." Other varieties of *quinoa* are bitter and have to be boiled several times, the water being frequently changed. The growing *quinoa* presents an attractive appearance; its leaves assume many colors.

As we went down the valley the evidences of extensive cultivation, both ancient and modern, steadily increased. Great numbers of old terraces were to be seen. There were many fields of wheat, some of them growing high up on the mountain side in what are called *temporales*, where, owing to the steep slope, there is little effort at tillage or cultivation, the planter trusting to luck to get some kind of a crop in reward for very little effort. On April 14th, just above Sicuani, we saw fields where *habas* beans had been gathered and the dried stalks piled in little stacks. At Occobamba, or the *pampa* where *oca* grows, we found fields of that useful tuber, now ripening. Near by were little thatched shelters, just erected for the temporary use of night watchmen during the harvest season.

The Peruvian highlanders whom we met by the roadside were different in feature, attitude, and clothing from those of the Titicaca Basin or even of Santa Rosa, which is not far away. They were typical Quichuas—peaceful agriculturists—usually spinning wool on the little hand spindles which have been used in the Andes from time immemorial. Their huts are built of adobe, the roofs thatched with coarse grass.

The Quichuas are brown in color. Their hair is straight and black. Gray hair is seldom seen. It is the custom among the men in certain localities to wear their hair long and braided. Beards are sparse or lacking. Bald heads are very rare. Teeth seem to be more enduring than with us. Throughout the Andes the frequency of well-preserved teeth was everywhere noteworthy except on sugar plantations, where there is opportunity to indulge freely in crude brown sugar nibbled from cakes or mixed with parched corn and eaten as a travel ration.

The Quichua face is broad and short. Its breadth is nearly the same as the Eskimo. Freckles are not common and appear to be limited to face and arms, in the few cases in which they were observed. On the other hand, a large proportion of the Indians are pock-marked and show the effects of living in a country which is "free from medical tyranny." There is no compulsory vaccination.

One hardly ever sees a fat Quichua. It is difficult to tell whether this is a racial characteristic or due rather to the lack of fat-producing foods in their diet. Although the Peruvian highlander has made the best use he could of the llama, he was never able to develop its slender legs and weak back sufficiently to use it for loads weighing more than eighty or a hundred pounds. Consequently, for the carrying of really heavy burdens he had to depend on himself. As a result, it is not surprising to learn from Dr. Ferris that while his arms are poorly developed, his shoulders are broader, his back muscles stronger, and the calves of his legs larger and more powerful than those of almost any other race.

The Quichuas are fond of shaking hands. When a visiting Indian joins a group he nearly always goes through the gentle ceremony with each person in turn. I do not know whether this was introduced by the Spaniards or comes down from prehistoric times. In any event, this handshaking in no way resembles the hearty clasp familiar to undergraduates at the beginning of the college year. As a matter of fact the Quichua handshake is extremely fishy and lacks cordiality. In testing the hand grip of the Quichuas by a dynamometer our surgeons found that the muscles of the forearm were poorly developed in the Quichua and the maximum grip was weak in both sexes, the average for the man being only about half of that found among American white adults of sedentary habits.

Dr. Alex Hrdlicka believes that the aboriginal races of North and South America were of the same stock. The wide differences in physiognomy observable among the different tribes in North and South America are perhaps due to their environmental history during the past 10,000 or 20,000 years. Mr. Frank Chapman, of the American Museum of Natural History, has pointed out the interesting biological fact that animals and birds found at sea level in the cold regions of Tierra del Fuego, while not found at sea level in Peru, do exist at very high altitudes, where the climate is similar to that with which they are acquainted. Similarly, it is interesting to learn that the inhabitants of the cold, lofty regions of southern Peru, living in towns and villages at altitudes of from 9000 to 14,000 feet above the sea, have physical peculiarities closely resembling those living at sea level in Tierra del Fuego, Alaska, and Labrador. Dr. Ferris says the Labrador Eskimo and the Quichua constitute the two "best-known short-stature races on the American continent."

So far as we could learn by questions and observation, about one quarter of the Quichuas are childless. In families which have children the average number is three or four. Large families are not common, although we generally learned that the living children in a family usually represented less than half of those which had been born. Infant mortality is very great. The proper feeding of children is not understood and it is a marvel how any of them manage to grow up at all.

Coughs and bronchial trouble are very common among the Indians. In fact, the most common afflictions of the tableland are those of the throat and lungs. Pneumonia is the most serious and most to be dreaded of all local diseases. It is really terrifying. Due to the rarity of the air and relative scarcity of oxygen, pneumonia is usually fatal at 8000 feet and is uniformly so at 11,000 feet. Patients are frequently ill only twenty-four hours. Tuberculosis is fairly common, its prevalence undoubtedly caused by the living conditions practiced among the highlanders, who are unwilling to sleep in a room which is not tightly closed and protected against any possible intrusion of fresh air. In the warmer valleys, where bodily comfort has led the natives to use huts of thatch and open reeds, instead of the air-tight hovels of the cold, bleak plateau, tuberculosis is seldom seen. Of course, there are no "boards of health," nor are the people bothered by being obliged to conform to any sanitary regulations. Water supplies are so often contaminated that the people have learned to avoid drinking it as far as possible. Instead, they eat quantities of soup.

In the market-place of Sicuani, the largest town in the valley, and the border-line between the potato-growing uplands and lowland maize fields, we attended the famous Sunday market. Many native "druggists" were present. Their stock usually consisted of "medicines," whose efficacy was learned by the Incas. There were forty or fifty kinds of simples and curiosities, cure-alls, and specifics. Fully half were reported to me as being "useful against fresh air" or the evil effects of drafts. The "medicines" included such minerals as iron ore and sulphur; such vegetables as dried seeds, roots, and the leaves of plants domesticated hundreds of years ago by the Incas or gathered in the tropical jungles of the lower Urubamba Valley; and such animals as starfish brought from the Pacific Ocean. Some of them were really useful herbs, while others have only a psychopathic effect on the patient. Each medicine was in an attractive little parti-colored woolen bag. The bags, differing in design and color, woven on miniature hand looms, were arranged side by side on the ground, the upper parts turned over and rolled down so as to disclose the contents.

Not many miles below Sicuani, at a place called Racche, are the remarkable ruins of the so-called Temple of Viracocha, described by Squier. At first sight Racche looks as though there were here a row of nine or ten lofty adobe piers, forty or fifty feet high! Closer inspection, however, shows them all to be parts of the central wall of a great temple. The wall is pierced with large doors and the spaces between the doors are broken by niches, narrower at the top than at the bottom. There are small holes in the doorposts for bar-holds. The base of the great wall is about five feet thick and is of stone. The ashlars are beautifully cut and, while not rectangular, are roughly squared and fitted together with most exquisite care, so as to insure their making a very firm foundation. Their surface is most attractive, but, strange to say, there is unmistakable evidence that the builders did not wish the stonework to show. This surface was at one time plastered with clay, a very significant fact. The builders wanted the wall to seem to be built entirely of adobe, yet, had the great clay wall rested on the ground, floods and erosion might have succeeded in undermining it. Instead, it rests securely on a beautifully built foundation of solid masonry. Even so, the great wall does not stand absolutely true, but leans slightly to the westward. The wall also seems to be less weathered on the west side. Probably the prevailing or strongest wind is from the east.

An interesting feature of the ruins is a round column about twenty feet high—a very rare occurrence in Inca architecture. It also is of adobe, on a stone foundation. There is only one column now standing. In Squier's day the remains of others were to be seen, but I could find no evidences of them. There was probably a double row of these columns to support the stringers and tiebeams of the roof. Apparently one end of a tiebeam rested on the circular column and the other end was embedded in the main wall. The holes where the tiebeams entered the wall have stone lintels.

Near the ruins of the great temple are those of other buildings, also unique, so far as I know. The base of the party wall, decorated with large niches, is of cut ashlars carefully laid; the middle course is of adobe, while the upper third is of rough, uncut stones. It looks very odd now but was originally covered with fine clay or stucco. In several cases the plastered walls are still standing, in fairly good condition, particularly where they have been sheltered from the weather.

The chief marvel of Racche, however, is the great adobe wall of the temple, which is nearly fifty feet high. It is slowly disintegrating, as might be expected. The wonder is that it should have stood so long in a rainy region without any roof or protecting cover. It is incredible that for at least five hundred years a wall of sun-dried clay should have been able to defy severe rainstorms. The lintels, made of hard-wood timbers and partially embedded in the wall, are all gone; yet the adobe remains. It would be very interesting to find out whether the water of the springs near the temple contains lime. If so this might have furnished natural calcareous cement in sufficient quantity to give the clay a particularly tenacious quality, able to resist weathering. The factors which have caused this extraordinary adobe wall to withstand the weather in such an exposed position for so many centuries, notwithstanding the heavy rains of each summer season from December to March, are worthy of further study.

It has been claimed that this temple was devoted to the worship of Viracocha, a great deity, the Jove or Zeus of the ancient pantheon. It seems to me more reasonable to suppose that a primitive folk constructed here a temple to the presiding divinity of the place, the god who gave them this precious clay. The principal industry of the neighboring village is still the manufacture of pottery. No better clay for ceramic purposes has been found in the Andes.

It would have been perfectly natural for the prehistoric potters to have desired to placate the presiding divinity, not so much perhaps out of gratitude for the clay as to avert his displeasure and fend off bad luck in baking pottery. It is well known that the best pottery of the Incas was extremely fine in texture. Students of ceramics are well aware of the uncertainty of the results of baking clay. Bad luck seems to come most unaccountably, even when the greatest pains are taken. Might it not have been possible that the people who were most concerned with creating pottery decided to erect this temple to insure success and get as much good luck as possible? Near the ancient temple is a small modern church with two towers. The churchyard appears to be a favorite place for baking pottery. Possibly the modern potters use the church to pray for success in their baking, just as the ancient potters used the great temple of Viracocha. The walls of the church are composed partly of adobe and partly of cut stones taken from the ruins.

Not far away is a fairly recent though prehistoric lava flow. It occurs to me that possibly this flow destroyed some of the clay beds from which the ancient potters got their precious materials. The temple may have been erected as a propitiatory offering to the god of volcanoes in the hope that the anger which had caused him to send the lava flow might be appeased. It may be that the Inca Viracocha, an unusually gifted ruler, was particularly interested in ceramics and was responsible for building the temple. If so, it would be natural for people who are devoted to ancestor worship to have here worshiped his memory.

[1] Fernando Montesinos, an ecclesiastical lawyer of the seventeenth century, appears to have gone to Peru in 1629 as the follower of that well-known viceroy, the Count of Chinchon, whose wife having contracted malaria was cured by the use of Peruvian bark or quinine and was instrumental in the introduction of this medicine into Europe, a fact which has been commemorated in the botanical name of the genus *cinchona*. Montesinos was well educated and appears to have given himself over entirely to historical research. He traveled extensively in Peru and wrote several books. His history of the Incas was spoiled by the introduction, in which, as might have been expected of an orthodox lawyer, he contended that Peru was peopled under the leadership of Ophir, the great-grandson of Noah! Nevertheless, one finds his work to be of great value and the late Sir Clements Markham, foremost of English students of Peruvian archeology, was inclined to place considerable credence in his statements. His account of pre-Hispanic Peru has recently been edited for the Hakluyt Society by Mr. Philip A. Means of Harvard University.

CHAPTER 7

The Valley of the Huatanay

✱

THE VALLEY OF THE HUATANAY is one of many valleys tributary to the Urubamba. It differs from them in having more arable land located under climatic conditions favorable for the raising of the food crops of the ancient Peruvians. Containing an area estimated at less than 160 square miles, it was the heart of the greatest empire that South America has ever seen. It is still intensively cultivated, the home of a large percentage of the people of this part of Peru. The Huatanay itself sometimes meanders through the valley in a natural manner, but at other times is seen to be confined within carefully built stone walls constructed by prehistoric agriculturists anxious to save their fields from floods and erosion. The climate is temperate. Extreme cold is unknown. Water freezes in the lowlands during the dry winter season, in June and July, and frost may occur any night in the year above 13,000 feet, but in general the climate may be said to be neither warm nor cold.

This rich valley was apportioned by the Spanish conquerors to soldiers who were granted large estates as well as the labor of the Indians living on them. This method still prevails and one may occasionally meet on the road wealthy landholders on their way to and from town. Although mules are essentially the most reliable saddle animals for work in the Andes, these landholders usually prefer horses, which are larger and faster, as well as being more gentle and better gaited. The gentry of the Huatanay Valley prefer a deep-seated saddle, over which is laid a heavy sheepskin or thick fur mat. The fashionable stirrups are pyramidal in shape, made of wood decorated with silver bands. Owing to the steepness of the roads, a crupper is considered necessary and is usually decorated with a broad, embossed panel, from which hang little trappings reminiscent of medieval harness. The bridle is usually made of carefully braided leather, decorated with silver and frequently furnished with an embossed leather eye shade or blinder, to indicate that the horse is high-spirited. This eye shade, which may be pulled down so as to blind both eyes completely, is more useful than a hitching post in persuading the horse to stand still.

The valley of the Huatanay River is divided into three parts, the basins of Lucre, Oropesa, and Cuzco. The basaltic cliffs near Oropesa divide the Lucre Basin from the Oropesa Basin. The pass at Angostura, or "the narrows," is the natural gateway between the Oropesa Basin and the Cuzco Basin. Each basin contains interesting ruins. In the Lucre Basin the most interesting are those of Rumiccolca and Piquillacta.

At the extreme eastern end of the valley, on top of the pass which leads to the Vilcanota is an ancient gateway called Rumiccolca (*Rumi* = "stone"; *ccolca* = "granary"). It is commonly supposed that this was an Inca fortress, intended to separate the chiefs of Cuzco from those of Vilcanota. It is now locally referred to as a "*fortaleza.*" The major part of the wall is well built of rough stones, laid in clay, while the sides of the gateway are faced with carefully cut andesite ashlars of an entirely different style. It is conceivable that some great chieftain built the rough wall in the days when the highlands were split up among many little independent rulers, and that later one of the Incas, no longer needing any fortifications between the Huatanay Valley and the Vilcanota Valley, tore down part of the wall and built a fine gateway. The faces of the ashlars are nicely finished except for several rough bosses or nubbins. They were probably used by the ancient masons in order to secure a better hold when finally adjusting the ashlars with small crowbars. It may have been the intention of the stone masons to remove these nubbins after the wall was completed. In one of the unfinished structures at Machu Picchu I noticed similar bosses. The name "Stone-granary" was probably originally applied to a neighboring edifice now in ruins.

On the rocky hillside above Rumiccolca are the ruins of many ancient terraces and some buildings. Not far from Rumiccolca, on the slopes of Mt. Piquillacta, are the ruins of an extensive city, also called Piquillacta. A large number of its houses have extraordinarily high walls. A high wall outside the city, and running north and south, was obviously built to protect it from enemies approaching from the Vilcanota Valley. In the other directions the slopes are so steep as to render a wall unnecessary. The walls are built of fragments of lava rock, with which the slopes of Mt. Piquillacta are covered. Cacti and thorny scrub are growing in the ruins, but the volcanic soil is rich enough to attract the attention of agriculturists, who come here from neighboring villages to cultivate their crops. The slopes above the city are still extensively cultivated, but without terraces. Wheat and barley are the principal crops.

As an illustration of the difficulty of identifying places in ancient Peru, it is worth noting that the gateway now called Rumiccolca is figured in Squier's "Peru" as "Piquillacta." On the other hand, the ruins of the large city, "covering thickly an area nearly a square mile," are called by Squier "the great Inca town of Muyna," a name also applied to the little lake which lies in the bottom of the Lucre Basin. As Squier came along the road from Racche he saw Mt. Piquillacta first, then the gateway, then Lake Muyna, then the ruins of the city. In each case the name of the most conspicuous, harmless, natural phenomenon seems to have been applied to ruins by those of whom he inquired. My own experience was different.

Dr. Aguilar, a distinguished professor in the University of Cuzco, who has a country place in the neighborhood and is very familiar with this region, brought me to this ancient city from the other direction. From him I learned that the city ruins are called Piquillacta, the name which is also applied to the mountain which lies to the eastward of the ruins and rises 1200 feet above them. Dr. Aguilar lives near Oropesa. As one comes from Oropesa, Mt. Piquillacta is a conspicuous point and is directly in line with the city ruins. Consequently, it would be natural for people viewing it from this direction to give to the ruins the name of the mountain rather than that of the lake. Yet the mountain may be named for the ruins. *Piqui* means "flea"; *llacta* means "town, city, country, district, or territory." Was this "The Territory of the Fleas" or was it "Flea Town"? And what was its name in the days of the Incas? Was the old name abandoned because it was considered unlucky?

Whatever the reason, it is a most extraordinary fact that we have here the evidences of a very large town, possibly pre-Inca, long since abandoned. There are scores of houses and numerous compounds laid out in regular fashion, the streets crossing each other at right angles, the whole covering an area considerably larger than the important town of Ollantaytambo. Not a soul lives here. It is true that across the Vilcanota to the east is a difficult, mountainous country culminating in Mt. Ausangate, the highest peak in the department. Yet Piquillacta is in the midst of a populous region. To the north lies the thickly settled valley of Pisac and Yucay; to the south, the important Vilcanota Valley with dozens of villages; to the west the densely populated valley of the Huatanay and Cuzco itself, the largest city in the highlands of Peru. Thousands of people live within a radius of twenty miles of Piquillacta, and the population is on the increase. It is perfectly easy of access and is less than a mile east of the railroad. Yet it is "*abandonado—desierto—despoblado*"! Undoubtedly here was once a large city of great importance. The reason for its being abandoned appears to be the absence of running water. Although Mt. Piquillacta is a large mass, nearly five miles long and two miles wide, rising to a point of 2000 feet above the Huatanay and Vilcanota rivers, it has no streams, brooks, or springs. It is an isolated, extinct volcano surrounded by igneous rocks, lavas, andesites, and basalts.

How came it that so large a city as Piquillacta could have been built on the slopes of a mountain which has no running streams? Has the climate changed so much since those days? If so, how is it that the surrounding region is still the populous part of southern Peru? It is inconceivable that so large a city could have been built and occupied on a plateau four hundred feet above the nearest water unless there was some way of providing it other than the arduous one of bringing every drop up the hill on the backs of men and llamas. If there were no places near here better provided with water than this site, one could understand that perhaps its inhabitants were obliged to depend entirely upon water carriers. On the contrary, within a radius of six miles there are half a dozen unoccupied sites near running streams. Until further studies can be made of this puzzling problem I believe that the answer lies in the ruins of Rumiccolca, which are usually thought of as a fortress.

Squier says that this "fortress" was "the southern limit of the dominions of the first Inca." "The fortress reaches from the mountain, on one side, to a high, rocky eminence on the other. It is popularly called 'El *Aqueducto*,' perhaps from some fancied resemblance to an aqueduct—but the name is evidently misapplied." Yet he admits that the cross-section of the wall, diminishing as it does "by graduations or steps on both sides," "might appear to conflict with the hypothesis of its being a work of defense or fortification" if it occupied "a different position." He noticed that "the top of the wall is throughout of the same level; becomes less in height as it approaches the hills on either hand and diminishes proportionately in thickness" as an aqueduct should do. Yet, so possessed was he by the "fortress" idea that he rejected not only local tradition as expressed in the native name, but even turned his back on the evidence of his own eyes. It seems to me that there is little doubt that instead of the ruins of Rumiccolca representing a fortification, we have here the remains of an ancient *azequia*, or aqueduct, built by some powerful chieftain to supply the people of Piquillacta with water.

A study of the topography of the region shows that the river which rises southwest of the village of Lucre and furnishes water power for its modern textile mills could have been used to supply such an *azequia*. The water, collected at an elevation of 10,700 feet, could easily have been brought six miles along the southern slopes of the Lucre Basin, around Mt. Rumiccolca and across the old road, on this aqueduct, at an elevation of about 10,600 feet. This would have permitted it to flow through some of the streets of Piquillacta and give the ancient city an adequate supply of water. The slopes of Rumiccolca are marked by many ancient terraces. Their upper limit corresponds roughly with the contour along which such an *azequia* would have had to pass. There is, in fact, a distinct line on the hillside which looks as though an *azequia* had once passed that way. In the valley back of Lucre are also faint indications of old *azequias*. There has been, however, a considerable amount of erosion on the hills, and if, as seems likely, the waterworks have been out of order for several centuries, it is not surprising that all traces of them have disappeared in places. I regret very much that circumstances over which I had no control prevented my making a thorough study of the possibilities of such a theory. It remains for some fortunate future investigator to determine who were the inhabitants of Piquillacta, how they secured their water supply, and why the city was abandoned.

Until then I suggest as a possible working hypothesis that we have at Piquillacta the remains of a pre-Inca city; that its chiefs and people cultivated the Lucre Basin and its tributaries; that as a community they were a separate political entity from the people of Cuzco; that the ruler of the Cuzco people, perhaps an Inca, finally became sufficiently powerful to conquer the people of the Lucre Basin, and removed the tribes which had occupied Piquillacta to a distant part of his domain, a system of colonization well known in the history of the Incas; that, after the people who had built and lived in Piquillacta departed, no subsequent dwellers in this region cared to reoccupy the site, and its aqueduct fell into decay. It is easy to believe that at first such a site would have been considered unlucky. Its houses, unfamiliar and unfashionable in design, would have been considered not desirable. Their high walls might have been used for a reconstructed city had there been plenty of water available. In any case, the ruins of the Lucre Basin offer a most fascinating problem.

In the Oropesa Basin the most important ruins are those of Tipon, a pleasant, well-watered valley several hundred feet above the village of Quispicanchi. They include carefully constructed houses of characteristic Inca construction, containing many symmetrically arranged niches with stone lintels. The walls of most of the houses are of rough stones laid in clay. Tipon was probably the residence of the principal chief of the Oropesa Basin. It commands a pleasant view of the village and of the hills to the south, which to-day are covered with fields of wheat and barley. At Tipon there is a nicely constructed fountain of cut stone. Some of the terraces are extremely well built, with roughly squared blocks fitting tightly together. Access from one terrace to another was obtained by steps made each of a single bonder projecting from the face of the terrace. Few better constructed terrace walls are to be seen anywhere. The terraces are still cultivated by the people of Quispicanchi. No one lives at Tipon now, although little shepherd boys and goatherds frequent the neighborhood. It is more convenient for the agriculturists to live at the edge of their largest fields, which are in the valley bottom, than to climb five hundred feet into the narrow valley and occupy the old buildings. Motives of security no longer require a residence here rather than in the open plain.

While I was examining the ruins and digging up a few attractive potsherds bearing Inca designs, Dr. Giesecke, the President of the University of Cuzco, who had accompanied me, climbed the mountain above Tipon with Dr. Aguilar and reported the presence of a fortification near its summit. My stay at Oropesa was rendered most comfortable and happy by the generous hospitality of Dr. Aguilar, whose *finca* is between Quispicanchi and Oropesa and commands a charming view of the valley.

From the Oropesa Basin, one enters the Cuzco Basin through an opening in the sandstone cliffs of Angostura near the modern town of San Geronimo. On the slopes above the south bank of the Huatanay, just beyond Angostura, are the ruins of a score or more of gable-roofed houses of characteristic Inca construction. The ancient buildings have doors, windows, and niches in walls of small stones laid in clay, the lintels having been of wood, now decayed. When we asked the name of these ruins we were told that it was Saylla, although that is the name of a modern village three miles away, down the Huatanay, in the Oropesa Basin. Like Piquillacta, old

Saylla has no water supply at present. It is not far from a stream called the Kkaira and could easily have been supplied with water by an *azequia* less than two miles in length brought along the 11,000 feet contour. It looks very much like the case of a village originally placed on the hills for the sake of comparative security and isolation and later abandoned through a desire to enjoy the advantages of living near the great highway in the bottom of the valley, after the Incas had established peace over the highlands. There may be another explanation.

It appears from Mr. Cook's studies that the deforestation of the Cuzco Basin by the hand of man, and modern methods of tillage on unterraced slopes, have caused an unusual amount of erosion to occur. Landslides are frequent in the rainy season.

Opposite Saylla is Mt. Picol, whose twin peaks are the most conspicuous feature on the north side of the basin. Waste material from its slopes is causing the rapid growth of a great gravel fan north of the village of San Geronimo. Professor Gregory noticed that the streams traversing the fan are even now engaged in burying ancient fields by "transporting gravel from the head of the fan to its lower margin," and that the lower end of the Cuzco Basin, where the Huatanay, hemmed in between the Angostura Narrows, cannot carry away the sediment as fast as it is brought down by its tributaries, is being choked up. If old Saylla represents a fortress set here to defend Cuzco against old Oropesa, it might very naturally have been abandoned when the rule of the Incas finally spread far over the Andes. On the other hand, it seems more likely that the people who built Saylla were farmers and that when the lower Cuzco Basin was filled up by aggradation, due to increased erosion, they abandoned this site for one nearer the arable lands. One may imagine the dismay with which the agricultural residents of these ancient houses saw their beautiful fields at the bottom of the hill, covered in a few days, or even hours, by enormous quantities of coarse gravel brought down from the steep slopes of Picol after some driving rainstorm. It may have been some such catastrophe that led them to take up their residence elsewhere. As a matter of fact we do not know when it was abandoned. Further investigation might point to its having been deserted when the Spanish village of San Geronimo was founded. However, I believe students of agriculture will agree with me that deforestation, increased erosion, and aggrading gravel banks probably drove the folk out of Saylla.

The southern rim of the Cuzco Basin is broken by no very striking peaks, although Huanacaurai (13,427 ft.), the highest point, is connected

in Inca tradition with some of the principal festivals and religious cele-
brations. The north side of the Huatanay Valley is much more irregular, rang-
ing from Ttica Ttica pass (12,000 ft.) to Mt. Pachatucsa (15,915 ft.), whose
five little peaks are frequently snow-clad. There is no permanent snow
either here or elsewhere in the Huatanay Valley.

The people of the Cuzco Basin are very short of fuel. There is no
native coal. What the railroad uses comes from Australia. Firewood is
scarce. The ancient forests disappeared long ago. The only trees in sight are
a few willows or poplars from Europe and one or two groves of eucalyptus,
also from Australia. Cuzco has been thought of and written of as being above
the tree line, but such is not the case. The absence of trees on the neighboring
hills is due entirely to the hand of man, the long occupation, the necessities of early agriculturists, who cleared the forests before the days of intensive terrace agriculture, and the firewood requirements of a large population.
The people of Cuzco do not dream of having enough fuel to make their
houses warm and comfortable. Only with difficulty can they get enough
for cooking purposes. They depend largely on fagots and straw which are
brought into town on the backs of men and animals.

In the fields of stubble left from the wheat and barley harvest we saw
many sheep feeding. They were thin and long-legged and many of the rams
had four horns, apparently due to centuries of inbreeding and the failure to
improve the original stock by the introduction of new and superior strains.

When one looks at the great amount of arable slopes on most of the
hills of the Cuzco Basin and the unusually extensive flat land near the
Huatanay, one readily understands why the heart of Inca Land witnessed
a concentration of population very unusual in the Andes. Most of the
important ruins are in the northwest quadrant of the basin either in the
immediate vicinity of Cuzco itself or on the "*pampas*" north of the city. The
reason is that the arable lands where most extensive potato cultivation could
be carried out are nearly all in this quadrant. In the midst of this potato country, at the foot of the pass that leads directly to Pisac and Paucartambo, is a
picturesque ruin which bears the native name of Pucará.

Pucará is the Quichua word for fortress and it needs but one glance at
the little hilltop crowned with a rectangular fortification to realize that the
term is justified. The walls are beautifully made of irregular blocks closely
fitted together. Advantage was taken of small cliffs on two sides of the hill
to strengthen the fortifications. We noticed openings or drains which had
been cut in the wall by the original builders in order to prevent the

accumulation of moisture on the terraced floor of the enclosed area, which is several feet above that of the sloping field outside. Similar conduits may be seen in many of the old walls in the city of Cuzco. Apparently, the ancient folk fully appreciated the importance of good drainage and took pains to secure it. At present Pucará is occupied by llama herdsmen and drovers, who find the enclosure a very convenient corral. Probably Pucará was built by the chief of a tribe of prehistoric herdsmen who raised root crops and kept their flocks of llamas and alpacas on the neighboring grassy slopes.

A short distance up the stream of the Lkalla Chaca, above Pucará, is a warm mineral spring. Around it is a fountain of cut stone. Near by are the ruins of a beautiful terrace, on top of which is a fine wall containing four large, ceremonial niches, level with the ground and about six feet high. The place is now called Tampu Machai. Polo de Ondegardo, who lived in Cuzco in 1560, while many of the royal family of the Incas were still alive, gives a list of the sacred or holy places which were venerated by all the Indians in those days. Among these he mentions that of Timpucpuquio, the "hot springs" near Tambo Machai, "called so from the manner in which the water boils up." The next *huaca*, or holy place, he mentions is Tambo Machai itself, "a house of the Inca Yupanqui, where he was entertained when he went to be married. It was placed on a hill near the road over the Andes. They sacrifice everything here except children."

The stonework of the ruins here is so excellent in character, the ashlars being very carefully fitted together, one may fairly assume a religious origin for the place. The Quichua word *macchini* means "to wash" or "to rinse a large narrow-mouthed pitcher." It may be that at Tampu Machai ceremonial purification of utensils devoted to royal or priestly uses was carried on. It is possible that this is the place where, according to Molina, all the youths of Cuzco who had been armed as knights in the great November festival came on the 21st day of the month to bathe and change their clothes. Afterwards they returned to the city to be lectured by their relatives. "Each relation that offered a sacrifice flogged a youth and delivered a discourse to him, exhorting him to be valiant and never to be a traitor to the Sun and the Inca, but to imitate the bravery and prowess of his ancestors."

Tampu Machai is located on a little bluff above the Lkalla Chaca, a small stream which finally joins the Huatanay near the town of San Sebastian. Before it reaches the Huatanay, the Lkalla Chaca joins the Cachimayo, famous as being so highly impregnated with salt as to have caused the rise

of extensive salt works. In fact, the Pizarros named the place Las Salinas, or
"the Salt Pits," on account of the salt pans with which, by a careful system
of terracing, the natives had filled the Cachimayo Valley. Prescott describes
the great battle which took place here on April 26, 1539, between the
forces of Pizarro and Almagro, the two leaders who had united for the
original conquest of Peru, but quarreled over the division of the territory.
Near the salt pans are many Inca walls and the ruins of structures, with
niches, called Rumihuasi, or "Stone House." The presence of salt in many of
the springs of the Huatanay Valley was a great source of annoyance to our
topographic engineers, who were frequently obliged to camp in districts
where the only water available was so saline as to spoil it for drinking purposes and ruin the tea.

The Cuzco Basin was undoubtedly once the site of a lake, "an ancient
water-body whose surface," says Professor Gregory, "lay well above the present site of San Sebastian and San Geronimo." This lake is believed to
have reached its maximum expansion in early Pleistocene times. Its rich
silts, so well adapted for raising maize, habas beans, and quinoa, have
always attracted farmers and are still intensively cultivated. It has been
named "Lake Morkill" in honor of that loyal friend of scientific research
in Peru, William L. Morkill, Esq., without whose untiring aid we could
never have brought our Peruvian explorations as far along as we did. In
pre-glacial times Lake Morkill fluctuated in volume. From time to time
parts of the shore were exposed long enough to enable plants to send their
roots into the fine materials and the sun to bake and crack the muds.
Mastodons grazed on its banks. "Lake Morkill probably existed during all
or nearly all of the glacial epoch." Its drainage was finally accomplished
by the Huatanay cutting down the sandstone hills, near Saylla, and devel-
oping the Angostura gorge.

In the banks of the Huatanay, a short distance below the city of
Cuzco, the stratified beds of the vanished Lake Morkill to-day contain
many fossil shells. Above these are gravels brought down by the floods
and landslides of more modern times, in which may be found potsherds
and bones. One of the chief affluents of the Huatanay is the
Chunchullumayo, which cuts off the southernmost third of Cuzco from
the center of the city. Its banks are terraced and are still used for gardens
and food crops. Here the hospitable Canadian missionaries have their
pleasant station, a veritable oasis of Anglo-Saxon cleanliness.

On a July morning in 1911, while strolling up the Ayahuaycco *quebrada*, an affluent of the Chunchullumayo, in company with Professor Foote and Surgeon Erving, my interest was aroused by the sight of several bones and potsherds exposed by recent erosion in the stratified gravel banks of the little gulch. Further examination showed that recent erosion had also cut through an ancient ash heap. On the side toward Cuzco I discovered a section of stone wall, built of roughly finished stones more or less carefully fitted together, which at first sight appeared to have been built to prevent further washing away of that side of the gulch. Yet above the wall and flush with its surface the bank appeared to consist of stratified gravel, indicating that the wall antedated the gravel deposits. Fifty feet farther up the *quebrada* another portion of wall appeared under the gravel bank. On top of the bank was a cultivated field! Half an hour's digging in the compact gravel showed that there was more wall underneath the field. Later investigation by Dr. Bowman showed that the wall was about three feet thick and nine feet in height, carefully faced on both sides with roughly cut stone and filled in with rubble, a type of stonework not uncommon in the foundations of some of the older buildings in the western part of the city of Cuzco.

Even at first sight it was obvious that this wall, built by man, was completely covered to a depth of six or eight feet by a compact water-laid gravel bank. This was sufficiently difficult to understand, yet a few days later, while endeavoring to solve the puzzle, I found something even more exciting. Half a mile farther up the gulch, the road, newly cut, ran close to the compact, perpendicular gravel bank. About five feet above the road I saw what looked like one of the small rocks which are freely interspersed throughout the gravels here. Closer examination showed it to be the end of a human femur. Apparently it formed an integral part of the gravel bank, which rose almost perpendicularly for seventy or eighty feet above it. Impressed by the possibilities in case it should turn out to be true that here, in the heart of Inca Land, a human bone had been buried under seventy-five feet of gravel, I refrained from disturbing it until I could get Dr. Bowman and Professor Foote, the geologist and the naturalist of the 1911 Expedition, to come with me to the Ayahuaycco *quebrada*. We excavated the femur and found behind it fragments of a number of other bones. They were excessively fragile. The femur was unable to support more than four inches of its own weight and broke off after the gravel had been partly removed. Although the gravel itself was somewhat damp the bones were dry and powdery, ashy gray in color. The bones were carried to the Hotel Central, where

CUZCO VALLEY, PIQUILLACTA

they were carefully photographed, soaked in melted vaseline, packed in cotton batting, and eventually brought to New Haven. Here they were examined by Dr. George F. Eaton, Curator of Osteology in the Peabody Museum. In the meantime Dr. Bowman had become convinced that the compact gravels of Ayahuaycco were of glacial origin.

When Dr. Eaton first examined the bone fragments he was surprised to find among them the bone of a horse. Unfortunately a careful examination of the photographs taken in Cuzco of all the fragments which were excavated by us on July 11th failed to reveal this particular bone. Dr. Bowman, upon being questioned, said that he had dug out one or two more bones in the cliff adjoining our excavation of July 11th and had added these to the original lot. Presumably this horse bone was one which he had added when the bones were packed. It did not worry him, however, and so sure was he of his interpretation of the gravel beds that he declared he did not care if we had found the bone of a Percheron stallion, he was sure that the age of the vertebrate remains might be "provisionally estimated at 20,000 to 40,000 years," until further studies could be made of the geology of the surrounding territory. In an article on the buried wall, Dr. Bowman came to the conclusion that "the wall is pre-Inca, that its relations to alluvial deposits which cover it indicate its erection before the alluvial slope in which it lies buried was formed, and that it represents the earliest type of architecture at present known in the Cuzco basin."

Dr. Eaton's study of the bones brought out the fact that eight of them were fragments of human bones representing at least three individuals, four were fragments of llama bones, one of the bone of a dog, and three were "bovine remains." The human remains agreed "in all essential respects" with the bones of modern Quichuas. Llama and dog might all have belonged to Inca, or even more recent times, but the bovine remains presented considerable difficulty. The three fragments were from bones which "are among the least characteristic parts of the skeleton." That which was of greatest interest was the fragment of a first rib, resembling the first rib of the extinct bison. Since this fragmentary bovine rib was of a form apparently characteristic of bisons and not seen in the domestic cattle of the United States, Dr. Eaton felt that it could not be denied "that the material examined suggests the possibility that some species of bison is here represented, yet it would hardly be in accordance with conservative methods to differentiate bison from domestic cattle solely by characters obtained from a study of the first ribs of a small number of individuals." Although staunchly supporting his theory of the age of the vertebrate remains, Dr. Bowman in his report on their geological relations admitted that the weakness of his case lay in the fact that the bovine remains were not sharply differentiated from the bones of modern cattle, and also in the possibility that "the bluff in which the bones were found may be faced by younger gravel and that the bones were found in a gravel veneer deposited during later periods of partial valley filling, ... although it still seems very unlikely."

Reports of glacial man in America have come from places as widely separated as California and Argentina. Careful investigation, however, has always thrown doubt on any great age being certainly attributable to any human remains. In view of the fragmentary character of the skeletal evidence, the fact that no proof of great antiquity could be drawn from the characters of the human skeletal parts, and the suggestion made by Dr. Bowman of the possibility that the gravels which contained the bones might be of a later origin than he thought, we determined to make further and more complete investigations in 1912. It was most desirable to clear up all doubts and dissolve all skepticism. I felt, perhaps mistakenly, that while a further study of the geology of the Cuzco Basin undoubtedly might lead Dr. Bowman to reverse his opinion, as was expected by some geologists, if it should lead him to confirm his original conclusions the same skeptics would be likely to continue their skepticism and say he was trying to bolster up his own previous opinions. Accordingly, I believed it preferable to take another geologist, whose independent testimony would give great weight to those conclusions should he find them confirmed by an exhaustive geological study of the Huatanay Valley. I asked Dr. Bowman's colleague, Professor Gregory, to make the necessary studies. At his request a very careful map of the Huatanay Valley was prepared under the direction of Chief Topographer Albert H. Bumstead. Dr. Eaton, who had had no opportunity of seeing Peru, was invited to accompany us and make a study of the bones of modern Peruvian cattle as well as of any other skeletal remains which might be found.

Furthermore, it seemed important to me to dig a tunnel into the Ayahuaycco hillside at the exact point from which we took the bones in 1911. So I asked Mr. K. C. Heald, whose engineering training had been in Colorado, to superintend it. Mr. Heald dug a tunnel eleven feet long, with a cross-section four and a half by three feet, into the solid mass of gravel. He expected to have to use timbering, but so firmly packed was the gravel that this was not necessary. No bones or artifacts were found—nothing but coarse gravel, uniform in texture and containing no unmistakable evidences of stratification. Apparently the bones had been in a land slip on the edge of an older, compact gravel mass.

In his studies of the Cuzco Basin Professor Gregory came to the conclusion that the Ayahuaycco gravel banks might have been repeatedly buried and reëxcavated many times during the past few centuries. He found evidence indicating periodic destruction and rebuilding of some gravel terraces, "even within the past one hundred years." Accordingly there was no longer any necessity to ascribe great antiquity to the bones or the wall which we found in the Ayahuaycco *quebrada*. Although the "Cuzco gravels are believed to have reached their greatest extent and thickness in late Pleistocene times," more recent deposits have, however, been superimposed on top and alongside of them. "Surface wash from the bordering slopes, controlled in amount and character by climatic changes, has probably been accumulating continuously since glacial times, and has greatly increased since human occupation began." "Geologic data do not require more than a few hundreds of years as the age of the human remains found in the Cuzco gravels."

But how about the "bison"? Soon after his arrival in Cuzco, Dr. Eaton examined the first ribs of carcasses of beef animals offered for sale in the public markets. He immediately became convinced that the "bison" was a Peruvian domestic ox. "Under the life-conditions prevailing in this part of the Andes, and possibly in correlation with the increased action of the respiratory muscles in a rarefied air, domestic cattle occasionally develop first ribs, closely approaching the form observed in bison." Such was the sad end of the "bison" and the "Cuzco man," who at one time I thought might be forty thousand years old, and now believe to have been two hundred years old, perhaps. The word *Ayahuaycco* in Quichua means "the valley of dead bodies" or "dead man's gulch." There is a story that it was used as a burial place for plague victims in Cuzco, not more than three generations ago!

CHAPTER 8

THE OLDEST CITY IN SOUTH AMERICA

✴

CUZCO, THE OLDEST CITY in South America, has changed completely since Squier's visit. In fact it has altered considerably since my own first impressions of it were published in "Across South America." To be sure, there are still the evidences of antiquity to be seen on every side; on the other hand there are corresponding evidences of advancement. Telephones, electric lights, street cars, and the "movies" have come to stay. The streets are cleaner. If the modern traveler finds fault with some of the conditions he encounters he must remember that many of the achievements of the people of ancient Cuzco are not yet duplicated in his own country nor have they ever been equaled in any other part of the world. And modern Cuzco is steadily progressing. The great square in front of the cathedral was completely metamorphosed by Prefect Nuñez in 1911; concrete walks and beds of bright flowers have replaced the market and the old cobblestone paving and made the plaza a favorite promenade of the citizens on pleasant evenings.

The principal market-place now is the Plaza of San Francisco. It is crowded with booths of every description. Nearly all of the food-stuffs and utensils used by the Indians may be bought here. Frequently thronged with Indians, buying and selling, arguing and jabbering, it affords, particularly in the early morning, a never-ending source of entertainment to one who is fond of the picturesque and interested in strange manners and customs.

The retail merchants of Cuzco follow the very old custom of congregating by classes. In one street are the dealers in hats; in another those who sell *coca*. The dressmakers and tailors are nearly all in one long arcade in a score or more of dark little shops. Their light seems to come entirely from the front door. The occupants are operators of American sewing-machines who not only make clothing to order, but always have on hand a large assortment of standard sizes and patterns. In another arcade are the shops of those who specialize in everything which appeals to the eye and the pocketbook of the *arriero*: richly decorated halters, which are intended to avert the Evil Eye from his best mules; leather knapsacks in which to carry his *coca* or other valuable articles; cloth cinches and leather bridles; rawhide lassos, with which he is more likely to make a diamond hitch than to rope a mule; flutes to while away the weary hours of his journey, and candles to be burned before his patron saint as he starts for some distant village; in a word, all the paraphernalia of his profession.

In order to learn more about the picturesque Quichuas who throng the streets of Cuzco it was felt to be important to secure anthropometric measurements of a hundred Indians. Accordingly, Surgeon Nelson set up a laboratory in the Hotel Central. His subjects were the unwilling victims of friendly *gendarmes* who went out into the streets with orders to bring for examination only pure-blooded Quichuas. Most of the Indians showed no resentment and were in the end pleased and surprised to find themselves the recipients of a small silver coin as compensation for loss of time.

One might have supposed that a large proportion of Dr. Nelson's subjects would have claimed Cuzco as their native place, but this was not the case. Actually fewer Indians came from the city itself than from relatively small towns like Anta, Huaracondo, and Maras. This may have been due to a number of causes. In the first place, the *gendarmes* may have preferred to arrest strangers from distant villages, who would submit more willingly. Secondly, the city folk were presumably more likely to be in their shops attending to their business or watching their wares in the plaza, an occupation which the *gendarmes* could not interrupt. On the other hand it is also probably true that the residents of Cuzco are of more mixed descent than those of remote villages, where even to-day one cannot find more than two or three individuals who speak Spanish. Furthermore, the attention of the *gendarmes* might have been drawn more easily to the quaintly caparisoned Indians temporarily in from the country, where city fashions do not prevail, than to those who through long residence in the city had learned to adopt a costume more in accordance with European notions. In 1870, according to Squier, seven eighths of the population of Cuzco were still pure Indian. Even to-day a large proportion of the individuals whom one sees in the streets appears to be of pure aboriginal ancestry. Of these we found that many are visitors from outlying villages. Cuzco is the Mecca of the most densely populated part of the Andes.

Probably a large part of its citizens are of mixed Spanish and Quichua ancestry. The Spanish *conquistadores* did not bring European women with them. Nearly all took native wives. The Spanish race is composed of such an extraordinary mixture of peoples from Europe and northern Africa, Celts, Iberians, Romans, and Goths, as well as Carthaginians, Berbers, and Moors, that the Hispanic peoples have far less antipathy toward intermarriage with the American race than have the Anglo-Saxons and Teutons of northern Europe. Consequently, there has gone on for centuries intermarriage of Spaniards and Indians with results which are difficult to determine. Some writers have said there were once 200,000 people in Cuzco. With primitive methods of transportation it would be very difficult to feed so many. Furthermore, in 1559, there were, according to Montesinos, only 20,000 Indians in Cuzco.

One of the charms of Cuzco is the juxtaposition of old and new. Street cars clanging over steel rails carry crowds of well-dressed Cuzceños past Inca walls to greet their friends at the railroad station. The driver is scarcely able by the most vigorous application of his brakes to prevent his mules from crashing into a compact herd of quiet, supercilious llamas sedately engaged in bringing small sacks of potatoes to the Cuzco market. The modern convent of La Merced is built of stones taken from ancient Inca structures. Fastened to ashlars which left the Inca stonemason's hands six or seven centuries ago, one sees a bill-board advertising Cuzco's largest moving-picture theater. On the 2d of July, 1915, the performance was for the benefit of the Belgian Red Cross! Gazing in awe at this sign were Indian boys from some remote Andean village where the custom is to wear ponchos with broad fringes, brightly colored, and knitted caps richly decorated with tasseled tops and elaborate ear-tabs, a costume whose design shows no trace of European influence. Side by side with these picturesque visitors was a barefooted Cuzco urchin clad in a striped jersey, cloth cap, coat, and pants of English pattern.

One sees electric light wires fastened to the walls of houses built four hundred years ago by the Spanish conquerors, walls which themselves rest on massive stone foundations laid by Inca masons centuries before the conquest. In one place telephone wires intercept one's view of the beautiful stone façade of an old Jesuit Church, now part of the University of Cuzco. It is built of reddish basalt from the quarries of Huaccoto, near the twin peaks of Mt. Picol. Professor Gregory says that this Huaccoto basalt has a softness and uniformity of texture which renders it peculiarly suitable for that elaborately carved stonework which was so greatly desired by ecclesiasti-cal architects of the sixteenth century. As compared with the dense dior-ite which was extensively used by the Incas, the basalt weathers far more rapidly. The rich red color of the weathered portions gives to the Jesuit Church an atmosphere of extreme age. The courtyard of the University, whose arcades echoed to the feet of learned Jesuit teachers long before Yale was founded, has recently been paved with concrete, transformed into a ten-nis court, and now echoes to the shouts of students to whom Dr. Giesecke, the successful president, is teaching the truth of the ancient axiom, "*Mens sana in corpore sano.*"

Modern Cuzco is a city of about 20,000 people. Although it is the political capital of the most important department in southern Peru, it had in 1911 only one hospital—a semi-public, non-sectarian organization on the west of the city, next door to the largest cemetery. In fact, so far away is it from everything else and so close to the cemetery that the funeral wreaths and the more prominent monuments are almost the only interesting things which the patients have to look at. The building has large courtyards and open colonnades, which would afford ideal conditions for patients able to take advantage of open-air treatment. At the time of Surgeon Erving's visit he found the patients were all kept in wards whose windows were small and practically always closed and shuttered, so that the atmosphere was close and the light insufficient. One could hardly imagine a stronger contrast than exists between such wards and those to which we are accustomed in the United States, where the maximum of sunlight and fresh air is sought and patients are encouraged to sit out-of-doors, and even have their cots on porches. There was no resident physician. The utmost care was taken throughout the hospital to have everything as dark as possible, thus con-forming to the ancient mountain traditions regarding the evil effects of sun-light and fresh air. Needless to say, the hospital has a high mortality and a very poor local reputation; yet it is the only hospital in the Department. Outside of Cuzco, in all the towns we visited, there was no provision for caring for the sick except in their own homes. In the larger places there are shops where some of the more common drugs may be obtained, but in the great majority of towns and villages no modern medicines can be purchased. No wonder President Giesecke, of the University, is urging his students to play football and tennis.

On the slopes of the hill which overshadows the University are the interesting terraces of Colcampata. Here, in 1571, lived Carlos Inca, a cousin of Inca Titu Cusi, one of the native rulers who succeeded in maintaining a precarious existence in the wilds of the Cordillera Uilcapampa after the Spanish Conquest. In the gardens of Colcampata is still preserved one of the most exquisite bits of Inca stonework to be seen in Peru. One wonders whether it is all that is left of a fine palace, or whether it represents the last efforts of a dying dynasty to erect a suitable residence for Titu Cusi's cousin. It is carefully preserved by Don Cesare Lomellini, the leading business man of Cuzco, a merchant prince of Italian origin, who is at once a banker, an exporter of hides and other country produce, and an importer of merchandise of every description, including pencils and sugar mills, lumber and hats, candy and hardware. He is also an amateur of Spanish colonial furniture as well as of the beautiful pottery of the Incas. Furthermore, he has always found time to turn aside from the pressing cares of his large business to assist our expeditions. He has frequently brought us in touch with the owners of country estates, or given us letters of introduction, so that our paths were made easy. He has provided us with storerooms for our equipment, assisted us in procuring trustworthy muleteers, seen to it that we were not swindled in local purchases of mules and pack saddles, given us invaluable advice in overcoming difficulties, and, in a word, placed himself wholly at our disposal, just as though we were his most desirable and best-paying clients. As a matter of fact, he never was willing to receive any compensation for the many favors he showed us. So important a factor was he in the success of our expeditions that he deserves to be gratefully remembered by all friends of exploration.

Above his country house at Colcampata is the hill of Sacsahuaman. It is possible to scramble up its face, but only by making more exertion than is desirable at this altitude, 11,900 feet. The easiest way to reach the famous "fortress" is by following the course of the little Tullumayu, "Feeble Stream," the easternmost of the three canalized streams which divide Cuzco into four parts. On its banks one first passes a tannery and then, a short distance up a steep gorge, the remains of an old mill. The stone flume and the adjoining ruins are commonly ascribed by the people of Cuzco to-day to the Incas, but do not look to me like Inca stonework. Since the Incas did not understand the mechanical principle of the wheel, it is hardly likely that

THE UNIVERSITY PATIO, UNIVERSITY OF PERU, CUZCO

they would have known how to make any use of water power. Finally, careful examination of the flume discloses the presence of lead cement, a substance unknown in Inca masonry.

A little farther up the stream one passes through a massive megalithic gateway and finds one's self in the presence of the astounding gray-blue Cyclopean walls of Sacsahuaman, described in "Across South America." Here the ancient builders constructed three great terraces, which extend one above another for a third of a mile across the hill between two deep gulches. The lowest terrace of the "fortress" is faced with colossal boulders, many of which weigh ten tons and some weigh more than twenty tons, yet all are fitted together with the utmost precision. I have visited Sacsahuaman repeatedly. Each time it invariably overwhelms and astounds. To a superstitious Indian who sees these walls for the first time, they must seem to have been built by gods.

About a mile northeast of Sacsahuaman are several small artificial hills, partly covered with vegetation, which seem to be composed entirely of gray-blue rock chips—chips from the great limestone blocks quarried here for the "fortress" and later conveyed with the utmost pains down to Sacsahuaman. They represent the labor of countless thousands of quarry-men. Even in modern times, with steam drills, explosives, steel tools, and light railways, these hills would be noteworthy, but when one pauses to consider that none of these mechanical devices were known to the ancient stonemasons and that these mountains of stone chips were made with stone tools and were all carried from the quarries by hand, it fairly staggers the imagination.

The ruins of Sacsahuaman represent not only an incredible amount of human labor, but also a very remarkable governmental organization. That thousands of people could have been spared from agricultural pursuits for so long a time as was necessary to extract the blocks from the quarries, hew them to the required shapes, transport them several miles over rough country, and bond them together in such an intricate manner, means that the leaders had the brains and ability to organize and arrange the affairs of a very large population. Such a folk could hardly have spent much time in drilling or preparing for warfare. Their building operations required infinite pains, endless time, and devoted skill. Such qualities could hardly have been called forth, even by powerful monarchs, had not the results been pleasing to the great majority of their people, people who were primarily agriculturists. They had learned to avert hunger and famine by relying on carefully built, stone-faced terraces, which would prevent their fields being carried off and spread over the plains of the Amazon. It seems to me possible that Sacsahuaman was built in accordance with their desires to please their gods. Is it not reasonable to suppose that a people to whom stone-faced terraces meant so much in the way of life-giving food should have sometimes built massive terraces of Cyclopean character, like Sacsahuaman, as an offering to the deity who first taught them terrace construction? This seems to me a more likely object for the gigantic labor involved in the construction of Sacsahuaman than its possible usefulness as a fortress. Equally strong defenses against an enemy attempting to attack the hilltop back of Cuzco might have been constructed of smaller stones in an infinitely shorter time, with far less labor and pains.

Such a display of the power to control the labor of thousands of individuals and force them to super-human efforts on an unproductive undertaking, which in its agricultural or strategic results was out of all proportion to the obvious cost, might have been caused by the supreme vanity of a great soldier. On the other hand, the ancient Peruvians were religious rather than warlike, more inclined to worship the sun than to fight great battles. Was Sacsahuaman due to the desire to please, at whatever cost, the god that fructified the crops which grew on terraces? It is not surprising that the Spanish conquerors, warriors themselves and descendants of twenty generations of a fighting race, accustomed as they were to the salients of European fortresses, should have looked upon Sacsahuaman as a fortress. To them the military use of its bastions was perfectly obvious. The value of its salients and reëntrant angles was not likely to be overlooked, for it had been only recently acquired by their crusading ancestors. The height and strength of its powerful walls enabled it to be of the greatest service to the soldiers of that day. They saw that it was virtually impregnable for any artillery with which they were familiar. In fact, in the wars of the Incas and those which followed Pizarro's entry into Cuzco, Sacsahuaman was repeatedly used as a fortress.

So it probably never occurred to the Spaniards that the Peruvians, who knew nothing of explosive powder or the use of artillery, did not construct Sacsahuaman in order to withstand such a siege as the fortresses of Europe were only too familiar with. So natural did it seem to the first Europeans who saw it to regard it as a fortress that it has seldom been thought of in any other way. The fact that the sacred city of Cuzco was more likely to be attacked by invaders coming up the valley, or even over the gentle slopes from the west, or through the pass from the north which for centuries has been used as part of the main highway of the central Andes, never seems to have troubled writers who regarded Sacsahuaman essentially as a fortress. It may be that Sacsahuaman was once used as a place where the votaries of the sun gathered at the end of the rainy season to celebrate the vernal equinox, and at the summer solstice to pray for the sun's return from his "farthest north." In any case I believe that the enormous cost of its construction shows that it was probably intended for religious rather than military purposes. It is more likely to have been an ancient shrine than a mighty fortress.

It now becomes necessary, in order to explain my explorations north of Cuzco, to ask the reader's attention to a brief account of the last four Incas who ruled over any part of Peru.

CHAPTER 9

THE LAST FOUR INCAS

✴

READERS OF PRESCOTT'S charming classic, "The Conquest of Peru," will remember that Pizarro, after killing Atahualpa, the Inca who had tried in vain to avoid his fate by filling a room with vessels of gold, decided to establish a native prince on the throne of the Incas to rule in accordance with the dictates of Spain. The young prince, Manco, a son of the great Inca Huayna Capac, named for the first Inca, Manco Ccapac, the founder of the dynasty, was selected as the most acceptable figurehead. He was a young man of ability and spirit. His induction into office in 1534 with appropriate ceremonies, the barbaric splendor of which only made the farce the more pitiful, did little to gratify his natural ambition. As might have been foreseen, he chafed under restraint, escaped as soon as possible from his attentive guardians, and raised an army of faithful Quichuas. There followed the siege of Cuzco, briefly characterized by Don Alonzo Enriques de Guzman, who took part in it, as "the most fearful and cruel war in the world." When in 1536 Cuzco was relieved by Pizarro's comrade, Almagro, and Manco's last chance of regaining the ancient capital of his ancestors failed, the Inca retreated to Ollantaytambo. Here, on the banks of the river Urubamba, Manco made a determined stand, but Ollantaytambo was too easily reached by Pizarro's mounted cavaliers. The Inca's followers, although aroused to their utmost endeavors by the presence of the magnificent stone edifices, fortresses, granaries, palaces, and hanging gardens of their ancestors, found it necessary to retreat. They fled in a northerly direction and made good their escape over snowy passes to Uiticos in the fastnesses of Uilcapampa, a veritable American Switzerland.

The Spaniards who attempted to follow Manco found his position practically impregnable. The citadel of Uilcapampa, a gigantic natural fortress defended by Nature in one of her profoundest moods, was only to be reached by fording dangerous torrents, or crossing the mountains by narrow defiles which themselves are higher than the most lofty peaks of Europe. It was hazardous for Hannibal and Napoleon to bring their armies through the comparatively low passes of the Alps. Pizarro found it impossible to follow the Inca Manco over the Pass of Panticalla, itself a snowy wilderness higher than the summit of Mont Blanc. In no part of the Peruvian Andes are there so many beautiful snowy peaks. Near by is the sharp, icy pinnacle of Mt. Veronica (elevation 19,342 ft.). Not far away is another magnificent snow-capped peak, Mt. Salcantay, 20,565 feet above the sea. Near Salcantay, is the sharp needle of Mt. Soray (19,435 ft.), while to the west of it are Panta (18,590 ft.) and Soiroccocha (18,197 ft.). On the shoulders of these mountains are unnamed glaciers and little valleys that have scarcely ever been seen except by some hardy prospector or inquisitive explorer. These valleys are to be reached only through passes where the traveler is likely to be waylaid by violent storms of hail and snow. During the rainy season a large part of Uilcapampa is absolutely impenetrable. Even in the dry season the difficulties of transportation are very great. The most sure-footed mule is sometimes unable to use the trails without assistance from man. It was an ideal place for the Inca Manco.

The *conquistador*, Cieza de Leon, who wrote in 1550 a graphic account of the wars of Peru, says that Manco took with him a "great quantity of treasure, collected from various parts...and many loads of rich clothing of wool, delicate in texture and very beautiful and showy." The Spaniards were absolutely unable to conceive of the ruler of a country traveling without rich "treasure." It is extremely doubtful whether Manco burdened himself with much gold or silver. Except for ornament there was little use to which he could have put the precious metals and they would have served only to arouse the cupidity of his enemies. His people had never been paid in gold or silver. Their labor was his due, and only such part of it as was needed to raise their own crops and make their own clothing was allotted to them; in fact, their lives were in his hands and the custom and usage of centuries made them faithful followers of their great chief. That Manco, however, actually did carry off with him beautiful textiles, and anything else which was useful, may be taken for granted. In Uiticos, safe from the armed forces of his enemies, the Inca was also able to enjoy the benefits of a delightful climate, and was in a well-watered region where corn, potatoes, both white and sweet, and the fruits of the temperate and sub-tropical regions easily grow. Using this as a base, he was accustomed to sally forth against the Spaniards frequently and in unexpected directions. His raids were usually successful. It was relatively easy for him, with a handful of followers, to dash out of the mountain fastnesses, cross the Apurimac River either by swimming or on primitive rafts, and reach the great road between Cuzco and Lima, the principal highway of Peru. Officials and merchants whose business led them over this route found it extremely precarious. Manco cheered his followers by making them realize that in these raids they were taking sweet revenge on the Spaniards for what they had done to Peru. It is interesting to note that Cieza de Leon justifies Manco in his attitude, for the Spaniards had indeed "seized his inheritance, forcing him to leave his native land, and to live in banishment."

Manco's success in securing such a place of refuge, and in using it as a base from which he could frequently annoy his enemies, led many of the *Orejones* of Cuzco to follow him. The Inca chiefs were called *Orejones*, "big ears," by the Spaniards because the lobes of their ears had been enlarged artificially to receive the great gold earrings which they were fond of wearing. Three years after Manco's retirement to the wilds of Uilcapampa there was born in Cuzco in the year 1539, Garcilasso Inca de la Vega, the son of an Inca princess and one of the *conquistadores*. As a small child Garcilasso heard of the activities of his royal relative. He left Peru as a boy and spent the rest of his life in Spain. After forty years in Europe he wrote, partly from memory, his "Royal Commentaries," an account of the country of his Indian ancestors. Of the Inca Manco, of whom he must frequently have heard uncomplimentary reports as a child, he speaks apologetically. He says: "In the time of Manco Inca, several robberies were committed on the road by his subjects; but still they had that respect for the Spanish Merchants that they let them go free and never pillaged them of their wares and merchandise, which were in no manner useful to them; howsoever they robbed the Indians of their cattle [llamas and alpacas], bred in the countrey.... The Inca lived in the Mountains, which afforded no tame Cattel; and only produced Tigers and Lions and Serpents of twenty-five and thirty feet long, with other venomous insects." (I am quoting from Sir Paul Rycaut's translation, published in London in 1688.) Garcilasso says Manco's soldiers took only "such food as they found in the hands of the Indians; which the Inca did usually call his own," saying, "That he who was Master of that whole Empire might lawfully challenge such a proportion thereof as was convenient to supply his necessary and natural support"—a reasonable apology; and yet personally I doubt whether Manco spared the Spanish merchants and failed to pillage them of their "wares and merchandise." As will be seen later, we found in Manco's palace some metal articles of European origin which might very well have been taken by Manco's raiders. Furthermore, it should be remembered that Garcilasso, although often quoted by Prescott, left Peru when he was sixteen years old and that his ideas were largely colored by his long life in Spain and his natural desire to extol the virtues of his mother's people, a brown race despised by the white Europeans for whom he wrote.

The methods of warfare and the weapons used by Manco and his followers at this time are thus described by Guzman. He says the Indians had no defensive arms such as helmets, shields, and armor, but used "lances, arrows, clubs, axes, halberds, darts, and slings, and another weapon which they call ayllas (the bolas), consisting of three round stones sewn up in leather, and each fastened to a cord a cubit long. They throw these at the horses, and thus bind their legs together; and sometimes they will fasten a man's arms to his sides in the same way. These Indians are so expert in the use of this weapon that they will bring down a deer with it in the chase. Their principal weapon, however, is the sling.... With it, they will hurl a huge stone with such force that it will kill a horse; in truth, the effect is little less great than that of an arquebus; and I have seen a stone, thus hurled from a sling, break a sword in two pieces which was held in a man's hand at a distance of thirty paces."

Manco's raids finally became so annoying that Pizarro sent a small force from Cuzco under Captain Villadiego to attack the Inca. Captain Villadiego found it impossible to use horses, although he realized that cavalry was the "important arm against these Indians." Confident in his strength and in the efficacy of his firearms, and anxious to enjoy the spoils of a successful raid against a chief reported to be traveling surrounded by his family "*and with rich treasure*," he pressed eagerly on, up through a lofty valley toward a defile in the mountains, probably the Pass of Panticalla. Here, fatigued and exhausted by their difficult march and suffering from the effects of the altitude (16,000 ft.), his men found themselves ambushed by the Inca, who with a small party, "little more than eighty Indians," "attacked the Christians, who numbered twenty-eight or thirty, and killed Captain Villadiego and all his men except two or three." To any one who has clambered over the passes of the Cordillera Uilcapampa it is not surprising that this military expedition was a failure or that the Inca, warned by keen-sighted Indians posted on appropriate vantage points, could have succeeded in defeating a small force of weary soldiers armed with the heavy blunderbuss of the seventeenth century. In a rocky pass, protected by huge boulders, and surrounded by quantities of natural ammunition for their slings, it must have been relatively simple for eighty Quichuas, who could "hurl a huge stone with such force that it would kill a horse," to have literally stoned to death Captain Villadiego's little company before they could have prepared their clumsy weapons for firing.

The fugitives returned to Cuzco and reported their misfortune. The importance of the reverse will be better appreciated if one remembers that the size of the force with which Pizarro conquered Peru was less than two hundred, only a few times larger than Captain Villadiego's company which had been wiped out by Manco. Its significance is further increased by the fact that the contemporary Spanish writers, with all their tendency to exaggerate, placed Manco's force at only "a little more than eighty Indians." Probably there were not even that many. The wonder is that the Inca's army was not reported as being several thousand.

Francisco Pizarro himself now hastily set out with a body of soldiers determined to punish this young Inca who had inflicted such a blow on the prestige of Spanish arms, "but this attempt also failed," for the Inca had withdrawn across the rivers and mountains of Uilcapampa to Uiticos, where, according to Cieza de Leon, he cheered his followers with the sight of the heads of his enemies. Unfortunately for accuracy, the custom of displaying on the ends of pikes the heads of one's enemies was European and not Peruvian. To be sure, the savage Indians of some of the Amazonian jungles do sometimes decapitate their enemies, remove the bones of the skull, dry the shrunken scalp and face, and wear the trophy as a mark of prowess just as the North American Indians did the scalps of their enemies. Such customs had no place among the peace-loving Inca agriculturists of central Peru. There were no Spaniards living with Manco at that time to report any such outrage on the bodies of Captain Villadiego's unfortunate men. Probably the *conquistadores* supposed that Manco did what the Spaniards would have done under similar circumstances.

Following the failure of Francisco Pizarro to penetrate to Uiticos, his brother, Gonzalo, "undertook the pursuit of the Inca and occupied some of his passes and bridges," but was unsuccessful in penetrating the mountain labyrinth. Being less foolhardy than Captain Villadiego, he did not come into actual conflict with Manco. Unable to subdue the young Inca or prevent his raids on travelers from Cuzco to Lima, Francisco Pizarro, "with the assent of the royal officers who were with him," established the city of Ayacucho at a convenient point on the road, so as to make it secure for travelers. Nevertheless, according to Montesinos, Manco caused the good people of Ayacucho quite a little trouble. Finally, Francisco Pizarro, "having taken one of Manco's wives prisoner with other Indians, stripped and flogged her, and then shot her to death with arrows."

Accounts of what happened in Uiticos under the rule of Manco are not very satisfactory. Father Calancha, who published in 1639 his "*Coronica Moralizada*," or "pious account of the missionary activities of the Augustinians" in Peru, says that the Inca Manco was obeyed by all the Indians who lived in a region extending "for two hundred leagues and more toward the east and toward the south, where there were innumerable Indians in various provinces." With customary monastic zeal and proper religious fervor, Father Calancha accuses the Inca of compelling the baptized Indians who fled to him from the Spaniards to abandon their new faith, torturing those who would no longer worship the old Inca "idols." This story need not be taken too literally, although undoubtedly the escaped Indians acted as though they had never been baptized.

Besides Indians fleeing from harsh masters, there came to Uilcapampa, in 1542, Gomez Perez, Diego Mendez, and half a dozen other Spanish fugitives, adherents of Almagro, "rascals," says Calancha, "worthy of Manco's favor." Obliged by the civil wars of the *conquistadores* to flee from the Pizarros, they were glad enough to find a welcome in Uiticos. To while away the time they played games and taught the Inca checkers and chess, as well as bowling-on-the-green and quoits. Montesinos says they also taught him to ride horseback and shoot an arquebus. They took their games very seriously and occasionally violent disputes arose, one of which, as we shall see, was to have fatal consequences. They were kept informed by Manco of what was going on in the viceroyalty. Although "encompassed within craggy and lofty mountains," the Inca was thoroughly cognizant of all those "revolutions" which might be of benefit to him.

Perhaps the most exciting news that reached Uiticos in 1544 was in regard to the arrival of the first Spanish viceroy. He brought the New Laws, a result of the efforts of the good Bishop Las Casas to alleviate the sufferings of the Indians. The New Laws provided, among other things, that

all the officers of the crown were to renounce their *repartimientos* or hold-
ings of Indian serfs, and that compulsory personal service was to be entirely
abolished. *Repartimientos* given to the conquerors were not to pass to their
heirs, but were to revert to the king. In other words, the New Laws gave evidence that the Spanish crown wished to be kind to the Indians and did not
approve of the Pizarros. This was good news for Manco and highly pleasing to the refugees. They persuaded the Inca to write a letter to the new
viceroy, asking permission to appear before him and offer his services to
the king. The Spanish refugees told the Inca that by this means he might
some day recover his empire, "or at least the best part of it." Their object in
persuading the Inca to send such a message to the viceroy becomes apparent when we learn that they "also wrote as from themselves desiring a pardon for what was past" and permission to return to Spanish dominions.

Gomez Perez, who seems to have been the active leader of the little
group, was selected to be the bearer of the letters from the Inca and the
refugees. Attended by a dozen Indians whom the Inca instructed to act as
his servants and bodyguard, he left Uilcapampa, presented his letters to the
viceroy, and gave him "a large relation of the State and Condition of the Inca,
and of his true and real designs to doe him service." "The Vice-king joyfully
received the news, and granted a full and ample pardon of all crimes, as
desired. And as to the Inca, he made many kind expressions of love and
respect, truly considering that the Interest of the Inca might be advantageous to him, both in War and Peace. And with this satisfactory answer
Gomez Perez returned both to the Inca and to his companions." The
refugees were delighted with the news and got ready to return to king and
country. Their departure from Uiticos was prevented by a tragic accident,
thus described by Garcilasso.

"The Inca, to humour the Spaniards and entertain himself with them,
had given directions for making a bowling-green; where playing one day
with Gomez Perez, he came to have some quarrel and difference with this
Perez about the measure of a Cast, which often happened between them;
for this Perez, being a person of a hot and fiery brain, without any judgment
or understanding, would take the least occasion in the world to contend
with and provoke the Inca.... Being no longer able to endure his rudeness,
the Inca punched him on the breast, and bid him to consider with whom
he talked. Perez, not considering in his heat and passion either his own safety
or the safety of his Companions, lifted up his hand, and with the bowl struck
the Inca so violently on the head, that he knocked him down. [He died three

days later.] The Indians hereupon, being enraged by the death of their Prince, joined together against Gomez and the Spaniards, who fled into a house, and with their Swords in their hands defended the door; the Indians set fire to the house, which being too hot for them, they sallied out into the Marketplace, where the Indians assaulted them and shot them with their Arrows until they had killed every man of them; and then afterwards, out of mere rage and fury they designed either to eat them raw as their custome was, or to burn them and cast their ashes into the river, that no sign or appearance might remain of them; but at length, after some consultation, they agreed to cast their bodies into the open fields, to be devoured by vultures and birds of the air, which they supposed to be the highest indignity and dishonour that they could show to their Corps." Garcilasso concludes: "I informed myself very perfectly from those chiefs and nobles who were present and eye-witnesses of the unparalleled piece of madness of that rash and hair-brained fool; and heard them tell this story to my mother and parents with tears in their eyes." There are many versions of the tragedy.[1] They all agree that a Spaniard murdered the Inca.

Thus, in 1545, the reign of an attractive and vigorous personality was brought to an abrupt close. Manco left three young sons, Sayri Tupac, Titu Cusi, and Tupac Amaru. Sayri Tupac, although he had not yet reached his majority, became Inca in his father's stead, and with the aid of regents reigned for ten years without disturbing his Spanish neighbors or being annoyed by them, unless the reference in Montesinos to a proposed burning of bridges near Abancay, under date of 1555, is correct. By a curious lapse Montesinos ascribes this attempt to the Inca Manco, who had been dead for ten years. In 1555 there came to Lima a new viceroy, who decided that it would be safer if young Sayri Tupac were within reach instead of living in the inaccessible wilds of Uilcapampa. The viceroy wisely undertook to accomplish this difficult matter through the Princess Beatrix Coya, an aunt of the Inca, who was living in Cuzco. She took kindly to the suggestion and dispatched to Uiticos a messenger, of the blood royal, attended by Indian servants. The journey was a dangerous one; bridges were down and the treacherous trails were well-nigh impassable. Sayri Tupac's regents permitted the messenger to enter Uilcapampa and deliver the viceroy's invitation, but were not inclined to believe that it was quite so attractive as appeared on the surface, even though brought to them by a kinsman. Accordingly, they kept the visitor as a hostage and sent a messenger of their own to Cuzco to see if any foul play could be discovered, and also to request that one John Sierra, a more trusted cousin, be sent to treat in this matter. All this took time.

In 1558 the viceroy, becoming impatient, dispatched from Lima Friar Melchior and one John Betanzos, who had married the daughter of the unfortunate Inca Atahualpa and pretended to be very learned in his wife's language. Montesinos says he was a "great linguist." They started off quite confidently for Uiticos, taking with them several pieces of velvet and damask, and two cups of gilded silver as presents. Anxious to secure the honor of being the first to reach the Inca, they traveled as fast as they could to the Chuquichaca bridge, "the key to the valley of Uiticos." Here they were detained by the soldiers of the regents. A day or so later John Sierra, the Inca's cousin from Cuzco, arrived at the bridge and was allowed to proceed, while the friar and Betanzos were still detained. John Sierra was welcomed by the Inca and his nobles, and did his best to encourage Sayri Tupac to accept the viceroy's offer. Finally John Betanzos and the friar were also sent for and admitted to the presence of the Inca, with the presents which the viceroy had sent. Sayri Tupac's first idea was to remain free and independent as he had hitherto done, so he requested the ambassadors to depart immediately with their silver gilt cups. They were sent back by one of the western routes across the Apurimac. A few days later, however, after John Sierra had told him some interesting stories of life in Cuzco, the Inca decided to reconsider the matter. His regents had a long debate, observed the flying of birds and the nature of the weather, but according to Garcilasso "made no inquiries of the devil." The omens were favorable and the regents finally decided to allow the Inca to accept the invitation of the viceroy.

Sayri Tupac, anxious to see something of the world, went directly to Lima, traveling in a litter made of rich materials, carried by relays chosen from the three hundred Indians who attended him. He was kindly received by the viceroy, and then went to Cuzco, where he lodged in his aunt's house. Here his relatives went to welcome him. "I, myself," says Garcilasso, "went in the name of my Father. I found him then playing a certain game used amongst the Indians.... I kissed his hands, and delivered my Message; he commanded me to sit down, and presently they brought two gilded cups of that Liquor, made of Mayz [chicha] which scarce contained four ounces of Drink; he took them both, and with his own Hand he gave one of them to me; he drank, and I pledged him, which as we have said, is the custom of Civility amongst them. This Ceremony being past, he asked me, Why I did not meet him at Uilcapampa. I answered him,

'Inca, as I am but a Youngman, the Governours make no account of me, to place me in such Ceremonies as these!' 'How', replied the Inca, 'I would rather have seen you than all the Friers and Fathers in Town.' As I was going away I made him a submissive bow and reverence, after the manner of the Indians, who are of his Alliance and Kindred, at which he was so much pleased, that he embraced me heartily, and with much affection, as appeared by his Countenance."

Sayri Tupac now received the sacred Red Fringe of Inca sovereignty, was married to a princess of the blood royal, joined her in baptism, and took up his abode in the beautiful valley of Yucay, a day's journey northeast of Cuzco, and never returned to Uiticos. His only daughter finally married a certain Captain Garcia, of whom more anon. Sayri Tupac died in 1560, leaving two brothers; the older, Titu Cusi Yupanqui, illegitimate, and the younger, Tupac Amaru, his rightful successor, an inexperienced youth.

The throne of Uiticos was seized by Titu Cusi. The new Inca seems to have been suspicious of the untimely death of Sayri Tupac, and to have felt that the Spaniards were capable of more foul play. So with his half-brother he stayed quietly in Uilcapampa. Their first visitor, so far as we know, was Diego Rodriguez de Figueroa, who wrote an interesting account of Uiticos and says he gave the Inca a pair of scissors. He was unsuccessful in his efforts to get Titu Cusi to go to Cuzco. In time there came an Augustinian missionary, Friar Marcos Garcia, who, six years after the death of Sayri Tupac, entered the rough country of Uilcapampa, "a land of moderate wealth, large rivers, and the usual rains," whose "forested mountains," says Father Calancha, "are magnificent." Friar Marcos had a hard journey. The bridges were down, the roads had been destroyed, and the passes blocked up. The few Indians who did occasionally appear in Cuzco from Uilcapampa said the friar could not get there "unless he should be able to change himself into a bird." However, with that courage and pertinacity which have marked so many missionary enterprises, Friar Marcos finally overcame all difficulties and reached Uiticos.

The missionary chronicler says that Titu Cusi was far from glad to see him and received him angrily. It worried him to find that a Spaniard had succeeded in penetrating his retreat. Besides, the Inca was annoyed to have any one preach against his "idolatries." Titu Cusi's own story, as written down by Friar Marcos, does not agree with Calancha's. Anyhow, Friar Marcos built a little church in a place called Puquiura, where many of the Inca's people were then living. "He planted crosses in the fields and on the mountains, these being the best things to frighten off devils." He "suffered many insults at the hands of the chiefs and principal followers of the Inca. Some of them did it to please the Devil, others to flatter the Inca, and many because they disliked his sermons, in which he scolded them for their vices and abominated among his converts the possession of four or six wives. So they punished him in the matter of food, and forced him to send to Cuzco for victuals. The Convent sent him hard-tack, which was for him a most delicious banquet."

Within a year or so another Augustinian missionary, Friar Diego Ortiz, left Cuzco alone for Uilcapampa. He suffered much on the road, but finally reached the retreat of the Inca and entered his presence in company with Friar Marcos. "Although the Inca was not too happy to see a new preacher, he was willing to grant him an entrance because the Inca...thought Friar Diego would not vex him nor take the trouble to reprove him. So the Inca gave him a license. They selected the town of Huarancalla, which was populous and well located in the midst of a number of other little towns and villages. There was a distance of two or three days journey from one Convent to the other. Leaving Friar Marcos in Puquiura, Friar Diego went to his new establishment and in a short time built a church, a house for himself, and a hospital,—all poor buildings made in a short time." He also started a school for children, and became very popular as he went about healing and teaching. He had an easier time than Friar Marcos, who, with less tact and no skill as a physician, was located nearer the center of the Inca cult.

The principal shrine of the Inca is described by Father Calancha as follows: "Close to Vitcos [or Uiticos] in a village called Chuquipalpa, is a House of the Sun, and in it a white rock over a spring of water where the Devil appears as a visible manifestation and was worshipped by those idolators. This was the principal *mochadero* of those forested mountains. The word 'mochadero'² is the common name which the Indians apply to their places of worship. In other words it is the only place where they practice the sacred ceremony of kissing. The origin of this, the principal part of their ceremonial, is that very practice which Job abominates when he solemnly clears himself of all offences before God and says to Him: 'Lord, all these punishments and even greater burdens would I have deserved had I done that which the blind Gentiles do when the sun rises resplendent or the moon shines clear and they exult in their hearts and extend their hands toward the sun and throw kisses to it, an act of very grave iniquity which is equivalent to denying the true God."

URUMBAMBA VALLEY NEAR MACHU PICCHU, PERU

Thus does the ecclesiastical chronicler refer to the practice in Peru of that particular form of worship of the heavenly bodies which was also widely spread in the East, in Arabia, and Palestine and was inveighed against by Mohammed as well as the ancient Hebrew prophets. Apparently this ceremony "of the most profound resignation and reverence" was practiced in Chuquipalpa, close to Uiticos, in the reign of the Inca Titu Cusi.

Calancha goes on to say: "In this white stone of the aforesaid House of the Sun, which is called Yurac Rumi [meaning, in Quichua, a white rock], there attends a Devil who is Captain of a legion. He and his legionaries show great kindness to the Indian idolators, but great terrors to the Catholics. They abuse with hideous cruelties the baptized ones who now no longer worship them with kisses, and many of the Indians have died from the horrible frights these devils have given them."

One day, when the Inca and his mother and their principal chiefs and counselors were away from Uiticos on a visit to some of their outlying estates, Friar Marcos and Friar Diego decided to make a spectacular attack on this particular Devil, who was at the great "white rock over a spring of water." The two monks summoned all their converts to gather at Puquiura, in the church or the neighboring plaza, and asked each to bring a stick of firewood in order that they might burn up this Devil who had tormented them. "An innumerable multitude" came together on the day appointed. The converted Indians were most anxious to get even with this Devil who had slain their friends and inflicted wounds on themselves; the doubters were curious to see the result; the Inca priests were there to see their god defeat the Christians'; while, as may readily be imagined, the rest of the population came to see the excitement. Starting out from Pucyura they marched to "the Temple of the Sun, in the village of Chuquipalpa, close to Uiticos."

Arrived at the sacred palisade, the monks raised the standard of the cross, recited their orisons, surrounded the spring, the white rock and the Temple of the Sun, and piled high the firewood. Then, having exorcised the locality, they called the Devil by all the vile names they could think of, to show their lack of respect, and finally commanded him never to return to this vicinity. Calling on Christ and the Virgin, they applied fire to the wood. "The poor Devil then fled roaring in a fury, and making the mountains to tremble."

It took remarkable courage on the part of the two lone monks thus to desecrate the chief shrine of the people among whom they were dwelling. It is almost incredible that in this remote valley, separated from their friends and far from the protecting hand of the Spanish viceroy, they should have dared to commit such an insult to the religion of their hosts. Of course, as soon as the Inca Titu Cusi heard of it, he was greatly annoyed. His mother was furious. They returned immediately to Pucyura. The chiefs wished to "slay the monks and tear them into small pieces," and undoubtedly would have done so had it not been for the regard in which Friar Diego was held. His skill in curing disease had so endeared him to the Indians that even the Inca himself dared not punish him for the attack on the Temple of the Sun. Friar Marcos, however, who probably originated the plan, and had done little to gain the good will of the Indians, did not fare so well. Calancha says he was stoned out of the province and the Inca threatened to kill him if he ever should return. Friar Diego, particularly beloved by those Indians who came from the fever-stricken jungles in the lower valleys, was allowed to remain, and finally became a trusted friend and adviser of Titu Cusi.

One day a Spaniard named Romero, an adventurous prospector for gold, was found penetrating the mountain valleys, and succeeded in getting permission from the Inca to see what minerals were there. He was too successful. Both gold and silver were found among the hills and he showed enthusiastic delight at his good fortune. The Inca, fearing that his reports might encourage others to enter Uilcapampa, put the unfortunate prospector to death, notwithstanding the protestations of Friar Diego. Foreigners were not wanted in Uilcapampa.

In the year 1570, ten years after the accession of Titu Cusi to the Inca throne in Uiticos, a new Spanish viceroy came to Cuzco. Unfortunately for the Incas, Don Francisco de Toledo, an indefatigable solider and administrator, was excessively bigoted, narrow-minded, cruel, and pitiless. Furthermore, Philip II and his Council of the Indies had decided that it would be worth while to make every effort to get the Inca out of Uiticos. For thirty-five years the Spanish conquerors had occupied Cuzco and the major portion of Peru without having been able to secure the submission of the Indians who lived in the province of Uilcapampa. It would be a great feather in the cap of Toledo if he could induce Titu Cusi to come and live where he would always be accessible to Spanish authority.

During the ensuing rainy season, after an unusually lively party, the Inca got soaked, had a chill, and was laid low. In the meantime the viceroy had picked out a Cuzco soldier, one Tilano de Anaya, who was well liked by the Inca, to try to persuade Titu Cusi to come to Cuzco. Tilano was instructed to go by way of Ollantaytambo and the Chuquichaca bridge. Luck was against him. Titu Cusi's illness was very serious. Friar Diego, his physician, had prescribed the usual remedies. Unfortunately, all the monk's skill was unavailing and his royal patient died. The "remedies" were held by Titu Cusi's mother and her counselors to be responsible. The poor friar had to suffer the penalty of death "for having caused the death of the Inca."

The third son of Manco, Tupac Amaru, brought up as a playfellow of the Virgins of the Sun in the Temple near Uiticos, and now happily married, was selected to rule the little kingdom. His brows were decked with the Scarlet Fringe of Sovereignty, but, thanks to the jealous fear of his powerful illegitimate brother, his training had not been that of a soldier. He was destined to have a brief, unhappy existence. When the young Inca's counselors heard that a messenger was coming from the viceroy, seven warriors were sent to meet him on the road. Tilano was preparing to spend the night at the Chuquichaca bridge when he was attacked and killed.

The viceroy heard of the murder of his ambassador at the same time that he learned of the martyrdom of Friar Diego. A blow had been struck at the very heart of Spanish domination; if the representatives of the Vice-Regent of Heaven and the messengers of the viceroy of Philip II were not inviolable, then who was safe? On Palm Sunday the energetic Toledo, surrounded by his council, determined to make war on the unfortunate young Tupac Amaru and give a reward to the soldier who would effect his capture. The council was of the opinion that "many Insurrections might be raised in that Empire by this young Heir." "Moreover it was alleged," says Garcilasso, ... "That by the Imprisonment of the Inca, all that *Treasure* might be discovered, which appertained to former kings, together with that Chain of Gold, which Huayna Capac commanded to be made for himself to wear on the great and solemn days of their Festival"! Furthermore, the "Chain of Gold with the remaining Treasure *belong'd* to his Catholic Majesty by right of Conquest"! Excuses were not wanting. The Incas must be exterminated.

The expedition was divided into two parts. One company was sent by way of Limatambo to Curahuasi, to head off the Inca in case he should cross the Apurimac and try to escape by one of the routes which had formerly been used by his father, Manco, in his marauding expeditions. The other company, under General Martin Hurtado and Captain Garcia, marched from Cuzco by way of Yucay and Ollantaytambo. They were more fortunate than Captain Villadiego whose force, thirty-five years before, had been met and destroyed at the pass of Panticalla. That was in the days of the active Inca Manco. Now there was no force defending this important pass. They descended the Lucumayo to its junction with the Urubamba and came to the bridge of Chuquichaca.

The narrow suspension bridge, built of native fibers, sagged deeply in the middle and swayed so threateningly over the gorge of the Urubamba that only one man could pass it at a time. The rapid river was too deep to be forded. There were no canoes. It would have been a difficult matter to have constructed rafts, for most of the trees that grow here are of hard wood and do not float. On the other side of the Urubamba was young Tupac Amaru, surrounded by his councilors, chiefs, and soldiers. The first hostile forces which in Pizarro's time had endeavored to fight their way into Uilcapampa had never been allowed by Manco to get as far as this. His youngest son, Tupac Amaru, had had no experience in these matters. The chiefs and nobles had failed to defend the pass; and they now failed to destroy the Chuquichaca bridge, apparently relying on their ability to take care of one Spanish soldier at a time and prevent the Spaniards from crossing the narrow, swaying structure. General Hurtado was not taking any such chances. He had brought with him one or two light mountain field pieces, with which the raw troops of the Inca were little acquainted. The sides of the valley at this point rise steeply from the river and the reverberations caused by gun fire would be fairly terrifying to those who had never heard anything like it before. A few volleys from the guns and the arquebuses, and the Indians fled pellmell in every direction, leaving the bridge undefended.

Captain Garcia, who had married the daughter of Sayri Tupac, was sent in pursuit of the Inca. His men found the road "narrow in the ascent, with forest on the right, and on the left a ravine of great depth." It was only a footpath, barely wide enough for two men to pass. Garcia, with customary Spanish bravery, marched at the head of his company. Suddenly out of the thick forest an Inca chieftain named Hualpa, endeavoring to protect the flight of Tupac Amaru, sprang on Garcia, held him so that he could not get at his sword and endeavored to hurl him over the cliff. The captain's life was saved by a faithful Indian servant who was following immediately behind him, carrying his sword. Drawing it from the scabbard "with much dexterity and animation," the Indian killed Hualpa and saved his master's life.

Garcia fought several battles, took some forts and succeeded in capturing many prisoners. From them it was learned that the Inca had "gone inland toward the valley of Simaponte; and that he was flying to the country of the Mañaries Indians, a warlike tribe and his friends, where *balsas* and canoes were posted to save him and enable him to escape." Nothing daunted by the dangers of the jungle nor the rapids of the river, Garcia finally managed to construct five rafts, on which he put some of his soldiers. Accompanying them himself, he descended the rapids, escaping death many times by swimming, and finally arrived at a place called Momori, only to find that the Inca, learning of their approach, had gone farther into the woods. Garcia followed hard after, although he and his men were by this time barefooted and suffering from want of food. They finally captured the Inca. Garcilasso says that Tupac Amaru, "considering that he had not People to make resistance, and that he was not conscious to himself of any Crime, or disturbance he had done or raised, suffered himself to be taken; choosing rather to entrust himself in the hands of the Spaniards, than to perish in those Mountains with Famine, or be drowned in those great Rivers.... The Spaniards in this manner seizing on the Inca, and on all the Indian Men and Women, who were in Company with him, amongst which was his Wife, two Sons, and a Daughter, returned with them in Triumph to Cuzco; to which place the Vice-King went, so soon as he was informed of the imprisonment of the poor Prince." A mock trial was held. The captured chiefs were tortured to death with fiendish brutality. Tupac Amaru's wife was mangled before his eyes. His own head was cut off and placed on a pole in the Cuzco Plaza. His little boys did not long survive. So perished the last of the Incas, descendants of the wisest Indian rulers America has ever seen.

BRIEF SUMMARY OF THE LAST FOUR INCAS

1534. The Inca *Manco* ascends the throne of his fathers.

1536. *Manco* flees from Cuzco to Uiticos and Uilcapampa.

1542. Promulgation of the "New Laws."

1545. Murder of *Manco* and accession of his son *Sayri Tupac.*

1555. *Sayri Tupac* goes to Cuzco and Yucay.

1560. Death of *Sayri Tupac.* His half brother *Titu Cusi* becomes Inca.

1566. Friar Marcos reaches Uiticos. Settles in Puquiura.

1566. Friar Diego joins him.

1568-9 (?). They burn the House of the Sun at Yurac Rumi in Chuquipalpa.

1571. *Titu Cusi* dies. Friar Diego suffers martyrdom. *Tupac Amaru* becomes Inca.

1572. Expedition of General Martin Hurtado and Captain Garcia de Loyola. Execution of *Tupac Amaru*.

[1] Another version of this event is that the quarrel was over a game of *chess* between the Inca and Diego Mendez, another of the refugees, who lost his temper and called the Inca a dog. Angered at the tone and language of his guest, the Inca gave him a blow with his fist. Diego Mendez thereupon drew a dagger and killed him. A totally different account from the one obtained by Garcilasso from his informants is that in a volume purporting to have been dictated to Friar Marcos by Manco's son, Titu Cusi, twenty years after the event. I quote from Sir Clements Markham's translation:

"After these Spaniards had been with my Father for several years in the said town of Viticos they were one day, with much good fellowship, playing at quoits with him; only them, my Father and me, who was then a boy [ten years old]. Without having any suspicion, although an Indian woman, named Banba, had said that the Spaniards wanted to murder the Inca, my Father was playing with them as usual. In this game, just as my Father was raising the quoit to throw, they all rushed upon him with knives, daggers and some swords. My Father, feeling himself wounded, strove to make some defence, but he was one and unarmed, and they were seven fully armed; he fell to the ground covered with wounds, and they left him for dead. I, being a little boy, and seeing my Father treated in this manner, wanted to go where he was to help him. But they turned furiously upon me, and hurled a lance which only just failed to kill me also. I was terrified and fled amongst some bushes. They looked for me, but could not find me. The Spaniards, seeing that my Father had ceased to breathe, went out of the gate, in high spirits, saying, 'Now that we have killed the Inca we have nothing to fear.' But at this moment the captain Rimachi Yupanqui arrived with some Antis, and presently chased them in such sort that, before they could get very far along a difficult road, they were caught and pulled from their horses. They all had to suffer very cruel deaths and some were burnt. Notwithstanding his wounds my Father lived for three days."

Another version is given by Montesinos in his *Anales*. It is more like Titu Cusi's.

[2] A Spanish derivative from the Quichua *mucha*, "a kiss." *Muchani* means "to adore, to reverence, to kiss the hands."

CHAPTER 10

SEARCHING FOR THE LAST INCA CAPITAL

✴

THE EVENTS DESCRIBED in the preceding chapter happened, for the most part, in Uiticos[1] and Uilcapampa, northwest of Ollantaytambo, about one hundred miles away from the Cuzco palace of the Spanish viceroy, in what Prescott calls "the remote fastnesses of the Andes." One looks in vain for Uiticos on modern maps of Peru, although several of the older maps give it. In 1625 "Viticos" is marked on de Laet's map of Peru as a mountainous province northeast of Lima and three hundred and fifty miles northwest of Vilcabamba! This error was copied by some later cartographers, including Mercator, until about 1740, when "Viticos" disappeared from all maps of Peru. The map makers had learned that there was no such place in that vicinity. Its real location was lost about three hundred years ago. A map published at Nuremberg in 1599 gives "Pincos" in the "Andes" mountains, a small range west of "Cusco." This does not seem to have been adopted by other cartographers; although a Paris map of 1739 gives "Picos" in about the same place. Nearly all the cartographers of the eighteenth century who give "Viticos" supposed it to be the name of a tribe, e.g., "Los Viticos" or "Les Viticos."

The largest official map of Peru, the work of that remarkable explorer, Raimondi, who spent his life crossing and recrossing Peru, does not contain the word Uiticos nor any of its numerous spellings, Viticos, Vitcos, Pitcos, or Biticos. Incidentally, it may seem strange that Uiticos could ever be written "Biticos." The Quichua language has no sound of V. The early Spanish writers, however, wrote the capital letter U exactly like a capital V.

In official documents and letters Uiticos became Viticos. The official readers, who had never heard the word pronounced, naturally used the V sound instead of the U sound. Both V and P easily become B. So Uiticos became Biticos and Uilcapampa became Vilcabamba.

Raimondi's marvelous energy led him to penetrate to more out-of-the-way Peruvian villages than any one had ever done before or is likely to do again. He stopped at nothing in the way of natural obstacles. In 1865 he went deep into the heart of Uilcapampa; yet found no Uiticos. He believed that the ruins of Choqquequirau represented the residence of the last Incas. This view had been held by the French explorer, Count de Sartiges, in 1834, who believed that Choqquequirau was abandoned when Sayri Tupac, Manco's oldest son, went to live in Yucay. Raimondi's view was also held by the leading Peruvian geographers, including Paz Soldan in 1877, and by Prefect Nuñez and his friends in 1909, at the time of my visit to Choqquequirau[2]. The only dissenter was the learned Peruvian historian, Don Carlos Romero, who insisted that the last Inca capital must be found elsewhere. He urged the importance of searching for Uiticos in the valleys of the rivers now called Vilcabamba and Urubamba. It was to be the work of the Yale Peruvian Expedition of 1911 to collect the geographical evidence which would meet the requirements of the chronicles and establish the whereabouts of the long-lost Inca capital.

That there were undescribed and unidentified ruins to be found in the Urubamba Valley was known to a few people in Cuzco, mostly wealthy planters who had large estates in the province of Convencion. One told us that he went to Santa Ana every year and was acquainted with a muleteer who had told him of some interesting ruins near the San Miguel bridge. Knowing the propensity of his countrymen to exaggerate, however, he placed little confidence in the story and, shrugging his shoulders, had crossed the bridge a score of times without taking the trouble to look into the matter. Another, Señor Pancorbo, whose plantation was in the Vilcabamba Valley, said that he had heard vague rumors of ruins in the valley above his plantation, particularly near Pucyura. If his story should prove to be correct, then it was likely that this might be the very Puquiura where Friar Marcos had established the first church in the "province of Uilcapampa." But that was "near" Uiticos and near a village called Chuquipalpa, where should be found the ruins of a Temple of the Sun, and in these ruins a "white rock over a spring of water." Yet neither these friendly planters nor the friends among whom they inquired had ever heard of Uiticos or a place called Chuquipalpa, or of such an interesting rock; nor had they themselves seen the ruins of which they had heard.

One of Señor Lomellini's friends, a talkative old fellow who had spent a large part of his life in prospecting for mines in the department of Cuzco, said that he had seen ruins "finer than Choqquequirau" at a place called Huayna Picchu; but he had never been to Choqquequirau. Those who knew him best shrugged their shoulders and did not seem to place much confidence in his word. Too often he had been over-enthusiastic about mines which did not "pan out." Yet his report resembled that of Charles Wiener, a French explorer, who, about 1875, in the course of his wanderings in the Andes, visited Ollantaytambo. While there he was told that there were fine ruins down the Urubamba Valley at a place called "Huaina-Picchu or Matcho-Picchu." He decided to go down the valley and look for these ruins. According to his text he crossed the Pass of Panticalla, descended the Lucumayo River to the bridge of Choqquechacca, and visited the lower Urubamba, returning by the same route. He published a detailed map of the valley. To one of its peaks he gives the name "Huaynapicchu, ele. 1815 m." and to another "Matchopicchu, ele. 1720 m." His interest in Inca ruins was very keen. He devotes pages to Ollantaytambo. He failed to reach Machu Picchu or to find any ruins of importance in the Urubamba or Vilcabamba valleys. Could we hope to be any more successful? Would the rumors that had reached us "pan out" as badly as those to which Wiener had listened so eagerly? Since his day, to be sure, the Peruvian Government had actually finished a road which led past Machu Picchu. On the other hand, a Harvard Anthropological Expedition, under the leadership of Dr. William C. Farrabee, had recently been over this road without reporting any ruins of importance. They were looking for savages and not ruins. Nevertheless, if Machu Picchu was "finer than Choqquequirau" why had no one pointed it out to them?

To most of our friends in Cuzco the idea that there could be anything finer than Choqquequirau seemed absurd. They regarded that "cradle of gold" as "the most remarkable archeological discovery of recent times." They assured us there was nothing half so good. They even assumed that we were secretly planning to return thither to *dig for buried treasure!* Denials were of no avail. To a people whose ancestors made fortunes out of lucky "strikes," and who themselves have been brought up on stories of enormous wealth still remaining to be discovered by some fortunate excavator, the question of *tesoro*—treasure, wealth, riches—is an ever-present source of conversation. Even the prefect of Cuzco was quite unable to conceive of my doing anything for the love of discovery. He was convinced that I should find great riches at Choqquequirau—and that I was in receipt of a very large salary! He refused to believe that the members of the Expedition received no more than their expenses. He told me confidentially that Professor Foote would sell his collection of insects for at least $10,000! Peruvians have not been accustomed to see any one do scientific work except as he was paid by the government or employed by a railroad or mining company. We have frequently found our work misunderstood and regarded with suspicion, even by the Cuzco Historical Society.

The valley of the Urubamba, or Uilcamayu, as it used to be called, may be reached from Cuzco in several ways. The usual route for those going to Yucay is northwest from the city, over the great Andean highway, past the slopes of Mt. Sencca. At Ttica-Ttica (12,000 ft.) the road crosses the lowest pass at the western end of the Cuzco Basin. At the last point from which one can see the city of Cuzco, all true Indians, whether on their way out of the valley or into it, pause, turn toward the east, facing the city, remove their hats and mutter a prayer. I believe that the words they use now are those of the "Ave Maria," or some other familiar orison of the Catholic Church. Nevertheless, the custom undoubtedly goes far back of the advent of the first Spanish missionaries. It is probably a relic of the ancient habit of worshiping the rising sun. During the centuries immediately preceding the conquest, the city of Cuzco was the residence of the Inca himself, that divine individual who was at once the head of Church and State. Nothing would have been more natural than for persons coming in sight of his residence to perform an act of veneration. This in turn might have led those leaving the city to fall into the same habit at the same point in the road. I have watched hundreds of travelers pass this point. None of those whose European costume proclaimed a white or mixed ancestry stopped to pray or make obeisance. On the other hand, all those, without exception, who were clothed in a native costume, which betokened that they considered themselves to be Indians rather than whites, paused for a moment, gazing at the ancient city, removed their hats, and said a short prayer.

Leaving Ttica-Ttica, we went northward for several leagues, passed the town of Chincheros, with its old Inca walls, and came at length to the edge of the wonderful valley of Yucay. In its bottom are great level terraces rescued from the Urubamba River by the untiring energy of the ancient folk.

On both sides of the valley the steep slopes bear many remains of narrow terraces, some of which are still in use. Above them are "*temporales*," fields of grain, resting like a patch-work quilt on slopes so steep it seems incredible they could be cultivated. Still higher up, their heads above the clouds, are the jagged snow-capped peaks. The whole offers a marvelous picture, rich in contrast, majestic in proportion. In Yucay once dwelt the Inca Manco's oldest son, Sayri Tupac, after he had accepted the viceroy's invitation to come under Spanish protection. Here he lived three years and here, in 1560, he died an untimely death under circumstances which led his brothers, Titu Cusi and Tupac Amaru, to think that they would be safer in Uiticos. We spent the night in Urubamba, the modern capital of the province, much favored by Peruvians of to-day because of its abundant water supply, delightful climate, and rich fruits. Cuzco, 11,000 feet, is too high to have charming surroundings, but two thousand feet lower, in the Urubamba Valley, there is everything to please the eye and delight the horticulturist.

Speaking of horticulturists reminds me of their enemies. Uru is the Quichua word for caterpillars or grubs, pampa means flat land. Urubamba is "flat-land-where-there-are-grubs-or-caterpillars." Had it been named by people who came up from a warm region where insects abound, it would hardly have been so denominated. Only people not accustomed to land where caterpillars and grubs flourished would have been struck by such a circumstance. Consequently, the valley was probably named by plateau dwellers who were working their way down into a warm region where butterflies and moths are more common. Notwithstanding its celebrated caterpillars, Urubamba's gardens to-day are full of roses, lilies, and other brilliant flowers. There are orchards of peaches, pears, and apples; there are fields where luscious strawberries are raised for the Cuzco market. Apparently, the grubs do not get everything.

The next day down the valley brought us to romantic Ollantaytambo, described in glowing terms by Castelnau, Marcou, Wiener, and Squier many years ago. It has lost none of its charm, even though Marcou's drawings are imaginary and Squier's are exaggerated. Here, as at Urubamba, there are flower gardens and highly cultivated green fields. The brooks are shaded by willows and poplars. Above them are magnificent precipices crowned by snow-capped peaks. The village itself was once the capital of an ancient principality whose history is shrouded in mystery. There are ruins of curious gabled buildings, storehouses, "prisons," or "monasteries," perched here and there on well-nigh inaccessible crags above the village. Below are broad terraces of unbelievable extent where abundant crops are still harvested; terraces which will stand for ages to come as monuments to the energy and skill of a bygone race. The "fortress" is on a little hill, surrounded by steep cliffs, high walls, and hanging gardens so as to be difficult of access. Centuries ago, when the tribe which cultivated the rich fields in this valley lived in fear and terror of their savage neighbors, this hill offered a place of refuge to which they could retire. It may have been fortified at that time. As centuries passed in which the land came under the control of the Incas, whose chief interest was the peaceful promotion of agriculture, it is likely that this fortress became a royal garden. The six great ashlars of reddish granite weighing fifteen or twenty tons each, and placed in line on the summit of the hill, were brought from a quarry several miles away with an immense amount of labor and pains. They were probably intended to be a record of the magnificence of an able ruler. Not only could he command the services of a sufficient number of men to extract these rocks from the quarry and carry them up an inclined plane from the bottom of the valley to the summit of the hill; he had to supply the men with food. The building of such a monument meant taking five hundred Indians away from their ordinary occupations as agriculturists. He must have been a very good administrator. To his people the magnificent megaliths were doubtless a source of pride. To his enemies they were a symbol of his power and might.

A league below Ollantaytambo the road forks. The right branch ascends a steep valley and crosses the pass of Panticalla near snow-covered Mt. Veronica. Near the pass are two groups of ruins. One of them, extravagantly referred to by Wiener as a "granite palace, whose appearance [*appareil*] resembles the more beautiful parts of Ollantaytambo," was only a storehouse. The other was probably a *tampu*, or inn, for the benefit of official travelers. All travelers in Inca times, even the bearers of burdens, were acting under official orders. Commercial business was unknown. The rights of personal property were not understood. No one had anything to sell; no one had any money to buy it with. On the other hand, the Incas had an elaborate system of tax collecting. Two thirds of the produce raised by their subjects was claimed by the civil and religious rulers. It was a reasonable provision of the benevolent despotism of the Incas that inhospitable regions like the Panticalla Pass near Mt. Veronica should be provided with suitable rest houses and storehouses. Polo de Ondegardo, an able and accomplished statesman, who was in office in Cuzco in 1560, says that the food of the *chasquis,* Inca post runners, was provided from official storehouses; "those who worked for the Inca's service, or for religion, never ate at their own expense." In Manco's day these buildings at Havaspampa probably sheltered the outpost which defeated Captain Villadiego.

Before the completion of the river road, about 1895, travelers from Cuzco to the lower Urubamba had a choice of two routes, one by way of the pass of Panticalla, followed by Captain Garcia in 1571, by General Miller in 1835, Castelnau in 1842, and Wiener in 1875; and one by way of the pass between Mts. Salcantay and Soray, along the Salcantay River to Huadquiña, followed by the Count de Sartiges in 1834 and Raimondi in 1865. Both of these routes avoid the highlands between Mt. Salcantay and Mt. Veronica and the lowlands between the villages of Piri and Huadquiña. This region was in 1911 undescribed in the geographical literature of southern Peru. We decided not to use either pass, but to go straight down the Urubamba river road. It led us into a fascinating country.

Two leagues beyond Piri, at Salapunco, the road skirts the base of precipitous cliffs, the beginnings of a wonderful mass of granite mountains which have made Uilcapampa more difficult of access than the surrounding highlands which are composed of schists, conglomerates, and limestone. Salapunco is the natural gateway to the ancient province, but it was closed for centuries by the combined efforts of nature and man. The Urubamba River, in cutting its way through the granite range, forms rapids too dangerous to be passable and precipices which can be scaled only with great effort and considerable peril. At one time a footpath probably ran near the river, where the Indians, by crawling along the face of the cliff and sometimes swinging from one ledge to another on hanging vines, were able to make their way to any of the alluvial terraces down the valley. Another path may have gone over the cliffs above the fortress, where we noticed, in various inaccessible places, the remains of walls built on narrow ledges. They were too narrow and too irregular to have been intended to support agricultural terraces. They may have been built to make the cliff more precipitous. They probably represent the foundations of an old trail. To defend these ancient paths we found that prehistoric man had built, at the foot of the precipices, close to the river, a small but powerful fortress whose ruins now pass by the name of Salapunco; *sala* = ruins; *punco* = gateway. Fashioned after famous Sacsahuaman and resembling it in the irregular character of the large ashlars and also by reason of the salients and reëntrant angles which enabled its defenders to prevent the walls being successfully scaled, it presents an interesting problem.

Commanding as it does the entrance to the valley of Torontoy, Salapunco may have been built by some ancient chief to enable him to levy tribute on all who passed. My first impression was that the fortress was placed here, at the end of the temperate zone, to defend the valleys of Urubamba and Ollantaytambo against savage enemies coming up from the forests of the Amazon. On the other hand, it is possible that Salapunco was built by the tribes occupying the fastnesses of Uilcapampa as an outpost to defend them against enemies coming down the valley from the direction of Ollantaytambo. They could easily have held it against a considerable force, for it is powerfully built and constructed with skill. Supplies from the plantations of Torontoy, lower down the river, might have reached it along the path which antedated the present government road. Salapunco may have been occupied by the troops of the Inca Manco when he established himself in Uiticos and ruled over Uilcapampa. He could hardly, however, have built a megalithic work of this kind. It is more likely that he would have destroyed the narrow trails than have attempted to hold the fort against the soldiers of Pizarro. Furthermore, its style and character seem to date it with the well-known megalithic structures of Cuzco and Ollantaytambo. This makes it seem all the more extraordinary that Salapunco could ever have been built as a defense against Ollantaytambo, unless it was built by folk who once occupied Cuzco and who later found a retreat in the canyons below here.

When we first visited Salapunco no megalithic remains had been reported as far down the valley as this. It never occurred to us that, in hunting for the remains of such comparatively recent structures as the Inca Manco had the force and time to build, we were to discover remains of a far more remote past. Yet we were soon to find ruins enough to explain why such a fortress as Salapunco might possibly have been built so as to defend Uilcapampa against Ollantaytambo and Cuzco and not those well-known Inca cities against the savages of the Amazon jungles.

Passing Salapunco, we skirted granite cliffs and precipices and entered a most interesting region, where we were surprised and charmed by the extent of the ancient terraces, their length and height, the presence of many Inca ruins, the beauty of the deep, narrow valleys, and the grandeur of the snow-clad mountains which towered above them. Across the river, near Quente, on top of a series of terraces, we saw the extensive ruins of

Patallacta (*pata* = height or terrace; *llacta* = town or city), an Inca town of great importance. It was not known to Raimondi or Paz Soldan, but is indicated on Wiener's map, although he does not appear to have visited it. We have been unable to find any reference to it in the chronicles. We spent several months here in 1915 excavating and determining the character of the ruins. In another volume I hope to tell more of the antiquities of this region. At present it must suffice to remark that our explorations near Patallacta disclosed no "white rock over a spring of water." None of the place names in this vicinity fit in with the accounts of Uiticos. Their identity remains a puzzle, although the symmetry of the buildings, their architectural idiosyncrasies such as niches, stone roof-pegs, bar-holds, and eye-bonders, indicate an Inca origin. At what date these towns and villages flourished, who built them, why they were deserted, we do not yet know; and the Indians who live hereabouts are ignorant, or silent, as to their history.

At Torontoy, the end of the cultivated temperate valley, we found another group of interesting ruins, possibly once the residence of an Inca chief. In a cave near by we secured some mummies. The ancient wrappings had been consumed by the natives in an effort to smoke out the vampire bats that lived in the cave. On the opposite side of the river are extensive terraces and above them, on a hilltop, other ruins first visited by Messrs. Tucker and Hendriksen in 1911. One of their Indian bearers, attempting to ford the rapids here with a large surveying instrument, was carried off his feet, swept away by the strong current, and drowned before help could reach him.

Near Torontoy is a densely wooded valley called the Pampa Ccahua. In 1915 rumors of Andean or "spectacled" bears having been seen here and of damage having been done by them to some of the higher crops, led us to go and investigate. We found no bears, but at an elevation of 12,000 feet were some very old trees, heavily covered with flowering moss not hitherto known to science. Above them I was so fortunate as to find a wild potato plant, the source from which the early Peruvians first developed many varieties of what we incorrectly call the Irish potato. The tubers were as large as peas.

Mr. Heller found here a strange little cousin of the kangaroo, a near relative of the coenolestes. It turned out to be new to science. To find a new genus of mammalian quadrupeds was an event which delighted Mr. Heller far more than shooting a dozen bears.[3]

GROSVENOR GLACIER AND MOUNT SALCANTAY, PERU

Torontoy is at the beginning of the Grand Canyon of the Urubamba, and such a canyon! The river "road" runs recklessly up and down rock stairways, blasts its way beneath overhanging precipices, spans chasms on frail bridges propped on rustic brackets against granite cliffs. Under dense forests, wherever the encroaching precipices permitted it, the land between them and the river was once terraced and cultivated. We found ourselves unexpectedly in a veritable wonderland. Emotions came thick and fast. We marveled at the exquisite pains with which the ancient folk had rescued incredibly narrow strips of arable land from the tumbling rapids. How could they ever have managed to build a retaining wall of heavy stones along the very edge of the dangerous river, which it is death to attempt to cross! On one sightly bend near a foaming waterfall some Inca chief built a temple, whose walls tantalize the traveler. He must pass by within pistol shot of the interesting ruins, unable to ford the intervening rapids. High up on the side of the canyon, five thousand feet above this temple, are the ruins of Corihuayrachina (*kori* = "gold"; *huayara* = "wind"; *huayrachina* = "a threshing-floor where winnowing takes place"). Possibly this was an ancient gold mine of the Incas. Half a mile above us on another steep slope, some modern pioneer had recently cleared the jungle from a fine series of ancient artificial terraces.

On the afternoon of July 23d we reached a hut called "*La Maquina*," where travelers frequently stop for the night. The name comes from the presence here of some large iron wheels, parts of a "machine" destined never to overcome the difficulties of being transported all the way to a sugar estate in the lower valley, and years ago left here to rust in the jungle. There was little fodder, and there was no good place for us to pitch our camp, so we pushed on over the very difficult road, which had been carved out of the face of a great granite cliff. Part of the cliff had slid off into the river and the breach thus made in the road had been repaired by means of a frail-looking rustic bridge built on a bracket composed of rough logs, branches, and reeds, tied together and surmounted by a few inches of earth and pebbles to make it seem sufficiently safe to the cautious cargo mules who picked their way gingerly across it. No wonder "the machine" rested where it did and gave its name to that part of the valley.

Dusk falls early in this deep canyon, the sides of which are considerably over a mile in height. It was almost dark when we passed a little sandy plain two or three acres in extent, which in this land of steep mountains is called a *pampa*. Were the dwellers on the *pampas* of Argentina—where a railroad can go for 250 miles in a straight line, except for the curvature of the earth—to see this little bit of flood-plain called Mandor Pampa, they would think some one had been joking or else grossly misusing a word which means to them illimitable space with not a hill in sight. However, to the ancient dwellers in this valley, where level land was so scarce that it was worth while to build high stone-faced terraces so as to enable two rows of corn to grow where none grew before, any little natural breathing space in the bottom of the canyon is called a *pampa*.

We passed an ill-kept, grass-thatched hut, turned off the road through a tiny clearing, and made our camp at the edge of the river Urubamba on a sandy beach. Opposite us, beyond the huge granite boulders which interfered with the progress of the surging stream, was a steep mountain clothed with thick jungle. It was an ideal spot for a camp, near the road and yet secluded. Our actions, however, aroused the suspicions of the owner of the hut, Melchor Arteaga, who leases the lands of Mandor Pampa. He was anxious to know why we did not stay at his hut like respectable travelers. Our *gendarme*, Sergeant Carrasco, reassured him. They had quite a long conversation. When Arteaga learned that we were interested in the architectural remains of the Incas, he said there were some very good ruins in this vicinity—in fact, some excellent ones on top of the opposite mountain, called Huayna Picchu, and also on a ridge called Machu Picchu. These were the very places Charles Wiener heard of at Ollantaytambo in 1875 and had been unable to reach. The story of my experiences on the following day will be found in a later chapter. Suffice it to say at this point that the ruins of Huayna Picchu turned out to be of very little importance, while those of Machu Picchu, familiar to readers of the "National Geographic Magazine," are as interesting as any ever found in the Andes.

When I first saw the remarkable citadel of Machu Picchu perched on a narrow ridge two thousand feet above the river, I wondered if it could be the place to which that old soldier, Baltasar de Ocampo, a member of Captain Garcia's expedition, was referring when he said: "The Inca Tupac Amaru was there in the fortress of Pitcos [Uiticos], which is on a very high mountain, whence the view commanded a great part of the province of Uilcapampa. Here there was an extensive level space, with very sumptuous and majestic buildings, erected with great skill and art, all the lintels of the doors, the principal as well as the ordinary ones, being of marble, elaborately carved." Could it be that "Picchu" was the modern variant of "Pitcos"? To be sure, the white granite of which the temples and palaces of Machu Picchu are constructed might easily pass for marble. The difficulty about fitting Ocampo's description to Machu Picchu, however, was that there was no difference between the lintels of the doors and the walls themselves. Furthermore, there is no "white rock over a spring of water" which Calancha says was "near Uiticos." There is no Pucyura in this neighborhood. In fact, the canyon of the Urubamba does not satisfy the geographical requirements of Uiticos. Although containing ruins of surpassing interest, Machu Picchu did not represent that last Inca capital for which we were searching. We had not yet found Manco's palace.

---

[1] Uiticos is probably derived from Uiticuni, meaning "to withdraw to a distance."

[2] Described in "Across South America."

[3] On the 1915 Expedition Mr. Heller captured twelve new species of mammals, but, as Mr. Oldfield Thomas says: "Of all the novelties, by far the most interesting is the new Marsupial....Members of the family were previously known from Colombia and Ecuador." Mr. Heller's discovery greatly extends the recent range of the kangaroo family.

CHAPTER II

THE SEARCH CONTINUED

★

MACHU PICCHU IS on the border-line between the temperate zone and the tropics. Camping near the bridge of San Miguel, below the ruins, both Mr. Heller and Mr. Cook found interesting evidences of this fact in the flora and fauna. From the point of view of historical geography, Mr. Cook's most important discovery was the presence here of *huilca*, a tree which does not grow in cold climates. The Quichua dictionaries tell us *huilca* is a "medicine, a purgative." An infusion made from the seeds of the tree is used as an enema. I am indebted to Mr. Cook for calling my attention to two articles by Mr. W. E. Safford in which it is also shown that from seeds of the *huilca* a powder is prepared, sometimes called *cohoba*. This powder, says Mr. Safford, is a narcotic snuff "inhaled through the nostrils by means of a bifurcated tube." "All writers unite in declaring that it induced a kind of intoxication or hypnotic state, accompanied by visions which were regarded by the natives as supernatural. While under its influence the necromancers, or priests, were supposed to hold communication with unseen powers, and their incoherent mutterings were regarded as prophecies or revelations of hidden things. In treating the sick the physicians made use of it to discover the cause of the malady or the person or spirit by whom the patient was bewitched." Mr. Safford quotes Las Casas as saying: "It was an interesting spectacle to witness how they took it and what they spake. The chief began the ceremony and while he was engaged all remained silent....When he had snuffed up the powder through his nostrils, he remained silent for a while with his head inclined to one side and his arms placed on his knees. Then he raised his face heavenward, uttering certain words which must have been his prayer to the true God, or to him whom he held as God; after which all responded, almost as we do when we say amen; and this they did with a loud voice or sound. Then they gave thanks and said to him certain complimentary things, entreating his benevolence and begging him to reveal to them what he had seen. He described to them his vision, saying that the Cemi [spirits] had spoken to him and had predicted good times or the contrary, or that children were to be born, or to die, or that there was to be some dispute with their neighbors, and other things which might come to his imagination, all disturbed with that intoxication."[1]

Clearly, from the point of view of priests and soothsayers, the place where *huilca* was first found and used in their incantations would be important. It is not strange to find therefore that the Inca name of this river was *Uilca-mayu*: the "huilca river." The *pampa* on this river where the trees grew would likely receive the name *Uilca pampa*. If it became an important city, then the surrounding region might be named *Uilcapampa* after it. This seems to me to be the most probable origin of the name of the province. Anyhow it is worth noting the fact that denizens of Cuzco and Ollantaytambo, coming down the river in search of this highly prized narcotic, must have found the first trees not far from Machu Picchu.

Leaving the ruins of Machu Picchu for later investigation, we now pushed on down the Urubamba Valley, crossed the bridge of San Miguel, passed the house of Señor Lizarraga, first of modern Peruvians to write his name on the granite walls of Machu Picchu, and came to the sugar-cane fields of Huadquiña. We had now left the temperate zone and entered the tropics.

At Huadquiña we were so fortunate as to find that the proprietress of the plantation, Señora Carmen Vargas, and her children, were spending the season here. During the rainy winter months they live in Cuzco, but when summer brings fine weather they come to Huadquiña to enjoy the free-and-easy life of the country. They made us welcome, not only with that hospitality to passing travelers which is common to sugar estates all over the world, but gave us real assistance in our explorations. Señora Carmen's estate covers more than two hundred square miles. Huadquiña is a splendid example of the ancient patriarchal system. The Indians who come from other parts of Peru to work on the plantation enjoy perquisites and wages unknown elsewhere. Those whose home is on the estate regard Señora Carmen with an affectionate reverence which she well deserves. All are welcome to bring her their troubles. The system goes back to the days when the spiritual, moral, and material welfare of the Indians was entrusted in *encomienda* to the lords of the *repartimiento* or allotted territory.

Huadquiña once belonged to the Jesuits. They planted the first sugar cane and established the mill. After their expulsion from the Spanish colonies at the end of the eighteenth century, Huadquiña was bought by a Peruvian. It was first described in geographical literature by the Count de Sartiges, who stayed here for several weeks in 1834 when on his way to Choqquequirau. He says that the owner of Huadquiña "is perhaps the only landed proprietor in the entire world who possesses on his estates all the products of the four parts of the globe. In the different regions of his domain he has wool, hides, horsehair, potatoes, wheat, corn, sugar, coffee, chocolate, *coca*, many mines of silver-bearing lead, and placers of gold." Truly a royal principality.

Incidentally it is interesting to note that although Sartiges was an enthusiastic explorer, eager to visit undescribed Inca ruins, he makes no mention whatever of Machu Picchu. Yet from Huadquiña one can reach Machu Picchu on foot in half a day without crossing the Urubamba River. Apparently the ruins were unknown to his hosts in 1834. They were equally unknown to our kind hosts in 1911. They scarcely believed the story I told them of the beauty and extent of the Inca edifices.[2] When my photographs were developed, however, and they saw with their own eyes the marvelous stonework of the principal temples, Señora Carmen and her family were struck dumb with wonder and astonishment. They could not understand how it was possible that they should have passed so close to Machu Picchu every year of their lives since the river road was opened without knowing what was there. They had seen a single little building on the crest of the ridge, but supposed that it was an isolated tower of no great interest or importance. Their neighbor, Lizarraga, near the bridge of San Miguel, had reported the presence of the ruins which he first visited in 1904, but, like our friends in Cuzco, they had paid little attention to his stories. We were soon to have a demonstration of the causes of such skepticism.

Our new friends read with interest my copy of those paragraphs of Calancha's "Chronicle" which referred to the location of the last Inca capital. Learning that we were anxious to discover Uiticos, a place of which they had never heard, they ordered the most intelligent tenants on the estate to come in and be questioned. The best informed of all was a sturdy *mestizo*, a trusted foreman, who said that in a little valley called Ccllumayu, a few hours' journey down the Urubamba, there were "important ruins" which had been seen by some of Señora Carmen's Indians. Even more interesting and thrilling was his statement that on a ridge up the Salcantay Valley was a place called Yurak Rumi (*yurak* = "white"; *rumi* = "stone") where some very interesting ruins had been found by his workmen when cutting trees for firewood. We all became excited over this, for among the paragraphs which I had copied from Calancha's "Chronicle" was the statement that "close to Uiticos" is the "white stone of the aforesaid house of the Sun which is called Yurak Rumi." Our hosts assured us that this must be the place, since no one hereabouts had ever heard of any other Yurak Rumi. The foreman, on being closely questioned, said that he had seen the ruins once or twice, that he had also been up the Urubamba Valley and seen the great ruins at Ollantaytambo, and that those which he had seen at Yurak Rumi were "as good as those at Ollantaytambo." Here was a definite statement made by an eyewitness. Apparently we were about to see that interesting rock where the last Incas worshiped. However, the foreman said that the trail thither was at present impassable, although a small gang of Indians could open it in less than a week. Our hosts, excited by the pictures we had shown them of Machu Picchu, and now believing that even finer ruins might be found on their own property, immediately gave orders to have the path to Yurak Rumi cleared for our benefit.

While this was being done, Señora Carmen's son, the manager of the plantation, offered to accompany us himself to Ccllumayu, where other "important ruins" had been found, which could be reached in a few hours without cutting any new trails. Acting on his assurance that we should not need tent or cots, we left our camping outfit behind and followed him to a small valley on the south side of the Urubamba. We found Ccllumayu to consist of two huts in a small clearing. Densely wooded slopes rose on all sides. The manager requested two of the Indian tenants to act as guides. With them, we plunged into the thick jungle and spent a long and fatiguing day searching in vain for ruins. That night the manager returned to Huadquiña, but Professor Foote and I preferred to remain in Ccllumayu and prosecute a more vigorous search on the next day. We shared a little thatched hut with our Indian hosts and a score of fat *cuys* (guinea pigs), the chief source of the Ccllumayu meat supply. The hut was built of rough wattles which admitted plenty of fresh air and gave us comfortable ventilation. Primitive little sleeping-platforms, also of wattles, constructed for the needs of short, stocky Indians, kept us from being overrun by inquisitive *cuys*, but could hardly be called as comfortable as our own folding cots which we had left at Huadquiña.

The next day our guides were able to point out in the woods a few piles of stones, the foundations of oval or circular huts which probably were built by some primitive savage tribe in prehistoric times. Nothing further could be found here of ruins, "important" or otherwise, although we spent three days at Ccllumayu. Such was our first disillusionment.

On our return to Huadquiña, we learned that the trail to Yurak Rumi would be ready "in a day or two." In the meantime our hosts became much interested in Professor Foote's collection of insects. They brought an unnamed scorpion and informed us that an orange orchard surrounded by high walls in a secluded place back of the house was "a great place for spiders." We found that their statement was not exaggerated and immediately engaged in an enthusiastic spider hunt. When these Huadquiña spiders were studied at the Harvard Museum of Comparative Zoölogy, Dr. Chamberlain found among them the representatives of four new genera and nineteen species hitherto unknown to science. As a reward of merit, he gave Professor Foote's name to the scorpion!

Finally the trail to Yurak Rumi was reported finished. It was with feelings of keen anticipation that I started out with the foreman to see those ruins which he had just revisited and now declared were "better than those of Ollantaytambo." It was to be presumed that in the pride of discovery he might have exaggerated their importance. Still it never entered my head what I was actually to find. After several hours spent in clearing away the dense forest growth which surrounded the walls I learned that this Yurak Rumi consisted of the ruins of a single little rectangular Inca storehouse. No effort had been made at beauty of construction. The walls were of rough, unfashioned stones laid in clay. The building was without a doorway, although it had several small windows and a series of ventilating shafts under the house. The lintels of the windows and of the small apertures leading into the subterranean shafts were of stone. There were no windows on the sunny north side or on the ends, but there were four on the south side through which it would have been possible to secure access to the stores of maize, potatoes, or other provisions placed here for safekeeping. It will be recalled that the Incas maintained an extensive system of public storehouses, not only in the centers of population, but also at strategic points on the principal trails. Yurak Rumi is on top of the ridge between the Salcantay and Huadquiña valleys, probably on an ancient road which crossed the province of Uilcapampa. As such it was interesting; but to compare it with Ollantaytambo, as the foreman had done, was to liken a cottage to a palace or a mouse to an elephant. It seems incredible that any-body having actually seen both places could have thought for a moment that one was "as good as the other." To be sure, the foreman was not a trained observer and his interest in Inca buildings was probably of the slight-est. Yet the ruins of Ollantaytambo are so well known and so impressive that even the most casual traveler is struck by them and the natives themselves are enormously proud of them. The real cause of the foreman's inaccuracy was probably his desire to please. To give an answer which will satisfy the questioner is a common trait in Peru as well as in many other parts of the world. Anyhow, the lessons of the past few days were not lost on us. We now understood the skepticism which had prevailed regarding Lizarraga's dis-coveries. It is small wonder that the occasional stories about Machu Picchu which had drifted into Cuzco had never elicited any enthusiasm nor even provoked investigation on the part of those professors and students in the University of Cuzco who were interested in visiting the remains of Inca civilization. They knew only too well the fondness of their countrymen for exaggeration and their inability to report facts accurately.

Obviously, we had not yet found Uiticos. So, bidding farewell to Señora Carmen, we crossed the Urubamba on the bridge of Colpani and proceeded down the valley past the mouth of the Lucumayo and the road from Panticalla, to the hamlet of Chauillay, where the Urubamba is joined by the Vilcabamba River.[3] Both rivers are restricted here to narrow gorges, through which their waters rush and roar on their way to the lower valley. A few rods from Chauillay was a fine bridge. The natives call it Chuquichaca! Steel and iron have superseded the old suspension bridge of huge cables made of vegetable fiber, with its narrow roadway of wattles supported by a network of vines. Yet here it was that in 1572 the military force sent by the viceroy, Francisco de Toledo, under the command of General Martin Hurtado and Captain Garcia, found the forces of the young Inca drawn up to defend Uiticos. It will be remembered that after a brief preliminary fire the forces of Tupac Amaru were routed without having destroyed the bridge and thus Captain Garcia was enabled to accomplish that which had proved too much for the famous Gonzalo Pizarro. Our inspection of the surroundings showed that Captain Garcia's companion, Baltasar de Ocampo, was correct when he said that the occupation of the bridge of Chuquichaca "was a measure of no small importance for the royal force." It certainly would have caused the Spaniards "great trouble" if they had had to rebuild it.

We might now have proceeded to follow Garcia's tracks up the Vilcabamba had we not been anxious to see the proprietor of the plantation of Santa Ana, Don Pedro Duque, reputed to be the wisest and ablest man in this whole province. We felt he would be able to offer us advice of prime importance in our search. So leaving the bridge of Chuquichaca, we continued down the Urubamba River which here meanders through a broad, fertile valley, green with tropical plantations. We passed groves of bananas and oranges, waving fields of green sugar cane, the hospitable dwellings of prosperous planters, and the huts of Indians fortunate enough to dwell in this tropical "Garden of Eden." The day was hot and thirst-provoking, so I stopped near some large orange trees loaded with ripe fruit and asked the Indian proprietress to sell me ten cents' worth. In exchange for the tiny silver *real* she dragged out a sack containing more than fifty oranges! I was fain to request her to permit us to take only as many as our pockets could hold; but she seemed so surprised and pained, we had to fill our saddle-bags as well.

At the end of the day we crossed the Urubamba River on a fine steel bridge and found ourselves in the prosperous little town of Quillabamba, the provincial capital. Its main street was lined with well-filled shops, evidence of the fact that this is one of the principal gateways to the Peruvian rubber country which, with the high price of rubber then prevailing, 1911, was the scene of unusual activity. Passing through Quillabamba and up a slight hill beyond it, we came to the long colonnades of the celebrated sugar estate of Santa Ana founded by the Jesuits, where all explorers who have passed this way since the days of Charles Wiener have been entertained. He says that he was received here "with a thousand signs of friendship" ("*mille témoignages d'amitié*"). We were received the same way. Even in a region where we had repeatedly received valuable assistance from government officials and generous hospitality from private individuals, our reception at Santa Ana stands out as particularly delightful.

Don Pedro Duque took great interest in enabling us to get all possible information about the little-known region into which we proposed to penetrate. Born in Colombia, but long resident in Peru, he was a gentleman of the old school, keenly interested, not only in the administration and economic progress of his plantation, but also in the intellectual movements of the outside world. He entered with zest into our historical-geographical studies. The name Uiticos was new to him, but after reading over with us our extracts from the Spanish chronicles he was sure that he could help us find it. And help us he did. Santa Ana is less than thirteen degrees south of the equator; the elevation is barely 2000 feet; the "winter" nights are cool; but the heat in the middle of the day is intense. Nevertheless, our host was so energetic that as a result of his efforts a number of the best-informed residents were brought to the conferences at the great plantation house. They told all they knew of the towns and valleys where the last four Incas had found a refuge, but that was not much. They all agreed that "if only Señor Lopez Torres were alive he could have been of great service" to us, as "he had prospected for mines and rubber in those parts more than any one else, and had once seen some Inca ruins in the forest!" Of Uiticos and Chuquipalpa and most of the places mentioned in the chronicles, none of Don Pedro's friends had ever heard. It was all rather discouraging, until one day, by the greatest good fortune, there arrived at Santa Ana another friend of Don Pedro's, the *teniente gobernador* of the village of Lucma in the valley of Vilcabamba—a crusty old fellow named Evaristo Mogrovejo. His brother, Pio Mogrovejo, had been a member of the party of energetic Peruvians who, in 1884, had searched for buried treasure at Choqquequirau and had left their names on its walls. Evaristo Mogrovejo could understand searching for buried treasure, but he was totally unable otherwise to comprehend our desire to find the ruins of the places mentioned by Father Calancha and the contemporaries of Captain Garcia. Had we first met Mogrovejo in Lucma he would undoubtedly have received us with suspicion and done nothing to further our quest. Fortunately for us, his official superior was the sub-prefect of the province of Convención, lived at Quillabamba near Santa Ana, and was a friend of Don Pedro's. The sub-prefect had received orders from his own official superior, the prefect of Cuzco, to take a personal interest in our undertaking, and accordingly gave particular orders to Mogrovejo to see to it that we were given every facility for finding the ancient ruins and identifying the places of historic interest. Although Mogrovejo declined to risk his skin in the savage wilderness of Conservidayoc, he carried out his orders faithfully and was ultimately of great assistance to us.

Extremely gratified with the result of our conferences in Santa Ana, yet reluctant to leave the delightful hospitality and charming conversation of our gracious host, we decided to go at once to Lucma, taking the road on the southwest side of the Urubamba and using the route followed by the pack animals which carry the precious cargoes of *coca* and *aguardiente* from Santa Ana to Ollantaytambo and Cuzco. Thanks to Don Pedro's energy, we made an excellent start; not one of those meant-to-be-early but really late-in-the-morning departures so customary in the Andes.

We passed through a region which originally had been heavily forested, had long since been cleared, and was now covered with bushes and second growth. Near the roadside I noticed a considerable number of land shells grouped on the under-side of overhanging rocks. As a boy in the Hawaiian Islands I had spent too many Saturdays collecting those beautiful and fascinating mollusks, which usually prefer the trees of upland valleys, to enable me to resist the temptation of gathering a large number of such as could easily be secured. None of the snails were moving. The dry season appears to be their resting period. Some weeks later Professor Foote and I passed through Maras and were interested to notice thousands of land shells, mostly white in color, on small bushes, where they seemed to be quietly sleeping. They were fairly "glued to their resting places"; clustered so closely in some cases as to give the stems of the bushes a ghostly appearance.

Our present objective was the valley of the river Vilcabamba. So far as we have been able to learn, only one other explorer had preceded us—the distinguished scientist Raimondi. His map of the Vilcabamba is fairly accurate. He reports the presence here of mines and minerals, but with the exception of an "abandoned *tampu*" at Maracnyoc ("the place which possesses a millstone"), he makes no mention of any ruins. Accordingly, although it seemed from the story of Baltasar de Ocampo and Captain Garcia's other contemporaries that we were now entering the valley of Uiticos, it was with feelings of considerable uncertainty that we proceeded on our quest. It may seem strange that we should have been in any doubt. Yet before our visit nearly all the Peruvian historians and geographers except Don Carlos Romero still believed that when the Inca Manco fled from Pizarro he took up his residence at Choqquequirau in the Apurimac Valley. The word *choqquequirau* means "cradle of gold" and this lent color to the legend that Manco had carried off with him from Cuzco great quantities of gold utensils and much treasure, which he deposited in his new capital. Raimondi, knowing that Manco had "retired to Uilcapampa," visited both the present villages of Vilcabamba and Pucyura and saw nothing of any ruins. He was satisfied that Choqquequirau was Manco's refuge because it was far enough from Pucyura to answer the requirements of Calancha that it was "two or three days' journey" from Uilcapampa to Puquiura.

A new road had recently been built along the river bank by the owner of the sugar estate at Paltaybamba, to enable his pack animals to travel more rapidly. Much of it had to be carved out of the face of a solid rock precipice and in places it pierces the cliffs in a series of little tunnels. My *gendarme* missed this road and took the steep old trail over the cliffs. As Ocampo said in his story of Captain Garcia's expedition, "the road was narrow in the ascent with forest on the right, and on the left a ravine of great depth." We reached Paltaybamba about dusk. The owner, Señor José S. Pancorbo, was absent, attending to the affairs of a rubber estate in the jungles of the river San Miguel. The plantation of Paltaybamba occupies the best lands in the lower Vilcabamba Valley, but lying, as it does, well off the main highway, visitors are rare and our arrival was the occasion for considerable excitement. We were not unexpected, however. It was Señor Pancorbo who had assured us in Cuzco that we should find ruins near Pucyura and he had told his major-domo to be on the look-out for us. We had a long talk with the manager of the plantation and his friends that evening. They had heard little of any ruins in this vicinity, but repeated one of the stories we had heard in Santa Ana, that way off somewhere in the *montaña* there was "an Inca city." All agreed that it was a very difficult place to reach; and none of them had ever been there. In the morning the manager gave us a guide to the next house up the valley, with orders that the man at that house should relay us to the next, and so on. These people, all tenants of the plantation, obligingly carried out their orders, although at considerable inconvenience to themselves.

The Vilcabamba Valley above Paltaybamba is very picturesque. There are high mountains on either side, covered with dense jungle and dark green foliage, in pleasing contrast to the light green of the fields of waving sugar cane. The valley is steep, the road is very winding, and the torrent of the Vilcabamba roars loudly, even in July. What it must be like in February, the rainy season, we could only surmise. About two leagues above Paltaybamba, at or near the spot called by Raimondi "Maracnyoc," an "abandoned *tampu*," we came to some old stone walls, the ruins of a place now called Huayara or "Hoyara." I believe them to be the ruins of the first Spanish settlement in this region, a place referred to by Ocampo, who says that the fugitives of Tupac Amaru's army were "brought back to the valley of Hoyara," where they were "settled in a large village, and a city of Spaniards was founded....This city was founded on an extensive plain near a river, with an admirable climate. From the river channels of water were taken for the service of the city, the water being very good." The water here is excellent, far better than any in the Cuzco Basin. On the plain near the river are some of the last cane fields of the plantation of Paltaybamba. "Hoyara" was abandoned after the discovery of gold mines several leagues farther up the valley, and the Spanish "city" was moved to the village now called Vilcabamba.

Our next stop was at Lucma, the home of *Teniente Gobernador* Mogrovejo. The village of Lucma is an irregular cluster of about thirty thatched-roofed huts. It enjoys a moderate amount of prosperity due to the fact of its being located near one of the gateways to the interior, the pass to the rubber estates in the San Miguel Valley. Here are "houses of refreshment" and two shops, the only ones in the region. One can buy cotton cloth, sugar, canned goods and candles. A picturesque belfry and a small church, old and somewhat out of repair, crown the small hill back of the village. There is little level land, but the slopes are gentle, and permit a considerable amount of agriculture.

There was no evidence of extensive terracing. Maize and alfalfa seemed to be the principal crops. Evaristo Mogrovejo lived on the little plaza around which the houses of the more important people were grouped. He had just returned from Santa Ana by the way of Idma, using a much worse trail than that over which we had come, but one which enabled him to avoid passing through Paltaybamba, with whose proprietor he was not on good terms. He told us stories of misadventures which had happened to travelers at the gates of Paltaybamba, stories highly reminiscent of feudal days in Europe, when provincial barons were accustomed to lay tribute on all who passed.

We offered to pay Mogrovejo a *gratificación* of a *sol*, or Peruvian silver dollar, for every ruin to which he would take us, and double that amount if the locality should prove to contain particularly interesting ruins. This aroused all his business instincts. He summoned his *alcaldes* and other well-informed Indians to appear and be interviewed. They told us there were "many ruins" hereabouts! Being a practical man himself, Mogrovejo had never taken any interest in ruins. Now he saw the chance not only to make money out of the ancient sites, but also to gain official favor by carrying out with unexampled vigor the orders of his superior, the sub-prefect of Quillabamba. So he exerted himself to the utmost in our behalf.

The next day we were guided up a ravine to the top of the ridge back of Lucma. This ridge divides the upper from the lower Vilcabamba. On all sides the hills rose several thousand feet above us. In places they were covered with forest growth, chiefly above the cloud line, where daily moisture encourages vegetation. In some of the forests on the more gentle slopes recent clearings gave evidence of enterprise on the part of the present inhabitants of the valley. After an hour's climb we reached what were unquestionably the ruins of Inca structures, on an artificial terrace which commands a magnificent view far down toward Paltaybamba and the bridge of Chuquichaca, as well as in the opposite direction. The contemporaries of Captain Garcia speak of a number of forts or *pucarás* which had to be stormed and captured before Tupac Amaru could be taken prisoner. This was probably one of those "fortresses." Its strategic position and the ease with which it could be defended point to such an interpretation. Nevertheless this ruin did not fit the "fortress of Pitcos," nor the "House of the Sun" near the "white rock over the spring." It is called *Incahuaracana*, "the place where the Inca shoots with a sling."

Incahuaracana consists of two typical Inca edifices—one of two rooms, about 70 by 20 feet, and the other, very long and narrow, 150 by 11 feet. The walls, of unhewn stone laid in clay, were not particularly well built and resemble in many respects the ruins at Choqquequirau. The rooms of the principal house are without windows, although each has three front doors and is lined with niches, four or five on a side. The long, narrow building was divided into three rooms, and had several front doors. A force of two hundred Indian soldiers could have slept in these houses without unusual crowding.

We left Lucma the next day, forded the Vilcabamba River and soon had an uninterrupted view up the valley to a high, truncated hill, its top partly covered with a scrubby growth of trees and bushes, its sides steep and rocky. We were told that the name of the hill was "Rosaspata," a word of modern hybrid origin—*pata* being Quichua for "hill," while *rosas* is the Spanish word for "roses." Mogrovejo said his Indians told him that on the "Hill of Roses" there were more ruins.

At the foot of the hill, and across the river, is the village of Pucyura. When Raimondi was here in 1865 it was but a "wretched hamlet with a paltry chapel." To-day it is more prosperous. There is a large public school here, to which children come from villages many miles away. So crowded is the school that in fine weather the children sit on benches out of doors. The boys all go barefooted. The girls wear high boots. I once saw them reciting a geography lesson, but I doubt if even the teacher knew whether or not this was the site of the first school in this whole region. For it was to "Puquiura" that Friar Marcos came in 1566. Perhaps he built the "*mezquina capilla*" which Raimondi scorned. If this were the "Puquiura" of Friar Marcos, then Uiticos must be near by, for he and Friar Diego walked with their famous procession of converts from "Puquiura" to the House of the Sun and the "white rock" which was "close to Uiticos."

Crossing the Vilcabamba on a footbridge that afternoon, we came immediately upon some old ruins that were not Incaic. Examination showed that they were apparently the remains of a very crude Spanish crushing mill, obviously intended to pulverize gold-bearing quartz on a considerable scale. Perhaps this was the place referred to by Ocampo, who says that the Inca Titu Cusi attended masses said by his friend Friar Diego in a chapel which is "near my houses and on my own lands, in the mining district of Puquiura, close to the ore-crushing mill of Don Christoval de Albornoz, Precentor that was of the Cuzco Cathedral."

One of the millstones is five feet in diameter and more than a foot thick. It lay near a huge, flat rock of white granite, hollowed out so as to enable the millstone to be rolled slowly around in a hollow trough. There was also a very large Indian mortar and pestle, heavy enough to need the services of four men to work it. The mortar was merely the hollowed-out top of a large boulder which projected a few inches above the surface of the ground. The pestle, four feet in diameter, was of the characteristic rocking-stone shape used from time immemorial by the Indians of the highlands for crushing maize or potatoes. Since no other ruins of a Spanish quartz-crushing plant have been found in this vicinity, it is probable that this once belonged to Don Christoval de Albornoz.

Near the mill the Tincochaca River joins the Vilcabamba from the southeast. Crossing this on a footbridge, I followed Mogrovejo to an old and very dilapidated structure in the saddle of the hill on the south side of Rosaspata. They called the place Uncapampa, or Inca pampa. It is probably one of the forts stormed by Captain Garcia and his men in 1571. The ruins represent a single house, 166 feet long by 33 feet wide. If the house had partitions they long since disappeared. There were six doorways in front, none on the ends or in the rear walls. The ruins resembled those of Incahuaracana, near Lucma. The walls had originally been built of rough stones laid in clay. The general finish was extremely rough. The few niches, all at one end of the structure, were irregular, about two feet in width and a little more than this in height. The one corner of the building which was still standing had a height of about ten feet. Two hundred Inca soldiers could have slept here also.

Leaving Uncapampa and following my guides, I climbed up the ridge and followed a path along its west side to the top of Rosaspata. Passing some ruins much overgrown and of a primitive character, I soon found myself on a pleasant *pampa* near the top of the mountain. The view from here com-

mands "a great part of the province of Uilcapampa." It is remarkably extensive on all sides; to the north and south are snow-capped mountains, to the
east and west, deep verdure-clad valleys.

Furthermore, on the north side of the *pampa* is an extensive level
space with a very sumptuous and majestic building "erected with great skill
and art, all the lintels of the doors, the principal as well as the ordinary ones,"
being of white granite elaborately cut. At last we had found a place which
seemed to meet most of the requirements of Ocampo's description of the
"fortress of Pitcos." To be sure it was not of "marble," and the lintels of the
doors were not "carved," in our sense of the word. They were, however, beautifully finished, as may be seen from the illustrations, and the white granite might easily pass for marble. If only we could find in this vicinity that
Temple of the Sun which Calancha said was "near" Uiticos, all doubts
would be at an end.

That night we stayed at Tincochaca, in the hut of an Indian friend of
Mogrovejo. As usual we made inquiries. Imagine our feelings when in
response to the oft-repeated question he said that in a neighboring valley
there was a great white rock over a spring of water! If his story should prove
to be true our quest for Uiticos was over. It behooved us to make a very careful study of what we had found.

---

[1] Mr. Safford says in his article on the "Identity of Cohoba" (*Journal of the Washington Academy of Sciences*,
Sept. 19, 1916): "The most remarkable fact connected with *Piptadenia peregrina*, or 'tree-tobacco' is that...the
source of its intoxicating properties still remains unknown." One of the bifurcated tubes, "in the first stages
of manufacture," was found at Machu Picchu.

[2] See the illustrations in Chapters XVII and XVIII.

[3] Since the historical Uilcapampa is not geographically identical with the modern Vilcabamba, the name
applied to this river and the old Spanish town at its source, I shall distinguish between the two by using
the correct, official spelling for the river and town, viz., Vilcabamba; and the phonetic spelling, Uilcapampa,
for the place referred to in the contemporary histories of the Inca Manco.

CHAPTER 12

THE FORTRESS OF UITICOS
AND THE HOUSE OF THE SUN

✦

WHEN THE VICEROY, Toledo, determined to conquer that last stronghold
of the Incas where for thirty-five years they had defied the supreme power
of Spain, he offered a thousand dollars a year as a pension to the soldier who
would capture Tupac Amaru. Captain Garcia earned the pension, but failed
to receive it; the "*mañana* habit" was already strong in the days of Philip II.
So the doughty captain filed a collection of testimonials with Philip's Royal
Council of the Indies. Among these is his own statement of what happened
on the campaign against Tupac Amaru. In this he says: "and having arrived
at the principal fortress, Guaynapucará ["the young fortress"], which the Incas
had fortified, we found it defended by the Prince Philipe Quispetutio, a son
of the Inca Titu Cusi, with his captains and soldiers. It is on a high eminence
surrounded with rugged crags and jungles, very dangerous to ascend and
almost impregnable. Nevertheless, with my aforesaid company of soldiers
I went up and gained the fortress, but only with the greatest possible labor
and danger. Thus we gained the province of Uilcapampa." The viceroy himself says this important victory was due to Captain Garcia's skill and courage
in storming the heights of Guaynapucará, "on Saint John the Baptist's day,
in 1572."

The "Hill of Roses" is indeed "a high eminence surrounded with
rugged crags." The side of easiest approach is protected by a splendid, long
wall, built so carefully as not to leave a single toe-hold for active besiegers.
The barracks at Uncapampa could have furnished a contingent to make an
attack on that side very dangerous. The hill is steep on all sides, and it would

have been extremely easy for a small force to have defended it. It was undoubtedly "almost impregnable." This was the feature Captain Garcia was most likely to remember.

On the very summit of the hill are the ruins of a partly enclosed compound consisting of thirteen or fourteen houses arranged so as to form a rough square, with one large and several small courtyards. The outside dimensions of the compound are about 160 feet by 145 feet. The builders showed the familiar Inca sense of symmetry in arranging the houses. Due to the wanton destruction of many buildings by the natives in their efforts at treasure-hunting, the walls have been so pulled down that it is impossible to get the exact dimensions of the buildings. In only one of them could we be sure that there had been any niches.

Most interesting of all is the structure which caught the attention of Ocampo and remained fixed in his memory. Enough remains of this building to give a good idea of its former grandeur. It was indeed a fit residence for a royal Inca, an exile from Cuzco. It is 245 feet by 43 feet. There were no windows, but it was lighted by thirty doorways, fifteen in front and the same in back. It contained ten large rooms, besides three hallways running from front to rear. The walls were built rather hastily and are not noteworthy, but the principal entrances, namely, those leading to each hall, are particularly well made; not, to be sure, of "marble" as Ocampo said—there is no marble in the province—but of finely cut ashlars of white granite. The lintels of the principal doorways, as well as of the ordinary ones, are also of solid blocks of white granite, the largest being as much as eight feet in length. The doorways are better than any other ruins in Uilcapampa except those of Machu Picchu, thus justifying the mention of them made by Ocampo, who lived near here and had time to become thoroughly familiar with their appearance. Unfortunately, a very small portion of the edifice was still standing. Most of the rear doors had been filled up with ashlars, in order to make a continuous fence. Other walls had been built from the ruins, to keep cattle out of the cultivated *pampa*. Rosaspata is at an elevation which places it on the borderland between the cold grazing country, with its root crops and sublimated pigweeds, and the temperate zone where maize flourishes.

On the south side of the hilltop, opposite the long palace, is the ruin of a single structure, 78 feet long and 35 feet wide, containing doors on both sides, no niches and no evidence of careful workmanship. It was probably a barracks for a company of soldiers.

The intervening "*pampa*" might have been the scene of those games of bowls and quoits, which were played by the Spanish refugees who fled from the wrath of Gonzalo Pizarro and found refuge with the Inca Manco. Here may have occurred that fatal game when one of the players lost his temper and killed his royal host.

Our excavations in 1915 yielded a mass of rough potsherds, a few Inca whirl-bobs and bronze shawl pins, and also a number of iron articles of European origin, heavily rusted—horseshoe nails, a buckle, a pair of scissors, several bridle or saddle ornaments, and three Jew's-harps. My first thought was that modern Peruvians must have lived here at one time, although the necessity of carrying all water supplies up the hill would make this unlikely. Furthermore, the presence here of artifacts of European origin does not of itself point to such a conclusion. In the first place, we know that Manco was accustomed to make raids on Spanish travelers between Cuzco and Lima. He might very easily have brought back with him a Spanish bridle. In the second place the musical instruments may have belonged to the refugees, who might have enjoyed whiling away their exile with melancholy twanging. In the third place the retainers of the Inca probably visited the Spanish market in Cuzco, where there would have been displayed at times a considerable assortment of goods of European manufacture. Finally Rodriguez de Figueroa speaks expressly of two pairs of scissors he brought as a present to Titu Cusi. That no such array of European artifacts has been turned up in the excavations of other important sites in the province of Uilcapampa would seem to indicate that they were abandoned before the Spanish Conquest or else were occupied by natives who had no means of accumulating such treasures.

Thanks to Ocampo's description of the fortress which Tupac Amaru was occupying in 1572 there is no doubt that this was the palace of the last Inca. Was it also the capital of his brothers, Titu Cusi and Sayri Tupac, and his father, Manco? It is astonishing how few details we have by which the Uiticos of Manco may be identified. His contemporaries are strangely silent. When he left Cuzco and sought refuge "in the remote fastnesses of the Andes," there was a Spanish soldier, Cieza de Leon, in the armies of Pizarro who had a genius for seeing and hearing interesting things and writing them down, and who tried to interview as many members of the royal family as he could;—Manco had thirteen brothers. Cieza de Leon says he was much disappointed not to be able to talk with Manco himself and his sons, but they had "retired into the provinces of Uiticos, which are in the most retired part of those regions, beyond the great Cordillera of the Andes."[1] The Spanish refugees who died as the result of the murder of Manco may not have known how to write. Anyhow, so far as we can learn they left no accounts from which any one could identify his residence.

Titu Cusi gives no definite clue, but the activities of Friar Marcos and Friar Diego, who came to be his spiritual advisers, are fully described by Calancha. It will be remembered that Calancha remarks that "close to Uiticos in a village called Chuquipalpa, is a House of the Sun and in it a white stone over a spring of water." Our guide had told us there was such a place close to the hill of Rosaspata.

On the day after making the first studies of the "Hill of Roses," I followed the impatient Mogrovejo—whose object was not to study ruins but to earn dollars for finding them—and went over the hill on its northeast side to the Valley of Los Andenes ("the Terraces"). Here, sure enough, was a large, white granite boulder, flattened on top, which had a carved seat or platform on its northern side. Its west side covered a cave in which were several niches. This cave had been walled in on one side. When Mogrovejo and the Indian guide said there was a manantial de agua ("spring of water") near by, I became greatly interested. On investigation, however, the "spring" turned out to be nothing but part of a small irrigating ditch. (Manantial means "spring"; it also means "running water"). But the rock was not "over the water." Although this was undoubtedly one of those huacas, or sacred boulders, selected by the Incas as the visible representations of the founders of a tribe and thus was an important accessory to ancestor worship, it was not the Yurak Rumi for which we were looking.

Leaving the boulder and the ruins of what possibly had been the house of its attendant priest, we followed the little water course past a large number of very handsomely built agricultural terraces, the first we had seen since leaving Machu Picchu and the most important ones in the valley. So scarce are andenes in this region and so noteworthy were these in particular that this vale has been named after them. They were probably built under the direction of Manco. Near them are a number of carved boulders, huacas. One had an intihuatana, or sundial nubbin, on it; another was carved in the shape of a saddle. Continuing, we followed a trickling stream through thick woods until we suddenly arrived at an open place called Ñusta Isppana. Here before us was a great white rock over a spring. Our guides had not misled us. Beneath the trees were the ruins of an Inca temple, flanking and partly enclosing the gigantic granite boulder, one end of which a small pool of running water. When we learned that the present name of this immediate vicinity is Chuquipalta our happiness was complete.

It was late on the afternoon of August 9, 1911, when I first saw this remarkable shrine. Densely wooded hills rose on every side. There was not a hut to be seen; scarcely a sound to be heard. It was an ideal place for practicing the mystic ceremonies of an ancient cult. The remarkable aspect of this great boulder and the dark pool beneath its shadow had caused this to become a place of worship. Here, without doubt, was "the principal *mochadero* of those forested mountains." It is still venerated by the Indians of the vicinity. At last we had found the place where, in the days of Titu Cusi, the Inca priests faced the east, greeted the rising sun, "extended their hands toward it," and "threw kisses to it," "a ceremony of the most profound resignation and reverence." We may imagine the sun priests, clad in their resplendent robes of office, standing on the top of the rock at the edge of its steepest side, their faces lit up with the rosy light of the early morning, awaiting the moment when the Great Divinity should appear above the eastern hills and receive their adoration. As it rose they saluted it and cried: "O Sun! Thou who art in peace and safety, shine upon us, keep us from sickness, and keep us in health and safety. O Sun! Thou who hast said let there be Cuzco and Tampu, grant that these children may conquer all other people. We beseech thee that thy children the Incas may be always conquerors, since it is for this that thou hast created them."

It was during Titu Cusi's reign that Friars Marcos and Diego marched over here with their converts from Puquiura, each carrying a stick of firewood. Calancha says the Indians worshiped the water as a divine thing, that the Devil had at times shown himself in the water. Since the surface of the little pool, as one gazes at it, does not reflect the sky, but only the overhanging, dark, mossy rock, the water looks black and forbidding, even to unsuperstitious Yankees. It is easy to believe that simple-minded Indian worshipers in this secluded spot could readily believe that they actually saw the Devil appearing "as a visible manifestation" in the water. Indians came from the most sequestered villages of the dense forests to worship here and to offer gifts and sacrifices. Nevertheless, the Augustinian monks here raised the standard of the cross, recited their orisons, and piled firewood all about the rock and temple. Exorcising the Devil and calling him by all the vile names they could think of, the friars commanded him never to return. Setting fire to the pile, they burned up the temple, scorched the rock, making a powerful impression on the Indians and causing the poor Devil to flee, "roaring in a fury." "The cruel Devil never more returned to the rock nor to this district." Whether the roaring which they heard was that of the Devil or of the flames we can only conjecture. Whether the conflagration temporarily dried up the swamp or interfered with the arrangements of the water supply so that the pool disappeared for the time being and gave the Devil no chance to appear in the water, where he had formerly been accustomed to show himself, is also a matter for speculation.

The buildings of the House of the Sun are in a very ruinous state, but the rock itself, with its curious carvings, is well preserved notwithstanding the great conflagration of 1570. Its length is fifty-two feet, its width thirty feet, and its height above the present level of the water, twenty-five feet. On the west side of the rock are seats and large steps or platforms. It was customary to kill llamas at these holy *huacas*. On top of the rock is a flattened place which may have been used for such sacrifices. From it runs a little crack in the boulder, which has been artificially enlarged and may have been intended to carry off the blood of the victim killed on top of the rock. It is still used for occult ceremonies of obscure origin which are quietly practiced here by the more superstitious Indian women of the valley, possibly in memory of the Ñusta or Inca princess for whom the shrine is named.

On the south side of the monolith are several large platforms and four or five small seats which have been cut in the rock. Great care was exercised in cutting out the platforms. The edges are very nearly square, level, and straight. The east side of the rock projects over the spring. Two seats have been carved immediately above the water. On the north side there are no seats. Near the water, steps have been carved. There is one flight of three and another of seven steps. Above them the rock has been flattened artificially and carved into a very bold relief. There are ten projecting square stones, like those usually called *intihuatana* or "places to which the sun is tied." In one line are seven; one is slightly apart from the six others. The other three are arranged in a triangular position above the seven. It is significant that these stones are on the northeast face of the rock, where they are exposed to the rising sun and cause striking shadows at sunrise.

Our excavations yielded no artifacts whatever and only a handful of very rough old potsherds of uncertain origin. The running water under the rock was clear and appeared to be a spring, but when we drained the swamp which adjoins the great rock on its northeastern side, we found that the spring was a little higher up the hill and that the water ran through the dark pool. We also found that what looked like a stone culvert on the borders of the little pool proved to be the top of the back of a row of seven or eight very fine stone seats. The platform on which the seats rested and the seats themselves are parts of three or four large rocks nicely fitted together. Some of the seats are under the black shadows of the overhanging rock. Since the pool was an object of fear and mystery the seats were probably used only by priests or sorcerers. It would have been a splendid place to practice divination. No doubt the devils "roared."

All our expeditions in the ancient province of Uilcapampa have failed to disclose the presence of any other "white rock over a spring of water" surrounded by the ruins of a possible "House of the Sun." Consequently it seems reasonable to adopt the following conclusions: *First*, Ñusta Isppana is the Yurak Rumi of Father Calancha. The Chuquipalta of to-day is the place to which he refers as Chuquipalpa. *Second*, Uiticos, "close to" this shrine, was once the name of the present valley of Vilcabamba between Tincochaca and Lucma. This is the "Viticos" of Cieza de Leon, a contemporary of Manco, who says that it was to the province of Viticos that Manco determined to retire when he rebelled against Pizarro, and that "having reached Viticos with a great quantity of treasure collected from various parts, together with his women and retinue, the king, Manco Inca, established himself in the strongest place he could find, whence he sallied forth many times and in many directions and disturbed those parts which were quiet, to do what harm he could to the Spaniards, whom he considered as cruel enemies." *Third*, the "strongest place" of Cieza, the Guaynapucará of Garcia, was Rosaspata, referred to by Ocampo as "the fortress of Pitcos," where, he says, "there was a level space with majestic buildings," the most noteworthy feature of which was that they had two kinds of doors and both kinds had white stone lintels. *Fourth*, the modern village of Pucyura in the valley of the river Vilcabamba is the Puquiura of Father Calancha, the site of the first mission church in this region, as assumed by Raimondi, although he was disappointed in the insignificance of the "wretched little village." The remains of the old quartz-crushing plant in Tincochaca, which has already been noted, the distance from the "House of the Sun," not too great for the religious procession, and the location of Pucyura near the fortress, all point to the correctness of this conclusion.

Finally, Calancha says that Friar Ortiz, after he had secured permission from Titu Cusi to establish the second missionary station in Uilcapampa, selected "the town of Huarancalla, which was populous and well located in the midst of a number of other little towns and villages. There was a dis-

tance of two or three days' journey from one convent to the other. Leaving
Friar Marcos in Puquiura, Friar Diego went to his new establishment, and
in a short time built a church." There is no "Huarancalla" to-day, nor any tradition of any, but in Mapillo, a pleasant valley at an elevation of about
10,000 feet, in the temperate zone where the crops with which the Incas
were familiar might have been raised, near pastures where llamas and
alpacas could have flourished, is a place called Huarancalque. The valley is
populous and contains a number of little towns and villages. Furthermore,
Huarancalque is two or three days' journey from Pucyura and is on the road
which the Indians of this region now use in going to Ayacucho. This was
undoubtedly the route used by Manco in his raids on Spanish caravans. The
Mapillo flows into the Apurimac near the mouth of the river Pampas. Not
far up the Pampas is the important bridge between Bombon and Ocros,
which Mr. Hay and I crossed in 1909 on our way from Cuzco to Lima. The
city of Ayacucho was founded by Pizarro, a day's journey from this bridge.
The necessity for the Spanish caravans to cross the river Pampas at this point
made it easy for Manco's foraging expeditions to reach them by sudden
marches from Uiticos down the Mapillo River by way of Huarancalque,
which is probably the "Huarancalla" of Calancha's "Chronicles." He must have
had rafts or canoes on which to cross the Apurimac, which is here very wide
and deep. In the valleys between Huarancalque and Lucma, Manco was cut
off from central Peru by the Apurimac and its magnificent canyon, which
in many places has a depth of over two miles. He was cut off from Cuzco
by the inhospitable snow fields and glaciers of Salcantay, Soray, and the adjacent ridges, even though they are only fifty miles from Cuzco. Frequently
all the passes are completely snow-blocked. Fatalities have been known even
in recent years. In this mountainous province Manco could be sure of
finding not only security from his Spanish enemies, but any climate that
he desired and an abundance of food for his followers. There seems to be
no reason to doubt that the retired region around the modern town of
Pucyura in the upper Vilcabamba Valley was once called Uiticos.

---

[1] In those days the term "Andes" appears to have been very limited in scope, and was applied only to the
high range north of Cuzco where lived the tribe called Antis. Their name was given to the range. Its culminating point was Mt. Salcantay.

CHAPTER 13

VILCABAMBA

★

ALTHOUGH THE REFUGE of Manco is frequently spoken of as Uiticos by the contemporary writers, the word Vilcabamba, or Uilcapampa, is used even more often. In fact Garcilasso, the chief historian of the Incas, himself the son of an Inca princess, does not mention Uiticos. Vilcabamba was the common name of the province. Father Calancha says it was a very large area, "covering fourteen degrees of longitude," about seven hundred miles wide. It included many savage tribes "of the far interior" who acknowledged the supremacy of the Incas and brought tribute to Manco and his sons. "The Mañaries and the Pilcosones came a hundred and two hundred leagues" to visit the Inca in Uiticos.

The name, Vilcabamba, is also applied repeatedly to a town. Titu Cusi says he lived there many years during his youth. Calancha says it was "two days' journey from Puquiura." Raimondi thought it must be Choqquequirau. Captain Garcia's soldiers, however, speak of it as being down in the warm valleys of the *montaña*, the present rubber country. On the other hand the only place which bears this name on the maps of Peru is near the source of the Vilcabamba River, not more than three or four leagues from Pucyura. We determined to visit it.

We found the town to lie on the edge of bleak upland pastures, 11,750 feet above the sea. Instead of Inca walls or ruins Vilcabamba has threescore solidly built Spanish houses. At the time of our visit they were mostly empty, although their roofs, of unusually heavy thatch, seemed to be in good repair. We stayed at the house of the *gobernador*,

Manuel Condoré. The nights were bitterly cold and we should have been most uncomfortable in a tent.

The *gobernador* said that the reason the town was deserted was that most of the people were now attending to their *chacras*, or little farms, and looking after their herds of sheep and cattle in the neighboring valleys. He said that only at special festival times, such as the annual visit of the priest, who celebrates mass in the church here, *once a year*, are the buildings fully occupied. In the latter part of the sixteenth century, gold mines were discovered in the adjacent mountains and the capital of the Spanish province of Vilcabamba was transferred from Hoyara to this place. Its official name, Condoré said, is still San Francisco de la Victoria de Vilcabamba, and as such it occurs on most of the early maps of Peru. The solidity of the stone houses was due to the prosperity of the gold diggers. The present air of desolation and absence of population is probably due to the decay of that industry.

The church is large. Near it, and slightly apart from the building, is a picturesque stone belfry with three old Spanish bells. Condoré said that the church was built at least three hundred years ago. It is probably the very structure whose construction was carefully supervised by Ocampo. In the negotiations for permission to move the municipality of San Francisco de la Victoria from Hoyara to the neighborhood of the mines, Ocampo, then one of the chief settlers, went to Cuzco as agent of the interested parties, to take the matter up with the viceroy. Ocampo's story is in part as follows:

"The change of site appeared convenient for the service of God our Lord and of his Majesty, and for the increase of his royal fifths, as well as beneficial to the inhabitants of the said city. Having examined the capitulations and reasons, the said Don Luis de Velasco [the viceroy] granted the licence to move the city to where it is now founded, ordering that it should have the title and name of the city of San Francisco of the Victory of Uilcapampa, which was its first name. By this change of site I, the said Baltasar de Ocampo, performed a great service to God our Lord and his Majesty. Through my care, industry and solicitude, a very good church was built, with its principal chapel and great doors." We found the walls to be heavy, massive, and well buttressed, the doors to be unusually large and the whole to show considerable "industry and solicitude."

The site was called "Onccoy, where the Spaniards who first discovered this land found the flocks and herds." Modern Vilcabamba is on grassy slopes, well suited for flocks and herds. On the steeper slopes potatoes are still raised, although the valley itself is given up to-day almost entirely to pasture lands. We saw horses, cattle, and sheep in abundance where the Incas must have pastured their llamas and alpacas. In the rocky cliffs near by are remains of the mines begun in Ocampo's day. There is little doubt that this was Onccoy, although that name is now no longer used here.

We met at the *gobernador's* an old Indian who admitted that an Inca had once lived on Rosaspata Hill. Of all the scores of persons whom we interviewed through the courtesy of the intelligent planters of the region or through the customary assistance of government officials, this Indian was the only one to make such an admission. Even he denied having heard of "Uiticos" or any of its variations. If we were indeed in the country of Manco and his sons, why should no one be familiar with that name?

Perhaps, after all, it is not surprising. The Indians of the highlands have now for so many generations been neglected by their rulers and brutalized by being allowed to drink all the alcohol they can purchase and to assimilate all the cocaine they can secure, through the constant chewing of *coca* leaves, that they have lost much if not all of their racial self-respect. It is the educated *mestizos* of the principal modern cities of Peru who, tracing their descent not only from the Spanish soldiers of the Conquest, but also from the blood of the race which was conquered, take pride in the achievements of the Incas and are endeavoring to preserve the remains of the wonderful civilization of their native ancestors. Until quite recently Vilcabamba was an unknown land to most of the Peruvians, even those who live in the city of Cuzco. Had the capital of the last four Incas been in a region whose climate appealed to Europeans, whose natural resources were sufficient to support a large population, and whose roads made transportation no more difficult than in most parts of the Andes, it would have been occupied from the days of Captain Garcia to the present by Spanish-speaking *mestizos*, who might have been interested in preserving the name of the ancient Inca capital and the traditions connected with it.

After the mines which attracted Ocampo and his friends "petered out," or else, with the primitive tools of the sixteenth century, ceased to yield adequate returns, the Spaniards lost interest in that remote region. The rude trails which connected Pucyura with Cuzco and civilization were at best dangerous and difficult. They were veritably impassable during a large part of the year even to people accustomed to Andean "roads."

The possibility of raising sugar cane and *coca* between Huadquiña and Santa Ana attracted a few Spanish-speaking people to live in the lower Urubamba Valley, notwithstanding the difficult transportation over the passes near Mts. Salcantay and Veronica; but there was nothing to lead any one to visit the upper Vilcabamba Valley or to desire to make it a place of residence. And until Señor Pancorbo opened the road to Lucma, Pucyura was extremely difficult of access. Nine generations of Indians lived and died in the province of Uilcapampa between the time of Tupac Amaru and the arrival of the first modern explorers. The great stone buildings constructed on the "Hill of Roses" in the days of Manco and his sons were allowed to fall into ruin. Their roofs decayed and disappeared. The names of those who once lived here were known to fewer and fewer of the natives. The Indians themselves had no desire to relate the story of the various forts and palaces to their Spanish landlords, nor had the latter any interest in hearing such tales. It was not until the renaissance of historical and geographical curiosity, in the nineteenth century, that it occurred to any one to look for Manco's capital. When Raimondi, the first scientist to penetrate Vilcabamba, reached Pucyura, no one thought to tell him that on the hilltop opposite the village once lived the last of the Incas and that the ruins of their palaces were still there, hidden underneath a thick growth of trees and vines.

A Spanish document of 1598 says the first town of "San Francisco de la Victoria de Vilcabamba" was in the "valley of Viticos." The town's long name became shortened to Vilcabamba. Then the river which flowed past was called the Vilcabamba, and is so marked on Raimondi's map. Uiticos had long since passed from the memory of man.

Furthermore, the fact that we saw no llamas or alpacas in the upland pastures, but only domestic animals of European origin, would also seem to indicate that for some reason or other this region had been abandoned by the Indians themselves. It is difficult to believe that if the Indians had inhabited these valleys continuously from Inca times to the present we should not have found at least a few of the indigenous American camels here. By itself, such an occurrence would hardly seem worth a remark, but taken in connection with the loss of traditions regarding Uiticos, it would seem to indicate that there must have been quite a long period of time in which no persons of consequence lived in this vicinity.

We are told by the historians of the colonial period that the mining operations of the first Spanish settlers were fatal to at least a million Indians. It is quite probable that the introduction of ordinary European contagious diseases, such as measles, chicken pox, and smallpox, may have had a great deal to do with the destruction of a large proportion of those unfortunates whose untimely deaths were attributed by historians to the very cruel practices of the early Spanish miners and treasure seekers. Both causes undoubtedly contributed to the result. There seems to be no question that the population diminished enormously in early colonial days. If this is true, the remaining population would naturally have sought regions where the conditions of existence and human intercourse were less severe and rigorous than in the valleys of Uiticos and Uilcapampa.

The students and travelers of the late nineteenth and early twentieth centuries, including such a careful observer as Bandelier, are of the opinion that the present-day population in the Andes of Peru and Bolivia is about as great as that at the time of the Conquest. In other words, with the decay of early colonial mining and the consequent disappearance of bad living conditions and forced labor at the mines, also with the rise of partial immunity to European diseases, and the more comfortable conditions of existence which have followed the coming of Peruvian independence, it is reasonable to suppose that the number of highland Indians has increased. With this increase has come a consequent crowding in certain localities. There would be a natural tendency to seek less crowded regions, even at the expense of using difficult mountain trails. This would lead to their occupying as remote and inaccessible a region as the ancient province of Uilcapampa. It is probable that after the gold mines ceased to pay, and before the demand for rubber caused the San Miguel Valley to be appropriated by the white man, there was a period of nearly three hundred years when no one of education or of intelligence superior to the ordinary Indian shepherd lived anywhere near Pucyura or Lucma. The adobe houses of these modern villages look fairly modern. They may have been built in the nineteenth century.

Such a theory would account for the very small amount of information prevailing in Peru regarding the region where we had been privileged to find so many ruins. This ignorance led the Peruvian geographers Raimondi and Paz Soldan to conclude that Choqquequirau, the only ruins reported between the Apurimac and the Urubamba, must have been the capital of the Incas who took refuge there. It also makes it seem more reasonable that the existence of Rosaspata and Ñusta Isppana should not have been known to Peruvian geographers and historians, or even to the government officials who lived in the adjacent villages.

We felt sure we had found Uiticos; nevertheless it was quite apparent that we had not yet found all the places which were called Vilcabamba. Examination of the writers of the sixteenth century shows that there may have been three places bearing that name; one spoken of by Calancha as Vilcabamba Viejo ("the old"), another also so called by Ocampo, and a third founded by the Spaniards, namely, the town we were now in. The story of the first is given in Calancha's account of the trials and tribulations of Friar Marcos and the martyrdom of Friar Diego Ortiz. The chronicler tells with considerable detail of their visit to "Vilcabamba Viejo." It was after the monks had already founded their religious establishment at Puquiura that they learned of the existence of this important religious center. They urged Titu Cusi to permit them to visit it. For a long time he refused. Its where-abouts remained unknown to them, but its strategic position as a religious stronghold led them to continue their demands. Finally, either to rid him-self of their importunities or because he imagined the undertaking might be made amusing, he yielded to their requests and bade them prepare for the journey. Calancha says that the Inca himself accompanied the two fri-ars, with a number of his captains and chieftains, taking them from Puquiura over a very rough and rugged road. The Inca, however, did not suffer from the character of the trail because, like the Roman generals of old, he was borne comfortably along in a litter by servants accustomed to this duty. The unfortunate missionaries were obliged to go on foot. The wet, rocky trail soon demoralized their foot-gear. When they came to a particularly bad place in the road, "*Ungacacha*," the trail went for some distance through water. The monks were forced to wade. The water was very cold. The Inca and his chief-tains were amused to see how the friars were hampered by their monastic garments while passing through the water. However, the monks persevered, greatly desiring to reach their goal, "on account of its being the largest city in which was the University of Idolatry, where lived the teachers who were wizards and masters of abomination." If one may judge by the name of the place, Uilcapampa, the wizards and sorcerers were probably aided by the powerful effects of the ancient snuff made from *huilca* seeds. After a three days' journey over very rough country, the monks arrived at their destination. Yet even then Titu Cusi was unwilling that they should live in the city, but ordered that the monks be given a dwelling outside, so that they might not witness the ceremonies and ancient rites which were practiced by the Inca and his captains and priests.

Nothing is said about the appearance of "Vilcabamba Viejo" and it is doubtful whether the monks were ever allowed to see the city, although they reached its vicinity. Here they stayed for three weeks and kept up their preaching and teaching. During their stay Titu Cusi, who had not wished to bring them here, got his revenge by annoying them in various ways. He was particularly anxious to make them break their vows of celibacy. Calancha says that after consultation with his priests and soothsayers Titu Cusi selected as tempters the most beautiful Indian women, including some individuals of the Yungas who were unusually attractive. It is possible that these women, who lived at the "University of Idolatry" in "Vilcabamba Viejo," were "Virgins of the Sun," who were under the orders of the Inca and his high priests and were selected from the fairest daughters of the empire. It is also evident that "Vilcabamba Viejo" was so constructed that the monks could be kept for three weeks in its vicinity without being able to see what was going on in the city or to describe the kinds of "abominations" which were practiced there, as they did those at the white rock of Chuquipalta. As will be shown later, it is possible that this Vilcabamba, referred to in Calancha's story as "Vilcabamba Viejo," was on the slopes of the mountain now called Machu Picchu.

In the meantime it was necessary to pursue the hunt for the ruins of Vilcabamba called "the old" by Ocampo, to distinguish it from the Spanish town of that name which he had helped to found after the capture of Tupac Amaru, and referred to merely as Vilcabamba by Captain Garcia and his companions in their accounts of the campaign.

CHAPTER 14

CONSERVIDAYOC

★

WHEN DON PEDRO DUQUE of Santa Ana was helping us to identify places mentioned in Calancha and Ocampo, the references to "Vilcabamba Viejo," or Old Uilcapampa, were supposed by two of his informants to point to a place called Conservidayoc. Don Pedro told us that in 1902 Lopez Torres, who had traveled much in the *montaña* looking for rubber trees, reported the discovery there of the ruins of an Inca city. All of Don Pedro's friends assured us that Conservidayoc was a terrible place to reach. "No one now living had been there." "It was inhabited by savage Indians who would not let strangers enter their villages."

When we reached Paltaybamba, Señor Pancorbo's manager confirmed what we had heard. He said further that an individual named Saavedra lived at Conservidayoc and undoubtedly knew all about the ruins, but was very averse to receiving visitors. Saavedra's house was extremely difficult to find. "No one had been there recently and returned alive." Opinions differed as to how far away it was.

Several days later, while Professor Foote and I were studying the ruins near Rosaspata, Señor Pancorbo, returning from his rubber estate in the San Miguel Valley and learning at Lucma of our presence near by, took great pains to find us and see how we were progressing. When he learned of our intention to search for the ruins of Conservidayoc, he asked us to desist from the attempt. He said Saavedra was "a very powerful man having many Indians under his control and living in grand state, with fifty servants, and not at all desirous of being visited by anybody." The Indians were "of the Campa tribe, very wild and extremely savage. They use poisoned arrows and are very hostile to strangers." Admitting that he had heard there were Inca ruins near Saavedra's station, Señor Pancorbo still begged us not to risk our lives by going to look for them.

By this time our curiosity was thoroughly aroused. We were familiar with the current stories regarding the habits of savage tribes who lived in the *montaña* and whose services were in great demand as rubber gatherers. We had even heard that Indians did not particularly like to work for Señor Pancorbo, who was an energetic, ambitious man, anxious to achieve many things, results which required more laborers than could easily be obtained. We could readily believe there might possibly be Indians at Conservidayoc who had escaped from the rubber estate of San Miguel. Undoubtedly, Señor Pancorbo's own life would have been at the mercy of their poisoned arrows. All over the Amazon Basin the exigencies of rubber gatherers had caused tribes visited with impunity by the explorers of the nineteenth century to become so savage and revengeful as to lead them to kill all white men in sight.

Professor Foote and I considered the matter in all its aspects. We finally came to the conclusion that in view of the specific reports regarding the presence of Inca ruins at Conservidayoc we could not afford to follow the advice of the friendly planter. We must at least make an effort to reach them, meanwhile taking every precaution to avoid arousing the enmity of the powerful Saavedra and his savage retainers.

On the day following our arrival at the town of Vilcabamba, the *gobernador*, Condoré, taking counsel with his chief assistant, had summoned the wisest Indians living in the vicinity, including a very picturesque old fellow whose name, Quispi Cusi, was strongly reminiscent of the days of Titu Cusi. It was explained to him that this was a very solemn occasion and that an official inquiry was in progress. He took off his hat—but not his knitted cap—and endeavored to the best of his ability to answer our questions about the surrounding country. It was he who said that the Inca Tupac Amaru once lived at Rosaspata. He had never heard of Uilcapampa Viejo, but he admitted that there were ruins in the *montaña* near Conservidayoc. Other Indians were questioned by Condoré. Several had heard of the ruins of Conservidayoc, but, apparently, none of them, nor any one in the village, had actually seen the ruins or visited their immediate vicinity. They all agreed that Saavedra's place was "at least four days' hard journey on foot in the *montaña* beyond Pampaconas." No village of that name appeared on any map of Peru, although it is frequently mentioned in the documents of the six-teenth century. Rodriguez de Figueroa, who came to seek an audience with Titu Cusi about 1565, says that he met Titu Cusi at a place called Banbaconas. He says further that the Inca came there from somewhere down in the dense forests of the *montaña* and presented him with a macaw and two hampers of peanuts—products of a warm region.

We had brought with us the large sheets of Raimondi's invaluable map which covered this locality. We also had the new map of South Peru and North Bolivia which had just been published by the Royal Geographical Society and gave a summary of all available information. The Indians said that Conservidayoc lay in a westerly direction from Vilcabamba, yet on Raimondi's map all of the rivers which rise in the mountains west of the town are short affluents of the Apurimac and flow southwest. We wondered whether the stories about ruins at Conservidayoc would turn out to be as barren of foundation as those we had heard from the trustworthy foreman at Huadquiña. One of our informants said the Inca city was called Espiritu Pampa, or the "Pampa of Ghosts." Would the ruins turn out to be "ghosts"? Would they vanish on the arrival of white men with cameras and steel meas-uring tapes?

No one at Vilcabamba had seen the ruins, but they said that at the vil-lage of Pampaconas, "about five leagues from here," there were Indians who had actually been to Conservidayoc. Our supplies were getting low. There were no shops nearer than Lucma; no food was obtainable from the natives. Accordingly, notwithstanding the protestations of the hospitable *gobernador*, we decided to start immediately for Conservidayoc.

At the end of a long day's march up the Vilcabamba Valley, Professor Foote, with his accustomed skill, was preparing the evening meal and we were both looking forward with satisfaction to enjoying large cups of our favorite beverage. Several years ago, when traveling on muleback across the great plateau of southern Bolivia, I had learned the value of sweet, hot tea as a stimulant and bracer in the high Andes. At first astonished to see how much tea the Indian *arrieros* drank, I learned from sad experience that it was far better than cold water, which often brings on mountain-sickness. This particular evening, one swallow of the hot tea caused consternation. It was the most horrible stuff imaginable. Examination showed small, oily par-ticles floating on the surface. Further investigation led to the discovery that one of our *arrieros* had that day placed our can of kerosene on top of one of the loads. The tin became leaky and the kerosene had dripped down into a food box. A cloth bag of granulated sugar had eagerly absorbed all the oil it could. There was no remedy but to throw away half of our supply. As I have said, the longer one works in the Andes the more desirable does sugar become and the more one seems to crave it. Yet we were unable to procure any here.

After the usual delays, caused in part by the difficulty of catching our mules, which had taken advantage of our historical investigations to stray far up the mountain pastures, we finally set out from the boundaries of known topography, headed for "Conservidayoc," a vague place surrounded with mystery; a land of hostile savages, albeit said to possess the ruins of an Inca town.

Our first day's journey was to Pampaconas. Here and in its vicinity the *gobernador* told us he could procure guides and the half-dozen carriers whose services we should require for the jungle trail where mules could not be used. As the Indians hereabouts were averse to penetrating the wilds of Conservidayoc and were also likely to be extremely alarmed at the sight of men in uniform, the two *gendarmes* who were now accompanying us were instructed to delay their departure for a few hours and not to reach Pampaconas with our pack train until dusk. The *gobernador* said that if the Indians of Pampaconas caught sight of any brass buttons coming over the hills they would hide so effectively that it would be impossible to secure any carriers. Apparently this was due in part to that love of freedom which had led them to abandon the more comfortable towns for a frontier village where landlords could not call on them for forced labor. Consequently, before the arrival of any such striking manifestations of official authority as our *gendarmes*, the *gobernador* and his friend Mogrovejo proposed to put in the day craftily commandeering the services of a half-dozen sturdy Indians. Their methods will be described presently.

Leaving modern Vilcabamba, we crossed the flat, marshy bottom of an old glaciated valley, in which one of our mules got thoroughly mired while searching for the succulent grasses which cover the treacherous bog. Fording the Vilcabamba River, which here is only a tiny brook, we climbed out of the valley and turned westward. On the mountains above us were vestiges of several abandoned mines. It was their discovery in 1572 or thereabouts which brought Ocampo and the first Spanish settlers to this valley. Raimondi says that he found here cobalt, nickel, silver-bearing copper ore, and lead sulphide. He does not mention any gold-bearing quartz. It may have been exhausted long before his day. As to the other minerals, the difficulties of transportation are so great that it is not likely that mining will be renewed here for many years to come.

At the top of the pass we turned to look back and saw a long chain of snow-capped mountains towering above and behind the town of Vilcabamba. We searched in vain for them on our maps. Raimondi, followed by the Royal Geographical Society, did not leave room enough for such a range to exist between the rivers Apurimac and Urubamba. Mr. Hendriksen determined our longitude to be 73° west, and our latitude to be 13° 8' south. Yet according to the latest map of this region, published in the preceding year, this was the very position of the river Apurimac itself, near its junction with the river Pampas. We ought to have been swimming "the Great Speaker." Actually we were on top of a lofty mountain pass surrounded by high peaks and glaciers. The mystery was finally solved by Mr. Bumstead in 1912, when he determined the Apurimac and the Urubamba to be thirty miles farther apart than any one had supposed. His surveys opened an unexplored region, 1500 square miles in extent, whose very existence had not been guessed before 1911. It proved to be one of the largest undescribed glaciated areas in South America. Yet it is less than a hundred miles from Cuzco, the chief city in the Peruvian Andes, and the site of a university for more than three centuries. That Uilcapampa could so long defy investigation and exploration shows better than anything else how wisely Manco had selected his refuge. It is indeed a veritable labyrinth of snow-clad peaks, unknown glaciers, and trackless canyons.

Looking west, we saw in front of us a great wilderness of deep green valleys and forest-clad slopes. We supposed from our maps that we were now looking down into the basin of the Apurimac. As a matter of fact, we were on the rim of the valley of the hitherto uncharted Pampaconas, a branch of the Cosireni, one of the affluents of the Urubamba. Instead of being the Apurimac Basin, what we saw was another unexplored region which drained into the Urubamba!

At the time, however, we did not know where we were, but understood from Condoré that somewhere far down in the *montaña* below us was Conservidayoc, the sequestered domain of Saavedra and his savage Indians. It seemed less likely than ever that the Incas could have built a town so far away from the climate and food to which they were accustomed. The "road" was now so bad that only with the greatest difficulty could we coax our sure-footed mules to follow it. Once we had to dismount, as the path led down a long, steep, rocky stairway of ancient origin. At last, rounding a hill, we came in sight of a lonesome little hut perched on a shoulder of the mountain. In front of it, seated in the sun on mats, were two women shelling corn. As soon as they saw the *gobernador* approaching, they stopped their work and began to prepare lunch. It was about eleven o'clock and they did not need to be told that Señor Condoré and his friends had not had anything but a cup of coffee since the night before. In order to meet the emergency of unexpected guests they killed four or five squealing *cuys* (guinea pigs), usually to be found scurrying about the mud floor of the huts of mountain Indians. Before long the savory odor of roast *cuy*, well basted, and cooked-to-a-turn on primitive spits, whetted our appetites.

In the eastern United States one sees guinea pigs only as pets or laboratory victims; never as an article of food. In spite of the celebrated dogma that "Pigs is Pigs," this form of "pork" has never found its way to our kitchens, even though these "pigs" live on a very clean, vegetable diet. Incidentally guinea pigs do not come from Guinea and are in no way related to pigs—Mr. Ellis Parker Butler to the contrary notwithstanding! They belong rather to the same family as rabbits and Belgian hares and have long been a highly prized article of food in the Andes of Peru. The wild species are of a grayish brown color, which enables them to escape observation in their natural habitat. The domestic varieties, which one sees in the huts of the Indians, are piebald, black, white, and tawny, varying from one another in color as much as do the llamas, which were also domesticated by the same race of people thousands of years ago. Although Anglo-Saxon "folkways," as Professor Sumner would say, permit us to eat and enjoy long-eared rabbits, we draw the line at short-eared rabbits, yet they were bred to be eaten.

I am willing to admit that this was the first time that I had ever knowingly tasted their delicate flesh, although once in the capital of Bolivia I thought the hotel kitchen had a diminishing supply! Had I not been very hungry, I might never have known how delicious a roast guinea pig can be. The meat is not unlike squab. To the Indians whose supply of animal food is small, whose fowls are treasured for their eggs, and whose thin sheep are more valuable as wool bearers than as mutton, the succulent guinea pig, "most prolific of mammals," as was discovered by Mr. Butler's hero, is a highly valued article of food, reserved for special occasions. The North American housewife keeps a few tins of sardines and cans of preserves on hand for emergencies. Her sister in the Andes similarly relies on fat little *cuys*.

After lunch, Condoré and Mogrovejo divided the extensive rolling countryside between them and each rode quietly from one lonesome farm to another, looking for men to engage as bearers. When they were so fortunate as to find the man of the house at home or working in his little *chacra* they greeted him pleasantly. When he came forward to shake hands, in the usual Indian manner, a silver dollar was unsuspectingly slipped into the palm of his right hand and he was informed that he had accepted pay for services which must now be performed. It seemed hard, but this was the only way in which it was possible to secure carriers.

During Inca times the Indians never received pay for their labor. A paternal government saw to it that they were properly fed and clothed and either given abundant opportunity to provide for their own necessities or else permitted to draw on official stores. In colonial days a more greedy and less paternal government took advantage of the ancient system and enforced it without taking pains to see that it should not cause suffering. Then, for generations, thoughtless landlords, backed by local authority, forced the Indians to work without suitably recompensing them at the end of their labors or even pretending to carry out promises and wage agreements. The peons learned that it was unwise to perform any labor without first having received a considerable portion of their pay. When once they accepted money, however, their own custom and the law of the land provided that they must carry out their obligations. Failure to do so meant legal punishment.

Consequently, when an unfortunate Pampaconas Indian found he had a dollar in his hand, he bemoaned his fate, but realized that service was inevitable. In vain did he plead that he was "busy," that his "crops needed attention," that his "family could not spare him," that "he lacked food for a journey." Condoré and Mogrovejo were accustomed to all varieties of excuses. They succeeded in "engaging" half a dozen carriers. Before dark we reached the village of Pampaconas, a few small huts scattered over grassy hillsides, at an elevation of 10,000 feet.

In the notes of one of the military advisers of Viceroy Francisco de Toledo is a reference to Pampaconas as a "high, cold place." This is correct. Nevertheless, I doubt if the present village is the Pampaconas mentioned in the documents of Garcia's day as being "an important town of the Incas." There are no ruins hereabouts. The huts of Pampaconas were newly built of stone and mud, and thatched with grass. They were occupied by a group of sturdy mountain Indians, who enjoyed unusual freedom from official or other interference and a good place in which to raise sheep and cultivate potatoes, on the very edge of the dense forest. We found that there was some excitement in the village because on the previous night a jaguar, or possibly a cougar, had come out of the forest, attacked, killed, and dragged off one of the village ponies.

We were conducted to the dwelling of a stocky, well-built Indian named Guzman, the most reliable man in the village, who had been selected to be the head of the party of carriers that was to accompany us to Conservidayoc. Guzman had some Spanish blood in his veins, although he did not boast of it. With his wife and six children he occupied one of the best huts. A fire in one corner frequently filled it with acrid smoke. It was very small and had no windows. At one end was a loft where family treasures could be kept dry and reasonably safe from molestation. Piles of sheep skins were arranged for visitors to sit upon. Three or four rude niches in the walls served in lieu of shelves and tables. The floor of well-trodden clay was damp. Three mongrel dogs and a flea-bitten cat were welcome to share the narrow space with the family and their visitors. A dozen hogs entered stealthily and tried to avoid attention by putting a muffler on involuntary grunts. They did not succeed and were violently ejected by a boy with a whip; only to return again and again, each time to be driven out as before, squealing loudly. Notwithstanding these interruptions, we carried on a most interesting conversation with Guzman. He had been to Conservidayoc and had himself actually seen ruins at Espiritu Pampa. At last the mythical "Pampa of Ghosts" began to take on in our minds an aspect of reality, even though we were careful to remind ourselves that another very trustworthy man had said he had seen ruins "finer than Ollantaytambo" near Huadquiña. Guzman did not seem to dread Conservidayoc as much as the other Indians, only one of whom had ever been there. To cheer them up we purchased a fat sheep, for which we paid fifty cents. Guzman immediately butchered it in preparation for the journey. Although it was August and the middle of the dry season, rain began to fall early in the afternoon. Sergeant Carrasco arrived after dark with our pack animals, but, missing the trail as he neared Guzman's place, one of the mules stepped into a bog and was extracted only with considerable difficulty.

We decided to pitch our small pyramidal tent on a fairly well-drained bit of turf not far from Guzman's little hut. In the evening, after we had had a long talk with the Indians, we came back through the rain to our comfortable little tent, only to hear various and sundry grunts emerging therefrom. We found that during our absence a large sow and six fat young pigs, unable to settle down comfortably at the Guzman hearth, had decided that our tent was much the driest available place on the mountain side and that our blankets made a particularly attractive bed. They had considerable difficulty in getting out of the small door as fast as they wished. Nevertheless, the pouring rain and the memory of comfortable blankets caused the pigs to return at intervals. As we were starting to enjoy our first nap, Guzman, with hospitable intent, sent us two bowls of steaming soup, which at first glance seemed to contain various sizes of white macaroni—a dish of which one of us was particularly fond. The white hollow cylinders proved to be extraordinarily tough, not the usual kind of macaroni. As a matter of fact, we learned that the evening meal which Guzman's wife had prepared for her guests was made chiefly of sheep's entrails!

Rain continued without intermission during the whole of a very cold and dreary night. Our tent, which had never been wet before, leaked badly; the only part which seemed to be thoroughly waterproof was the floor. As day dawned we found ourselves to be lying in puddles of water. Everything was soaked. Furthermore, rain was still falling. While we were discussing the situation and wondering what we should cook for breakfast, the faithful Guzman heard our voices and immediately sent us two more bowls of hot soup, which were this time more welcome, even though among the bountiful corn, beans, and potatoes we came unexpectedly upon fragments of the teeth and jaws of the sheep. Evidently in Pampaconas nothing is wasted.

We were anxious to make an early start for Conservidayoc, but it was first necessary for our Indians to prepare food for the ten days' journey ahead of them. Guzman's wife, and I suppose the wives of our other carriers, spent the morning grinding chuño (frozen potatoes) with a rocking stone pestle on a flat stone mortar, and parching or toasting large quantities of sweet corn in a terra-cotta olla. With chuño and tostado, the body of the sheep, and a small quantity of coca leaves, the Indians professed themselves to be perfectly contented. Of our own provisions we had so small a quantity that we were unable to spare any. However, it is doubtful whether the Indians would have liked them as much as the food to which they had long been accustomed.

Toward noon, all the Indian carriers but one having arrived, and the rain having partly subsided, we started for Conservidayoc. We were told that it would be possible to use the mules for this day's journey. San Fernando, our first stop, was "seven leagues" away, far down in the densely wooded Pampaconas Valley. Leaving the village we climbed up the mountain back of Guzman's hut and followed a faint trail by a dangerous and precarious route along the crest of the ridge. The rains had not improved the path. Our saddle mules were of little use. We had to go nearly all the way on foot. Owing to cold rain and mist we could see but little of the deep canyon which opened below us, and into which we now began to descend through the clouds by a very steep, zigzag path, four thousand feet to a hot tropical valley. Below the clouds we found ourselves near a small abandoned clearing. Passing this and fording little streams, we went along a very narrow path, across steep slopes, on which maize had been planted. Finally we came to another little clearing and two extremely primitive little shanties, mere shelters not deserving to be called huts; and this was San Fernando, the end of the mule trail. There was scarcely room enough in them for our six carriers. It was with great difficulty we found and cleared a place for our tent, although its floor was only seven feet square. There was no really flat land at all.

At 8:30 P.M. August 13, 1911, while lying on the ground in our tent, I noticed an earthquake. It was felt also by the Indians in the near-by shelter, who from force of habit rushed out of their frail structure and made a great disturbance, crying out that there was a *temblor*. Even had their little thatched roof fallen upon them, as it might have done during the stormy night which followed, they were in no danger; but, being accustomed to the stone walls and red tiled roofs of mountain villages where earthquakes sometimes do very serious harm, they were greatly excited. The motion seemed to me to be like a slight shuffle from west to east, lasting three or four seconds, a gentle rocking back and forth, with eight or ten vibrations. Several weeks later, near Huadquiña, we happened to stop at the Colpani telegraph office. The operator said he had felt two shocks on August 13th—one at five o'clock, which had shaken the books off his table and knocked over a box of insulators standing along a wall which ran north and south. He said the shock which I had felt was the lighter of the two.

During the night it rained hard, but our tent was now adjusting itself to the "dry seasons" and we were more comfortable. Furthermore, camping out at 10,000 feet above sea level is very different from camping at 6000 feet. This elevation, similar to that of the bridge of San Miguel, below Machu Picchu, is on the lower edge of the temperate zone and the beginning of the torrid tropics. Sugar cane, peppers, bananas, and grenadillas grow here as well as maize, squashes, and sweet potatoes. None of these things will grow at Pampaconas. The Indians who raise sheep and white potatoes in that cold region come to San Fernando to make *chacras* or small clearings. The three or four natives whom we found here were so alarmed by the sight of brass buttons that they disappeared during the night rather than take the chance of having a silver dollar pressed into their hands in the morning! From San Fernando, we sent one of our *gendarmes* back to Pampaconas with the mules. Our carriers were good for about fifty pounds apiece.

Half an hour's walk brought us to Vista Alegre, another little clearing on an alluvial fan in the bend of the river. The soil here seemed to be very rich. In the *chacra* we saw corn stalks eighteen feet in height, near a gigantic tree almost completely enveloped in the embrace of a *mato-palo*, or parasitic fig tree. This clearing certainly deserves its name, for it commands a "charming view" of the green Pampaconas Valley. Opposite us rose abruptly a heavily forested mountain, whose summit was lost in the clouds a mile above. To circumvent this mountain the river had been flowing in a westerly direction; now it gradually turned to the northward. Again we were mystified; for, by Raimondi's map, it should have gone southward.

We entered a dense jungle, where the narrow path became more and more difficult for our carriers. Crawling over rocks, under branches, along slippery little cliffs, on steps which had been cut in earth or rock, over a trail which not even dogs could follow unassisted, slowly we made our way down the valley. Owing to the heat, humidity, and the frequent showers, it was mid-afternoon before we reached another little clearing called Pacaypata. Here, on a hillside nearly a thousand feet above the river, our men decided to spend the night in a tiny little shelter six feet long and five feet wide. Professor Foote and I had to dig a shelf out of the steep hillside in order to pitch our tent.

The next morning, not being detained by the vagaries of a mule train, we made an early start. As we followed the faint little trail across the gulches tributary to the river Pampaconas, we had to negotiate several unusually steep descents and ascents. The bearers suffered from the heat. They found it more and more difficult to carry their loads. Twice we had to cross the rapids of the river on primitive bridges which consisted only of a few little logs lashed together and resting on slippery boulders.

By one o'clock we found ourselves on a small plain (ele. 4500 ft.) in dense woods surrounded by tree ferns, vines, and tangled thickets, through which it was impossible to see for more than a few feet. Here Guzman told us we must stop and rest a while, as we were now in the territory of *los salvajes*, the savage Indians who acknowledged only the rule of Saavedra and resented all intrusion. Guzman did not seem to be particularly afraid, but said that we ought to send ahead one of our carriers, to warn the savages that we were coming on a friendly mission and were not in search of rubber gatherers; otherwise they might attack us, or run away and disappear into the jungle. He said we should never be able to find the ruins without their help. The carrier who was selected to go ahead did not relish his task. Leaving his pack behind, he proceeded very quietly and cautiously along the trail and was lost to view almost immediately. There followed an exciting half-hour while we waited, wondering what attitude the savages would take toward us, and trying to picture to ourselves the mighty potentate, Saavedra, who had been described as sitting in the midst of savage luxury, "surrounded by fifty servants," and directing his myrmidons to checkmate our desires to visit the Inca city on the "pampa of ghosts."

Suddenly, we were startled by the crackling of twigs and the sound of a man running. We instinctively held our rifles a little tighter in readiness for whatever might befall—when there burst out of the woods a pleasant-faced young Peruvian, quite conventionally clad, who had come in haste from Saavedra, his father, to extend to us a most cordial welcome! It seemed scarcely credible, but a glance at his face showed that there was no ambush in store for us. It was with a sigh of relief that we realized there was to be no shower of poisoned arrows from the impenetrable thickets. Gathering up our packs, we continued along the jungle trail, through woods which gradually became higher, deeper, and darker, until presently we saw sunlight ahead and, to our intense astonishment, the bright green of waving sugar cane. A few moments of walking through the cane fields found us at a large comfortable hut, welcomed very simply and modestly by Saavedra himself. A more pleasant and peaceable little man it was never my good fortune to meet. We looked furtively around for his fifty savage servants, but all we saw was his good-natured Indian wife, three or four small children, and a wild-eyed maid-of-all-work, evidently the only savage present. Saavedra said some called this place "Jesús Maria" because they were so surprised when they saw it.

It is difficult to describe our feelings as we accepted Saavedra's invitation to make ourselves at home, and sat down to an abundant meal of boiled chicken, rice, and sweet cassava (*manioc*). Saavedra gave us to understand that we were not only most welcome to anything he had, but that he would do everything to enable us to see the ruins, which were, it seemed, at Espiritu Pampa, some distance farther down the valley, to be reached only by a hard trail passable for barefooted savages, but scarcely available for us unless we chose to go a good part of the distance on hands and knees. The next day, while our carriers were engaged in clearing this trail, Professor

Foote collected a large number of insects, including eight new species of moths and butterflies.

I inspected Saavedra's plantation. The soil having lain fallow for centuries, and being rich in humus, had produced more sugar cane than he could grind. In addition to this, he had bananas, coffee trees, sweet potatoes, tobacco, and peanuts. Instead of being "a very powerful chief having many Indians under his control"—a kind of "Pooh-Bah"—he was merely a pioneer. In the utter wilderness, far from any neighbors, surrounded by dense forests and a few savages, he had established his home. He was not an Indian potentate, but only a frontiersman, soft-spoken and energetic, an ingenious carpenter and mechanic, a modest Peruvian of the best type.

Owing to the scarcity of arable land he was obliged to cultivate such *pampas* as he could find—one an alluvial fan near his house, another a natural terrace near the river. Back of the house was a thatched shelter under which he had constructed a little sugar mill. It had a pair of hardwood rollers, each capable of being turned, with much creaking and cracking, by a large, rustic wheel made of roughly hewn timbers fastened together with wooden pins and lashed with thongs, worked by hand and foot power. Since Saavedra had been unable to coax any pack animals over the trail to Conservidayoc he was obliged to depend entirely on his own limited strength and that of his active son, aided by the uncertain and irregular services of such savages as wished to work for sugar, trinkets, or other trade articles. Sometimes the savages seemed to enjoy the fun of climbing on the great creaking treadwheel, as though it were a game. At other times they would disappear in the woods.

Near the mill were some interesting large pots which Saavedra was using in the process of boiling the juice and making crude sugar. He said he had found the pots in the jungle not far away. They had been made by the Incas. Four of them were of the familiar *aryballus* type. Another was of a closely related form, having a wide mouth, pointed base, single incised, conventionalized, animal-head nubbin attached to the shoulder, and band-shaped handles attached vertically below the median line. Although capable of holding more than ten gallons, this huge pot was intended to be carried on the back and shoulders by means of a rope passing through the handles and around the nubbin. Saavedra said that he had found near his house several bottle-shaped cists lined with stones, with a flat stone on top—evidently ancient graves. The bones had entirely disappeared. The cover of one of the graves had been pierced; the hole covered with a thin sheet of beaten silver. He had also found a few stone implements and two or three small bronze Inca axes.

On the *pampa*, below his house, Saavedra had constructed with infinite labor another sugar mill. It seemed strange that he should have taken the trouble to make two mills; but when one remembered that he had no pack animals and was usually obliged to bring the cane to the mill on his own back and the back of his son, one realized that it was easier, while the cane was growing, to construct a new mill near the cane field than to have to carry the heavy bundles of ripe cane up the hill. He said his hardest task was to get money with which to send his children to school in Cuzco and to pay his taxes. The only way in which he could get any cash was by making *chancaca*, crude brown sugar, and carrying it on his back, fifty pounds at a time, three hard days' journey on foot up the mountain to Pampaconas or Vilcabamba, six or seven thousand feet above his little plantation. He said he could usually sell such a load for five *soles*, equivalent to two dollars and a half! His was certainly a hard lot, but he did not complain, although he smilingly admitted that it was very difficult to keep the trail open, since the jungle grew so fast and the floods in the river continually washed away his little rustic bridges. His chief regret was that as the result of a recent revolution, with which he had had nothing to do, the government had decreed that all firearms should be turned in, and so he had lost the one thing he needed to enable him to get fresh meat in the forest.

In the clearing near the house we were interested to see a large turkey-like bird, the *pava de la montaña*, glossy black, its most striking feature a high, coral red comb. Although completely at liberty, it seemed to be thoroughly domesticated. It would make an attractive bird for introduction into our Southern States.

Saavedra gave us some very black leaves of native tobacco, which he had cured. An inveterate smoker who tried it in his pipe said it was without exception the strongest stuff he ever had encountered!

So interested did I become in talking with Saavedra, seeing his plantation, and marveling that he should be worried about taxes and have to obey regulations in regard to firearms, I had almost forgotten about the wild Indians. Suddenly our carriers ran toward the house in a great flurry of excitement, shouting that there was a "savage" in the bushes near by. The "wild man" was very timid, but curiosity finally got the better of fear and he summoned up sufficient courage to accept Saavedra's urgent invitation that he come out and meet us. He proved to be a miserable specimen, suffering from a very bad cold in his head. It has been my good fortune at one time or another to meet primitive folk in various parts of America and the Pacific, but this man was by far the dirtiest and most wretched savage that I have ever seen.

He was dressed in a long, filthy tunic which came nearly to his ankles. It was made of a large square of coarsely woven cotton cloth, with a hole in the middle for his head. The sides were stitched up, leaving holes for the arms. His hair was long, unkempt, and matted. He had small, deep-set eyes, cadaverous cheeks, thick lips, and a large mouth. His big toes were unusually long and prehensile. Slung over one shoulder he carried a small knapsack made of coarse fiber net. Around his neck hung what at first sight seemed to be a necklace composed of a dozen stout cords securely knotted together. Although I did not see it in use, I was given to understand that when climbing trees, he used this stout loop to fasten his ankles together and thus secure a tighter grip for his feet.

By evening two other savages had come in; a young married man and his little sister. Both had bad colds. Saavedra told us that these Indians were Pichanguerras, a subdivision of the Campa tribe. Saavedra and his son spoke a little of their language, which sounded to our unaccustomed ears like a succession of low grunts, breathings, and gutturals. It was pieced out by signs. The long tunics worn by the men indicated that they had one or more wives. Before marrying they wear very scanty attire—nothing more than a few rags hanging over one shoulder and tied about the waist. The long tunic, a comfortable enough garment to wear during the cold nights, and their only covering, must impede their progress in the jungle; yet they live partly by hunting, using bows and arrows. We learned that these Pichanguerras had run away from the rubber country in the lower valleys; that they found it uncomfortably cold at this altitude, 4500 feet, but preferred freedom in the higher valleys to serfdom on a rubber estate.

Saavedra said that he had named his plantation *Conservidayoc*, because it was in truth "a spot where one may be preserved from harm." Such was the home of the potentate from whose abode "no one had been known to return alive."

CHAPTER 15

The Pampa of Ghosts

✶

Two days later we left Conservidayoc for Espiritu Pampa by the trail which Saavedra's son and our Pampaconas Indians had been clearing. We emerged from the thickets near a promontory where there was a fine view down the valley and particularly of a heavily wooded alluvial fan just below us. In it were two or three small clearings and the little oval huts of the savages of Espiritu Pampa, the "Pampa of Ghosts."

On top of the promontory was the ruin of a small, rectangular building of rough stone, once probably an Inca watch-tower. From here to Espiritu Pampa our trail followed an ancient stone stairway, about four feet in width and nearly a third of a mile long. It was built of uncut stones. Possibly it was the work of those soldiers whose chief duty it was to watch from the top of the promontory and who used their spare time making roads. We arrived at the principal clearing just as a heavy thunder-shower began. The huts were empty. Obviously their occupants had seen us coming and had disappeared in the jungle. We hesitated to enter the home of a savage without an invitation, but the terrific downpour overcame our scruples, if not our nervousness. The hut had a steeply pitched roof. Its sides were made of small logs driven endwise into the ground and fastened together with vines. A small fire had been burning on the ground. Near the embers were two old black ollas of Inca origin.

In the little *chacra*, cassava, *coca*, and sweet potatoes were growing in haphazard fashion among charred and fallen tree trunks; a typical *milpa* farm. In the clearing were the ruins of eighteen or twenty circular houses arranged in an irregular group. We wondered if this could be the "Inca city" which Lopez Torres had reported. Among the ruins we picked up several fragments of Inca pottery. There was nothing Incaic about the buildings. One was rectangular and one was spade-shaded, but all the rest were round. The buildings varied in diameter from fifteen to twenty feet. Each had but a single opening. The walls had tumbled down, but gave no evidence of careful construction. Not far away, in woods which had not yet been cleared by the savages, we found other circular walls. They were still standing to a height of about four feet. If the savages have extended their *milpa* clearings since our visit, the falling trees have probably spoiled these walls by now. The ancient village probably belonged to a tribe which acknowledged allegiance to the Incas, but the architecture of the buildings gave no indication of their having been constructed by the Incas themselves. We began to wonder whether the "Pampa of Ghosts" really had anything important in store for us. Undoubtedly this alluvial fan had been highly prized in this country of terribly steep hills. It must have been inhabited, off and on, for many centuries. Yet this was not an "Inca city."

While we were wondering whether the Incas themselves ever lived here, there suddenly appeared the naked figure of a sturdy young savage, armed with a stout bow and long arrows, and wearing a fillet of bamboo. He had been hunting and showed us a bird he had shot. Soon afterwards there came the two adult savages we had met at Saavedra's, accompanied by a cross-eyed friend, all wearing long tunics. They offered to guide us to other ruins. It was very difficult for us to follow their rapid pace. Half an hour's scramble through the jungle brought us to a *pampa* or natural terrace on the banks of a little tributary of the Pampaconas. They called it Eromboni. Here we found several old artificial terraces and the rough foundations of a long, rectangular building 192 feet by 24 feet. It might have had twenty-four doors, twelve in front and twelve in back, each three and a half feet wide. No lintels were in evidence. The walls were only a foot high. There was very little building material in sight. Apparently the structure had never been completed. Near by was a typical Inca fountain with three stone spouts, or conduits. Two hundred yards beyond the water-carrier's rendezvous, hidden behind a curtain of hanging vines and thickets so dense we could not see more than a few feet in any direction, the savages showed us the ruins of a group of stone houses whose walls were still standing in fine condition.

One of the buildings was rounded at one end. Another, standing by itself at the south end of a little *pampa*, had neither doors nor windows. It was rectangular. Its four or five niches were arranged with unique irregularity. Furthermore, they were two feet deep, an unusual dimension. Probably this was a storehouse. On the east side of the *pampa* was a structure, 120 feet long by 21 feet wide, divided into five rooms of unequal size. The walls were of rough stones laid in adobe. Like some of the Inca buildings at Ollantaytambo, the lintels of the doors were made of three or four narrow uncut ashlars. Some rooms had niches. On the north side of the *pampa* was another rectangular building. On the west side was the edge of a stone-faced terrace. Below it was a partly enclosed fountain or bathhouse, with a stone spout and a stone-lined basin. The shapes of the houses, their general arrangement, the niches, stone roof-pegs and lintels, all point to Inca builders. In the buildings we picked up several fragments of Inca pottery.

Equally interesting and very puzzling were half a dozen crude Spanish roofing tiles, baked red. All the pieces and fragments we could find would not have covered four square feet. They were of widely different sizes, as though some one had been experimenting. Perhaps an Inca who had seen the new red tiled roofs of Cuzco had tried to reproduce them here in the jungle, but without success.

At dusk we all returned to Espiritu Pampa. Our faces, hands, and clothes had been torn by the jungle; our feet were weary and sore. Nevertheless the day's work had been very satisfactory and we prepared to enjoy a good night's rest. Alas, we were doomed to disappointment. During the day some one had brought to the hut eight tame but noisy macaws. Furthermore, our savage helpers determined to make the night hideous with cries, tom-toms, and drums, either to discourage the visits of hostile Indians or jaguars, or for the purpose of exorcising the demons brought by the white men, or else to cheer up their families, who were undoubtedly hiding in the jungle near by.

The next day the savages and our carriers continued to clear away as much as possible of the tangled growth near the best ruins. In this process, to the intense surprise not only of ourselves, but also of the savages, they discovered, just below the "bathhouse" where we had stood the day before, the well-preserved ruins of two buildings of superior construction, well fitted with stone-pegs and numerous niches, very symmetrically arranged. These houses stood by themselves on a little artificial terrace. Fragments of characteristic Inca pottery were found on the floor, including pieces of a large *aryballus*.

Nothing gives a better idea of the density of the jungle than the fact that the savages themselves had often been within five feet of these fine walls without being aware of their existence.

Encouraged by this important discovery of the most characteristic Inca ruins found in the valley, we continued the search, but all that any one was able to find was a carefully built stone bridge over a brook. Saavedra's son questioned the savages carefully. They said they knew of no other antiquities.

Who built the stone buildings of Espiritu Pampa and Eromboni Pampa? Was this the "Vilcabamba Viejo" of Father Calancha, that "University of Idolatry where lived the teachers who were wizards and masters of abomination," the place to which Friar Marcos and Friar Diego went with so much suffering? Was there formerly on this trail a place called Ungacacha where the monks had to wade, and amused Titu Cusi by the way they handled their monastic robes in the water? They called it a "three days' journey over rough country." Another reference in Father Calancha speaks of Puquiura as being "two long days' journey from Vilcabamba." It took us five days to go from Espiritu Pampa to Pucyura, although Indians, unencumbered by burdens, and spurred on by necessity, might do it in three. It is possible to fit some other details of the story into this locality, although there is no place on the road called Ungacacha. Nevertheless it does not seem to me reasonable to suppose that the priests and Virgins of the Sun (the personnel of the "University of Idolatry") who fled from cold Cuzco with Manco and were established by him somewhere in the fastnesses of Uilcapampa would have cared to live in the hot valley of Espiritu Pampa. The difference in climate is as great as that between Scotland and Egypt, or New York and Havana. They would not have found in Espiritu Pampa the food which they liked. Furthermore, they could have found the seclusion and safety which they craved just as well in several other parts of the province, particularly at Machu Picchu, together with a cool, bracing climate and food-stuffs more nearly resembling those to which they were accustomed. Finally Calancha says "Vilcabamba the Old" was "the largest city" in the province, a term far more applicable to Machu Picchu or even to Choqquequirau than to Espiritu Pampa.

On the other hand there seems to be no doubt that Espiritu Pampa in the *montaña* does meet the requirements of the place called Vilcabamba by the companions of Captain Garcia. They speak of it as the town and valley to which Tupac Amaru, the last Inca, escaped after his forces lost the "young fortress" of Uiticos. Ocampo, doubtless wishing to emphasize the difference between it and his own metropolis, the Spanish town of Vilcabamba, calls the refuge of Tupac "Vilcabamba the old." Ocampo's new "Vilcabamba" was not in existence when Friar Marcos and Friar Diego lived in this province.

HIRAM BINGHAM STANDS ATOP A STONE BRIDGE AT
ESPIRITU PAMPA, PERU, THE SITE BINGHAM ORIGINALLY
THOUGHT TO BE THE REMAINS OF VILCABAMBA

If Calancha wrote his chronicles from their notes, the term "old" would not apply to Espiritu Pampa, but to an older Vilcabamba than either of the places known to Ocampo.

The ruins are of late Inca pattern, not of a kind which would have required a long period to build. The unfinished building may have been under construction during the latter part of the reign of Titu Cusi. It was Titu Cusi's desire that Rodriguez de Figueroa should meet him at Pampaconas. The Inca evidently came from a Vilcabamba down in the *montaña*, and, as has been said, brought Rodriguez a present of a macaw and two hampers of peanuts, articles of trade still common at Conservidayoc. There appears to me every reason to believe that the ruins of Espiritu Pampa are those of one of the favorite residences of this Inca—the very Vilcabamba, in fact, where he spent his boyhood and from which he journeyed to meet Rodriguez in 1565.[1]

In 1572, when Captain Garcia took up the pursuit of Tupac Amaru after the victory of Vilcabamba, the Inca fled "inland toward the valley of Simaponte...to the country of the Mañaries Indians, a warlike tribe and his friends, where *balsas* and canoes were posted to save him and enable him to escape." There is now no valley in this vicinity called Simaponte, so far as we have been able to discover. The Mañaries Indians are said to have lived on the banks of the lower Urubamba. In order to reach their country Tupac Amaru probably went down the Pampaconas from Espiritu Pampa. From the "Pampa of Ghosts" to canoe navigation would have been but a short journey. Evidently his friends who helped him to escape were canoe-men. Captain Garcia gives an account of the pursuit of Tupac Amaru in which he says that, not deterred by the dangers of the jungle or the river, he constructed five rafts on which he put some of his soldiers and, accompanying them himself, went down the rapids, escaping death many times by swimming, until he arrived at a place called Momori, only to find that the Inca, learning of his approach, had gone farther into the woods. Nothing daunted, Garcia followed him, although he and his men now had to go on foot and barefooted, with hardly anything to eat, most of their provisions having been lost in the river, until they finally caught Tupac and his friends; a tragic ending to a terrible chase, hard on the white man and fatal for the Incas.

It was with great regret that I was now unable to follow the Pampaconas River to its junction with the Urubamba. It seemed possible that the Pampaconas might be known as the Sirialo, or the Coribeni, both of which were believed by Dr. Bowman's canoe-men to rise in the mountains of Vilcabamba. It was not, however, until the summer of 1915 that we were able definitely to learn that the Pampaconas was really a branch of the Cosireni. It seems likely that the Cosireni was once called the "Simaponte." Whether the Comberciato is the "Momori" is hard to say.

To be the next to follow in the footsteps of Tupac Amaru and Captain Garcia was the privilege of Messrs. Heller, Ford, and Maynard. They found that the unpleasant features had not been exaggerated. They were tormented by insects and great quantities of ants—a small red ant found on tree trunks, and a large black one, about an inch in length, frequently seen among the leaves on the ground. The bite of the red ant caused a stinging and burning for about fifteen minutes. One of their carriers who was bitten in the foot by a black ant suffered intense pain for a number of hours. Not only his foot, but also his leg and hip were affected. The savages were both fishermen and hunters; the fish being taken with nets, the game killed with bows and arrows. Peccaries were shot from a blind made of palm leaves a few feet from a runway. Fishing brought rather meager results. Three Indians fished all night and caught only one fish, a perch weighing about four pounds.

The temperature was so high that candles could easily be tied in knots. Excessive humidity caused all leather articles to become blue with mould. Clouds of flies and mosquitoes increased the likelihood of spreading communicable jungle fevers.

The river Comberciato was reached by Mr. Heller at a point not more than a league from its junction with the Urubamba. The lower course of the Comberciato is not considered dangerous to canoe navigation, but the valley is much narrower than the Cosireni. The width of the river is about 150 feet and its volume is twice that of the Cosireni. The climate is very trying. The nights are hot. Insect pests are numerous. Mr. Heller found that "the forest was filled with annoying, though sting-less, bees which persisted in attempting to roost on the countenance of any human being available." On the banks of the Comberciato he found several families of savages. All the men were keen hunters and fishermen. Their weapons consisted of powerful bows made from the wood of a small palm and long arrows made of reeds and finished with feathers arranged in a spiral.

Monkeys were abundant. Specimens of six distinct genera were found, including the large red howler, inert and easily located by its deep, roaring bellow which can be heard for a distance of several miles; the giant black spider monkey, very alert, and, when frightened, fairly flying through the branches at astonishing speed; and a woolly monkey, black in color, and very intelligent in expression, frequently tamed by the savages, who "enjoy having them as pets but are not averse to eating them when food is scarce." "The flesh of monkeys is greatly appreciated by these Indians, who preserved what they did not require for immediate needs by drying it over the smoke of a wood fire."

On the Cosireni Mr. Maynard noticed that one of his Indian guides carried a package, wrapped in leaves, which on being opened proved to contain forty or fifty large hairless grubs or caterpillars. The man finally bit their heads off and threw the bodies into a small bag, saying that the grubs were considered a great delicacy by the savages.

The Indians we met at Espiritu Pampa closely resembled those seen in the lower valley. All our savages were bareheaded and barefooted. They live so much in the shelter of the jungle that hats are not necessary. Sandals or shoes would only make it harder to use the slippery little trails. They had seen no strangers penetrate this valley for about ten years, and at first kept their wives and children well secluded. Later, when Messrs. Hendriksen and Tucker were sent here to determine the astronomical position of Espiritu Pampa, the savages permitted Mr. Tucker to take photographs of their families. Perhaps it is doubtful whether they knew just what he was doing. At all events they did not run away and hide.

All the men and older boys wore white fillets of bamboo. The married men had smeared paint on their faces, and one of them was wearing the characteristic lip ornament of the Campas. Some of the children wore no clothing at all. Two of the wives wore long tunics like the men. One of them had a truly savage face, daubed with paint. She wore no fillet, had the best tunic, and wore a handsome necklace made of seeds and the skins of small birds of brilliant plumage, a work of art which must have cost infinite pains and the loss of not a few arrows. All the women carried babies in little hammocks slung over the shoulder. One little girl, not more than six years old, was carrying on her back a child of two, in a hammock supported from her head by a tump-line. It will be remembered that forest Indians nearly always use tump-lines so as to allow their hands free play. One of the wives was fairer than the others and looked as though she might have had a Spanish ancestor. The most savage-looking of the women was very scantily clad, wore a necklace of seeds, a white lip ornament, and a few rags tied around her waist. All her children were naked. The children of the woman with the handsome necklace were clothed in pieces of old tunics, and one of them, evidently her mother's favorite, was decorated with bird skins and a necklace made from the teeth of monkeys.

Such were the people among whom Tupac Amaru took refuge when he fled from Vilcabamba. Whether he partook of such a delicacy as monkey meat, which all Amazonian Indians relish, but which is not eaten by the highlanders, may be doubted. Garcilasso speaks of Tupac Amaru's preferring to entrust himself to the hands of the Spaniards "rather than to perish of famine." His Indian allies lived perfectly well in a region where monkeys abound. It is doubtful whether they would ever have permitted Captain Garcia to capture the Inca had they been able to furnish Tupac with such food as he was accustomed to.

At all events our investigations seem to point to the probability of this valley having been an important part of the domain of the last Incas. It would have been pleasant to prolong our studies, but the carriers were anxious to return to Pampaconas. Although they did not have to eat monkey meat, they were afraid of the savages and nervous as to what use the latter might some day make of the powerful bows and long arrows.

At Conservidayoc Saavedra kindly took the trouble to make some sugar for us. He poured the syrup in oblong moulds cut in a row along the side of a big log of hard wood. In some of the moulds his son placed handfuls of nicely roasted peanuts. The result was a confection or "emergency ration" which we greatly enjoyed on our return journey.

At San Fernando we met the pack mules. The next day, in the midst of continuing torrential tropical downpours, we climbed out of the hot valley to the cold heights of Pampaconas. We were soaked with perspiration and drenched with rain. Snow had been falling above the village; our teeth chattered like castanets. Professor Foote immediately commandeered Mrs. Guzman's fire and filled our tea kettle. It may be doubted whether a more wretched, cold, wet, and bedraggled party ever arrived at Guzman's hut; certainly nothing ever tasted better than that steaming hot sweet tea.

---

[1] Titu Cusi was an illegitimate son of Manco. His mother was not of royal blood and may have been a native of the warm valleys.

CHAPTER 16

THE STORY OF TAMPU-TOCCO,
A LOST CITY OF THE FIRST INCAS

✳

IT WILL BE REMEMBERED that while on the search for the capital of the last Incas we had found several groups of ruins which we could not fit entirely into the story of Manco and his sons. The most important of these was Machu Picchu. Many of its buildings are far older than the ruins of Rosaspata and Espiritu Pampa. To understand just what we may have found at Machu Picchu it is now necessary to tell the story of a celebrated city, whose name, Tampu-tocco, was not used even at the time of the Spanish Conquest as the cognomen of any of the Inca towns then in existence. I must draw the reader's attention far away from the period when Pizarro and Manco, Toledo and Tupac Amaru were the protagonists, back to events which occurred nearly seven hundred years before their day. The last Incas ruled in Uiticos between 1536 and 1572. The last Amautas flourished about 800 A.D.

The Amautas had been ruling the Peruvian highlands for about sixty generations, when, as has been told in Chapter VI, invaders came from the south and east. The Amautas had built up a wonderful civilization. Many of the agricultural and engineering feats which we ordinarily assign to the Incas were really achievements of the Amautas. The last of the Amautas was Pachacuti VI, who was killed by an arrow on the battle-field of La Raya. The historian Montesinos, whose work on the antiquities of Peru has recently been translated for the Hakluyt Society by Mr. P. A. Means, of Harvard University, tells us that the followers of Pachacuti VI fled with his body to "Tampu-tocco." This, says the historian, was "a healthy place" where there was a cave in which they hid the Amauta's body. Cuzco, the finest and most important of all their cities, was sacked. General anarchy prevailed throughout the ancient empire. The good old days of peace and plenty disappeared before the invader. The glory of the old empire was destroyed, not to return for several centuries. In these dark ages, resembling those of European medieval times which followed the Germanic migrations and the fall of the Roman Empire, Peru was split up into a large number of small independent units. Each district chose its own ruler and carried on depredations against its neighbors. The effects of this may still be seen in the ruins of small fortresses found guarding the way into isolated Andean valleys.

Montesinos says that those who were most loyal to the Amautas were few in number and not strong enough to oppose their enemies successfully. Some of them, probably the principal priests, wise men, and chiefs of the ancient régime, built a new city at "Tampu-tocco." Here they kept alive the memory of the Amautas and lived in such a relatively civilized manner as to draw to them, little by little, those who wished to be safe from the prevailing chaos and disorder and the tyranny of the independent chiefs or "robber barons." In their new capital, they elected a king, Titi Truaman Quicho.

The survivors of the old régime enjoyed living at Tampu-tocco, because there never have been any earthquakes, plagues, or tremblings there. Furthermore, if fortune should turn against their new young king, Titi Truaman, and he should be killed, they could bury him in a very sacred place, namely, the cave where they hid the body of Pachacuti VI.

Fortune was kind to the founders of the new kingdom. They had chosen an excellent place of refuge where they were not disturbed. To their ruler, the king of Tampu-tocco, and to his successors nothing worth recording happened for centuries. During this period several of the kings wished to establish themselves in ancient Cuzco, where the great Amautas had reigned, but for one reason or another were obliged to forego their ambitions.

One of the most enlightened rulers of Tampu-tocco was a king called Tupac Cauri, or Pachacuti VII. In his day people began to write on the leaves of trees. He sent messengers to the various parts of the highlands, asking the tribes to stop worshiping idols and animals, to cease practicing evil customs which had grown up since the fall of the Amautas, and to return to the ways of their ancestors. He met with little encouragement. On the contrary, his ambassadors were killed and little or no change took place. Discouraged by the failure of his attempts at reformation and desirous of learning its cause, Tupac Cauri was told by his soothsayers that the matter which most displeased the gods was the invention of writing. Thereupon he forbade anybody to practice writing, under penalty of death. This mandate was observed with such strictness that the ancient folk never again used letters. Instead, they used *quipus*, strings and knots. It was supposed that the gods were appeased, and every one breathed easier. No one realized how near the Peruvians as a race had come to taking a most momentous step.

This curious and interesting tradition relates to an event supposed to have occurred many centuries before the Spanish Conquest. We have no ocular evidence to support it. The skeptic may brush it aside as a story intended to appeal to the vanity of persons with Inca blood in their veins; yet it is not told by the half-caste Garcilasso, who wanted Europeans to admire his maternal ancestors and wrote his book accordingly, but is in the pages of that careful investigator Montesinos, a pure-blooded Spaniard. As a matter of fact, to students of Sumner's "Folkways," the story rings true. Some young fellow, brighter than the rest, developed a system of ideographs which he scratched on broad, smooth leaves. It worked. People were beginning to adopt it. The conservative priests of Tampu-tocco did not like it. There was danger lest some of the precious secrets, heretofore handed down orally to the neophytes, might become public property. Nevertheless, the invention was so useful that it began to spread. There followed some extremely unlucky event—the ambassadors were killed, the king's plans miscarried. What more natural than that the newly discovered ideographs should be blamed for it? As a result, the king of Tampu-tocco, instigated thereto by the priests, determined to abolish this new thing. Its usefulness had not yet been firmly established. In fact it was inconvenient; the leaves withered, dried, and cracked, or blew away, and the writings were lost. Had the new invention been permitted to exist a little longer, some one would have commenced to scratch ideographs on rocks. Then it would have persisted. The rulers and priests, however, found that the important records of tribute and taxes could be kept perfectly well by means of the *quipus*. And the "job" of those whose duty it was to remember what each string stood for was assured. After all there is nothing unusual about Montesinos's story. One has only to look at the history of Spain itself to realize that royal bigotry and priestly intolerance have often crushed new ideas and kept great nations from making important advances.

Montesinos says further that Tupac Cauri established in Tampu-tocco a kind of university where boys were taught the use of *quipus*, the method of counting and the significance of the different colored strings, while their fathers and older brothers were trained in military exercises—in other words, practiced with the sling, the bolas and the war-club; perhaps also with bows and arrows. Around the name of Tupac Cauri, or Pachacuti VII, as he wished to be called, is gathered the story of various intellectual movements which took place in Tampu-tocco.

Finally, there came a time when the skill and military efficiency of the little kingdom rose to a high plane. The ruler and his councilors, bearing in mind the tradition of their ancestors who centuries before had dwelt in Cuzco, again determined to make the attempt to reëstablish themselves there. An earthquake, which ruined many buildings in Cuzco, caused rivers to change their courses, destroyed towns, and was followed by the outbreak of a disastrous epidemic. The chiefs were obliged to give up their plans, although in healthy Tampu-tocco there was no pestilence. Their kingdom became more and more crowded. Every available square yard of arable land was terraced and cultivated. The men were intelligent, well organized, and accustomed to discipline, but they could not raise enough food for their families; so, about 1300 A.D., they were forced to secure arable land by conquest, under the leadership of the energetic ruler of the day. His name was Manco Ccapac, generally called the first Inca, the ruler for whom the Manco of 1536 was named.

There are many stories of the rise of the first Inca. When he had grown to man's estate, he assembled his people to see how he could secure new lands for them. After consultation with his brothers, he determined to set out with them "toward the hill over which the sun rose," as we are informed by Pachacuti Yamqui Salcamayhua, an Indian who was a descendant of a long line of Incas, whose great-grandparents lived in the time of the Spanish Conquest, and who wrote an account of the antiquities of Peru in 1620. He gives the history of the Incas as it was handed down to the descendants of the former rulers of Peru. In it we read that Manco Ccapac and his brothers finally succeeded in reaching Cuzco and settled there. With the return of the descendants of the Amautas to Cuzco there ended the glory of Tampu-tocco. Manco married his own sister in order that he might not lose caste and that no other family be elevated by this marriage to be on an equality with his. He made good laws, conquered many provinces, and is regarded as the founder of the Inca dynasty. The highlanders came under his sway and brought him rich presents. The Inca, as Manco Ccapac now came to be known, was recognized as the most powerful chief, the most valiant fighter, and the most lucky warrior in the Andes. His captains and soldiers were brave, well disciplined, and well armed. All his affairs prospered greatly. "*Afterward he ordered works to be executed at the place of his birth, consisting of a masonry wall with three windows, which were emblems of the house of his fathers whence he descended. The first window was called Tampu-tocco.*" I quote from Sir Clements Markham's translation.

The Spaniards who asked about Tampu-tocco were told that it was at or near Paccaritampu, a small town eight or ten miles south of Cuzco. I learned that ruins are very scarce in its vicinity. There are none in the town. The most important are the ruins of Maucallacta, an Inca village, a few miles away. Near it I found a rocky hill consisting of several crags and large rocks, the surface of one of which is carved into platforms and two sleeping pumas. It is called Puma Urco. Beneath the rocks are some caves. I was told they had recently been used by political refugees. There is enough about the caves and the characteristics of the ruins near Paccaritampu to lend color to the story told to the early Spaniards. Nevertheless, it would seem as if Tampu-tocco must have been a place more remote from Cuzco and better defended by Nature from any attacks on that side. How else would it have been possible for the disorganized remnant of Pachacuti VI's army to have taken refuge there and set up an independent kingdom in the face of the warlike invaders from the south? A few men might have hid in the caves of Puma Urco, but Paccaritampu is not a natural citadel.

The surrounding region is not difficult of access. There are no precipices between here and the Cuzco Basin. There are no natural defenses against such an invading force as captured the capital of the Amautas. Furthermore, *tampu* means "a place of temporary abode," or "a tavern," or "an improved piece of ground" or "farm far from a town"; *tocco* means "window." There is an old tavern at Maucallacta near Paccaritampu, but there are no windows in the building to justify the name of "window tavern" or "place of temporary abode" (or "farm far from a town") "noted for its windows." There is nothing of a "masonry wall with three windows" corresponding to Salcamayhua's description of Manco Ccapac's memorial at his birthplace. The word "Tampu-tocco" does not occur on any map I have been able to consult, nor is it in the exhaustive gazetteer of Peru compiled by Paz Soldan.

CHAPTER 17

MACHU PICCHU

✱

IT WAS IN JULY, 1911, that we first entered that marvelous canyon of the Urubamba, where the river escapes from the cold regions near Cuzco by tearing its way through gigantic mountains of granite. From Torontoy to Colpani the road runs through a land of matchless charm. It has the majestic grandeur of the Canadian Rockies, as well as the startling beauty of the Nuuanu Pali near Honolulu, and the enchanting vistas of the Koolau Ditch Trail on Maui. In the variety of its charms and the power of its spell, I know of no place in the world which can compare with it. Not only has it great snow peaks looming above the clouds more than two miles overhead; gigantic precipices of many-colored granite rising sheer for thousands of feet above the foaming, glistening, roaring rapids; it has also, in striking contrast, orchids and tree ferns, the delectable beauty of luxurious vegetation, and the mysterious witchery of the jungle. One is drawn irresistibly onward by ever-recurring surprises through a deep, winding gorge, turning and twisting past overhanging cliffs of incredible height. Above all, there is the fascination of finding here and there under the swaying vines, or perched on top of a beetling crag, the rugged masonry of a bygone race; and of trying to understand the bewildering romance of the ancient builders who ages ago sought refuge in a region which appears to have been expressly designed by Nature as a sanctuary for the oppressed, a place where they might fearlessly and patiently give expression to their passion for walls of enduring beauty. Space forbids any attempt to describe in detail the constantly changing panorama, the rank

Melchor Arteaga crossing a log bridge over the Urubamba River

tropical foliage, the countless terraces, the towering cliffs, the glaciers peeping out between the clouds.

We had camped at a place near the river, called Mandor Pampa. Melchor Arteaga, proprietor of the neighboring farm, had told us of ruins at Machu Picchu, as was related in Chapter 10.

The morning of July 24th dawned in a cold drizzle. Arteaga shivered and seemed inclined to stay in his hut. I offered to pay him well if he would show me the ruins. He demurred and said it was too hard a climb for such a wet day. When he found that we were willing to pay him a *sol*, three or four times the ordinary daily wage in this vicinity, he finally agreed to guide us to the ruins. No one supposed that they would be particularly interesting. Accompanied by Sergeant Carrasco I left camp at ten o'clock and went some distance upstream. On the road we passed a venomous snake which recently had been killed. This region has an unpleasant notoriety for being the favorite haunt of "vipers." The lance-headed or yellow viper, commonly known as the fer-de-lance, a very venomous serpent capable of making considerable springs when in pursuit of its prey, is common hereabouts. Later two of our mules died from snake-bite.

After a walk of three quarters of an hour the guide left the main road and plunged down through the jungle to the bank of the river. Here there was a primitive "bridge" which crossed the roaring rapids at its narrowest part, where the stream was forced to flow between two great boulders. The bridge was made of half a dozen very slender logs, some of which were not long enough to span the distance between the boulders. They had been spliced and lashed together with vines. Arteaga and Carrasco took off their shoes and crept gingerly across, using their somewhat prehensile toes to keep from slipping. It was obvious that no one could have lived for an instant in the rapids, but would immediately have been dashed to pieces against granite boulders. I am frank to confess that I got down on hands and knees and crawled across, six inches at a time. Even after we reached the other side I could not help wondering what would happen to the "bridge" if a particularly heavy shower should fall in the valley above. A light rain had fallen during the night. The river had risen so that the bridge was already threatened by the foaming rapids. It would not take much more rain to wash away the bridge entirely. If this should happen during the day it might be very awkward. As a matter of fact, it did happen a few days later and the next explorers to attempt to cross the river at this point found only one slender log remaining.

Leaving the stream, we struggled up the bank through a dense jungle, and in a few minutes reached the bottom of a precipitous slope. For an hour and twenty minutes we had a hard climb. A good part of the distance we went on all fours, sometimes hanging on by the tips of our fingers. Here and there, a primitive ladder made from the roughly hewn trunk of a small tree was placed in such a way as to help one over what might otherwise have proved to be an impassable cliff. In another place the slope was covered with slippery grass where it was hard to find either handholds or footholds. The guide said that there were lots of snakes here. The humidity was great, the heat was excessive, and we were not in training.

Shortly after noon we reached a little grass-covered hut where several good-natured Indians, pleasantly surprised at our unexpected arrival, welcomed us with dripping gourds full of cool, delicious water. Then they set before us a few cooked sweet potatoes, called here *cumara*, a Quichua word identical with the Polynesian *kumala*, as has been pointed out by Mr. Cook.

Apart from the wonderful view of the canyon, all we could see from our cool shelter was a couple of small grass huts and a few ancient stone-faced terraces. Two pleasant Indian farmers, Richarte and Alvarez, had chosen this eagle's nest for their home. They said they had found plenty of terraces here on which to grow their crops and they were usually free

STONE RUINS AT MACHU PICCHU

from undesirable visitors. They did not speak Spanish, but through Sergeant Carrasco I learned that there were more ruins "a little farther along." In this country one never can tell whether such a report is worthy of credence. "He may have been lying" is a good footnote to affix to all hearsay evidence. Accordingly, I was not unduly excited, nor in a great hurry to move. The heat was still great, the water from the Indian's spring was cool and delicious, and the rustic wooden bench, hospitably covered immediately after my arrival with a soft, woolen poncho, seemed most comfortable. Furthermore, the view was simply enchanting. Tremendous green precipices fell away to the white rapids of the Urubamba below. Immediately in front, on the north side of the valley, was a great granite cliff rising 2000 feet sheer. To the left was the solitary peak of Huayna Picchu, surrounded by seemingly inaccessible precipices. On all sides were rocky cliffs. Beyond them cloud-capped mountains rose thousands of feet above us.

The Indians said there were two paths to the outside world. Of one we had already had a taste; the other, they said, was more difficult—a perilous path down the face of a rocky precipice on the other side of the ridge. It was their only means of egress in the wet season, when the bridge over which we had come could not be maintained. I was not surprised to learn that they went away from home only "about once a month."

STAIRCASE AT MACHU PICCHU

A VIEW OF HUAYANU PICCHU PEAK, WHICH OVERLOOKS MACHU PICCHU

Richarte told us that they had been living here four years. It seems probable that, owing to its inaccessibility, the canyon had been unoccupied for several centuries, but with the completion of the new government road settlers began once more to occupy this region. In time somebody clambered up the precipices and found on the slopes of Machu Picchu, at an elevation of 9000 feet above the sea, an abundance of rich soil conveniently situated on artificial terraces, in a fine climate. Here the Indians had finally cleared off some ruins, burned over a few terraces, and planted crops of maize, sweet and white potatoes, sugar cane, beans, peppers, tree tomatoes, and gooseberries. At first they appropriated some of the ancient houses and replaced the roofs of wood and thatch. They found, however, that there were neither springs nor wells near the ancient buildings. An ancient aqueduct which had once brought a tiny stream to the citadel had long since disappeared beneath the forest, filled with earth washed from the upper terraces. So, abandoning the shelter of the ruins, the Indians were now enjoying the convenience of living near some springs in roughly built thatched huts of their own design.

Without the slightest expectation of finding anything more interesting than the stone-faced terraces of which I already had a glimpse, and the ruins of two or three stone houses such as we had encountered at various places on the road between Ollantaytambo and Torontoy, I finally left the cool shade

TERRACES AT PISAC, PERU, BELOW THE CITADEL OF MACHU PICCHU

of the pleasant little hut and climbed farther up the ridge and around a slight promontory. Arteaga had "been here once before," and decided to rest and gossip with Richarte and Alvarez in the hut. They sent a small boy with me as a guide.

Hardly had we rounded the promontory when the character of the stonework began to improve. A flight of beautifully constructed terraces, each two hundred yards long and ten feet high, had been recently rescued from the jungle by the Indians. A forest of large trees had been chopped down and burned over to make a clearing for agricultural purposes. Crossing these terraces, I entered the untouched forest beyond, and suddenly found myself in a maze of beautiful granite houses! They were covered with trees and moss and the growth of centuries, but in the dense shadow, hiding in bamboo thickets and tangled vines, could be seen, here and there, walls of white granite ashlars most carefully cut and exquisitely fitted together. Buildings with windows were frequent. Here at least was a "place far from town and conspicuous for its windows."

Under a carved rock the little boy showed me a cave beautifully lined with the finest cut stone. It was evidently intended to be a Royal Mausoleum. On top of this particular boulder a semicircular building had been constructed. The wall followed the natural curvature of the rock and was keyed to it by one of the finest examples of masonry I have ever seen. This beautiful wall, made of carefully matched ashlars of pure white granite, especially selected for its fine grain, was the work of a master artist. The interior surface of the wall was broken by niches and square stone-pegs. The exterior surface was perfectly simple and unadorned. The lower courses, of particularly large ashlars, gave it a look of solidity. The upper courses, diminishing in size toward the top, lent grace and delicacy to the structure. The flowing lines, the symmetrical arrangement of the ashlars, and the gradual gradation of the courses, combined to produce a wonderful effect, softer and more pleasing than that of the marble temples of the Old World. Owing to the absence of mortar, there are no ugly spaces between the rocks. They might have grown together.

The elusive beauty of this chaste, undecorated surface seems to me to be due to the fact that the wall was built under the eye of a master mason who knew not the straight edge, the plumb rule, or the square. He had no instruments of precision, so he had to depend on his eye. He had a good eye, an artistic eye, an eye for symmetry and beauty of form. His product received none of the harshness of mechanical and mathematical accuracy. The apparently rectangular blocks are not really rectangular. The apparently straight lines of the courses are not actually straight in the exact sense of that term.

To my astonishment I saw that this wall and its adjoining semicircular temple over the cave were as fine as the finest stonework in the far-famed Temple of the Sun in Cuzco. Surprise followed surprise in bewildering succession. I climbed a marvelous great stairway of large granite blocks, walked along a *pampa* where the Indians had a small vegetable garden, and came into a little clearing. Here were the ruins of two of the finest structures I have ever seen in Peru. Not only were they made of selected blocks of beautifully grained white granite; their walls contained ashlars of Cyclopean size, ten feet in length, and higher than a man. The sight held me spellbound.

Each building had only three walls and was entirely open on the side toward the clearing. The principal temple was lined with exquisitely made niches, five high up at each end, and seven on the back wall. There were seven courses of ashlars in the end walls. Under the seven rear niches was a rectangular block fourteen feet long, probably a sacrificial altar. The building did not look as though it had ever had a roof. The top course of beautifully smooth ashlars was not intended to be covered.

The other temple is on the east side of the *pampa*. I called it the

Temple of the Three Windows. Like its neighbor, it is unique among Inca ruins. Its eastern wall, overlooking the citadel, is a massive stone framework for three conspicuously large windows, obviously too large to serve any useful purpose, yet most beautifully made with the greatest care and solidity. This was clearly a ceremonial edifice of peculiar significance. Nowhere else in Peru, so far as I know, is there a similar structure conspicuous as "a masonry wall with three windows."

These ruins have no other name than that of the mountain on the slopes of which they are located. Had this place been occupied uninterruptedly, like Cuzco and Ollantaytambo, Machu Picchu would have retained its ancient name, but during the centuries when it was abandoned, its name was lost. Examination showed that it was essentially a fortified place, a remote fastness protected by natural bulwarks, of which man took advantage to create the most impregnable stronghold in the Andes. Our subsequent excavations and the clearing made in 1912, to be described in a subsequent volume, has shown that this was the chief place in Uilcapampa.

It did not take an expert to realize, from the glimpse of Machu Picchu on that rainy day in July, 1911, when Sergeant Carrasco and I first saw it, that here were most extraordinary and interesting ruins. Although the ridge had been partly cleared by the Indians for their fields of maize, so much of it was still underneath a thick jungle growth—some walls were actually supporting trees ten and twelve inches in diameter—that it was impossible to determine just what would be found here. As soon as I could get hold of Mr. Tucker, who was assisting Mr. Hendriksen, and Mr. Lanius, who had gone down the Urubamba with Dr. Bowman, I asked them to make a map of the ruins. I knew it would be a difficult undertaking and that it was essential for Mr. Tucker to join me in Arequipa not later than the first of October for the ascent of Coropuna. With the hearty aid of Richarte and Alvarez, the surveyors did better than I expected. In the ten days while they were at the ruins they were able to secure data from which Mr. Tucker afterwards prepared a map which told better than could any words of mine the importance of this site and the necessity for further investigation.

With the possible exception of one mining prospector, no one in Cuzco had seen the ruins of Machu Picchu or appreciated their importance. No one had any realization of what an extraordinary place lay on top of the ridge. It had never been visited by any of the planters of the lower Urubamba Valley who annually passed over the road which winds through the canyon two thousand feet below.

SACRED PLAZA, MACHU PICCHU

It seems incredible that this citadel, less than three days' journey from Cuzco, should have remained so long undescribed by travelers and comparatively unknown even to the Peruvians themselves. If the *conquistadores* ever saw this wonderful place, some reference to it surely would have been made; yet nothing can be found which clearly refers to the ruins of Machu Picchu. Just when it was first seen by a Spanish-speaking person is uncertain. When the Count de Sartiges was at Huadquiña in 1834 he was looking for ruins; yet, although so near, he heard of none here. From a crude scrawl on the walls of one of the finest buildings, we learned that the ruins were visited in 1902 by Lizarraga, lessee of the lands immediately below the bridge of San Miguel. This is the earliest local record. Yet some one must have visited Machu Picchu long before that; because in 1875, as has been said, the French explorer Charles Wiener heard in Ollantaytambo of there being ruins at "Huaina-Picchu or Matcho-Picchu." He tried to find them. That he failed was due to there being no road through the canyon of Torontoy and the necessity of making a wide detour through the pass of Panticalla and the Lucumayo Valley, a route which brought him to the Urubamba River at the bridge of Chuquichaca, twenty-five miles below Machu Picchu.

It was not until 1890 that the Peruvian Government, recognizing the needs of the enterprising planters who were opening up the lower valley of the Urubamba, decided to construct a mule trail along the banks of the river through the grand canyon to enable the much-desired *coca* and *aguardiente* to be shipped from Huadquiña, Maranura, and Santa Ana to Cuzco more quickly and cheaply than formerly. This road avoids the necessity of carrying the precious cargoes over the dangerous snowy passes of Mt. Veronica and Mt. Salcantay, so vividly described by Raimondi, de Sartiges, and others. The road, however, was very expensive, took years to build, and still requires frequent repair. In fact, even to-day travel over it is often suspended for several days or weeks at a time, following some tremendous avalanche. Yet it was this new road which had led Melchor Arteaga to build his hut near the arable land at Mandor Pampa, where he could raise food for his family and offer rough shelter to passing travelers. It was this new road which brought Richarte, Alvarez, and their enterprising friends into this little-known region, gave them the opportunity of occupying the ancient terraces of Machu Picchu, which had lain fallow for centuries, encouraged them to keep open a passable trail over the precipices, and made it feasible for us to reach the ruins. It was this new road which offered us in 1911 a virgin field between Ollantaytambo and Huadquiña and enabled us to learn that the Incas, or their predecessors, had once lived here in the remote fastnesses of the Andes, and had left stone witnesses of the magnificence and beauty of their ancient civilization, more interesting and extensive than any which have been found since the days of the Spanish Conquest of Peru.

CHAPTER 18

THE ORIGIN OF MACHU PICCHU

✳

SOME OTHER DAY I hope to tell of the work of clearing and excavating Machu Picchu, of the life lived by its citizens, and of the ancient towns of which it was the most important. At present I must rest content with a discussion of its probable identity. Here was a powerful citadel tenable against all odds, a stronghold where a mere handful of defenders could prevent a great army from taking the place by assault. Why should any one have desired to be so secure from capture as to have built a fortress in such an inaccessible place?

The builders were not in search of fields. There is so little arable land here that every square yard of earth had to be terraced in order to provide food for the inhabitants. They were not looking for comfort or convenience. Safety was their primary consideration. They were sufficiently civilized to practice intensive agriculture, sufficiently skillful to equal the best masonry the world has ever seen, sufficiently ingenious to make delicate bronzes, and sufficiently advanced in art to realize the beauty of simplicity. What could have induced such a people to select this remote fastness of the Andes, with all its disadvantages, as the site for their capital, unless they were fleeing from powerful enemies.

The thought will already have occurred to the reader that the Temple of the Three Windows at Machu Picchu fits the words of that native writer who had "heard from a child the most ancient traditions and histories," including the story already quoted from Sir Clements Markham's translation that Manco Ccapac, the first Inca, "ordered works to be executed at the place of his birth; consisting of a masonry wall with three windows, which were emblems of the house of his fathers whence he descended. The first window was called 'Tampu-tocco.'" Although none of the other chroniclers gives the story of the first Inca ordering a memorial wall to be built at the place of his birth, they nearly all tell of his having come from a place called Tampu-tocco, "an inn or country place remarkable for its windows." Sir Clements Markham, in his "Incas of Peru," refers to Tampu-tocco as "the hill with the three openings or windows."

The place assigned by all the chroniclers as the location of the traditional Tampu-tocco, as has been said, is Paccaritampu, about nine miles southwest of Cuzco. Paccaritampu has some interesting ruins and caves, but careful examination shows that while there are more than three openings to its caves, there are no windows in its buildings. The buildings of Machu Picchu, on the other hand, have far more windows than any other important ruin in Peru. The climate of Paccaritampu, like that of most places in the highlands, is too severe to invite or encourage the use of windows. The climate of Machu Picchu is mild, consequently the use of windows was natural and agreeable.

So far as I know, there is no place in Peru where the ruins consist of anything like a "masonry wall with three windows" of such a ceremonial character as is here referred to, except at Machu Picchu. It would certainly seem as though the Temple of the Three Windows, the most significant structure within the citadel, is the building referred to by Pachacuti Yamqui Salcamayhua.

The principal difficulty with this theory is that while the first meaning of *tocco* in Holguin's standard Quichua dictionary is "*ventana*" or "window," and while "window" is the *only* meaning given this important word in Markham's revised Quichua dictionary (1908), a dictionary compiled from many sources, the second meaning of *tocco* given by Holguin is "*alacena*," "a cupboard set in a wall." Undoubtedly this means what we call, in the ruins of the houses of the Incas, a niche. Now the drawings, crude as they are, in Sir Clements Markham's translation of the Salcamayhua manuscript, do give the impression of niches rather than of windows. Does *Tampu-tocco* mean a *tampu* remarkable for its niches? At Paccaritampu there do not appear to be any particularly fine niches; while at Machu Picchu, on the other hand, there are many very beautiful niches, especially in the cave which has been referred to as a "Royal Mausoleum." As a matter of fact, nearly all the finest ruins of the Incas have excellent niches. Since niches were so common a feature of Inca architecture, the chances are that Sir Clements is right in translating Salcamayhua as he did and in calling Tampu-tocco "the hill with the three openings or windows." In any case Machu Picchu fits the story far better than does Paccaritampu. However, in view of the fact that the early writers all repeat the story that Tampu-tocco was at Paccaritampu, it would be absurd to say that they did not know what they were talking about, even though the actual remains at or near Paccaritampu do not fit the requirements.

It would be easier to adopt Paccaritampu as the site of Tampu-tocco were it not for the legal records of an inquiry made by Toledo at the time when he put the last Inca to death. Fifteen Indians, descended from those who used to live near Las Salinas, the important salt works near Cuzco, on being questioned, agreed that they had heard their fathers and grandfathers repeat the tradition that when the first Inca, Manco Ccapac, captured their lands, he came from Tampu-tocco. They did not say that the first Inca came from Paccaritampu, which, it seems to me, would have been a most natural thing for them to have said if this were the general belief of the natives. In addition there is the still older testimony of some Indians born before the arrival of the first Spaniards, who were examined at a legal investigation in 1570. A chief, aged ninety-two, testified that Manco Ccapac came out of a cave called Tocco, and that he was lord of the town near that cave. Not one of the witnesses stated that Manco Ccapac came from Paccaritampu, although it is difficult to imagine why they should not have done so if, as the contemporary historians believed, this was really the original Tampu-tocco. The chroniclers were willing enough to accept the interesting cave near Paccaritampu as the place where Manco Ccapac was born, and from which he came to conquer Cuzco. Why were the sworn witnesses so reticent? It seems hardly possible that they should have forgotten where Tampu-tocco was supposed to have been. Was their reticence due to the fact that its actual whereabouts had been successfully kept secret? Manco Ccapac's home was that Tampu-tocco to which the followers of Pachacuti VI fled with his body after the overthrow of the old régime, a very secluded and holy place. Did they know it was in the same fastnesses of the Andes to which in the days of Pizarro the young Inca Manco had fled from Cuzco? Was this the cause of their reticence?

Certainly the requirements of Tampu-tocco are met at Machu Picchu. The splendid natural defenses of the Grand Canyon of the Urubamba made it an ideal refuge for the descendants of the Amautas during the centuries

VIEW FROM THE TOP OF MT. MACHU PICCHU TO RAPIDS OF URUBAMBA BELOW

of lawlessness and confusion which succeeded the barbarian invasions from the plains to the east and south. The scarcity of violent earthquakes and also its healthfulness, both marked characteristics of Tampu-tocco, are met at Machu Picchu. It is worth noting that the existence of Machu Picchu might easily have been concealed from the common people. At the time of the Spanish Conquest its location might have been known only to the Inca and his priests.

So, notwithstanding the belief of the historians, I feel it is reasonable to conclude that the first name of the ruins at Machu Picchu was Tampu-tocco. Here Pachacuti VI was buried; here was the capital of the little kingdom where during the centuries between the Amautas and the Incas there was kept alive the wisdom, skill, and best traditions of the ancient folk who had developed the civilization of Peru.

It is well to remember that the defenses of Cuzco were of little avail before the onslaught of the war-like invaders. The great organization of farmers and masons, so successful in its ability to perform mighty feats of engineering with primitive tools of wood, stone, and bronze, had crumbled away before the attacks of savage hordes who knew little of the arts of peace. The defeated leaders had to choose a region where they might live in safety from their fierce enemies. Furthermore, in the environs of Machu Picchu they found every variety of climate—valleys so low as to produce the precious *coca, yucca,* and *plantain,* the fruits and vegetables of the tropics; slopes high enough to be suitable for many varieties of maize, *quinoa,* and other cereals, as well as their favorite root crops, including both sweet and white potatoes, *oca, añu,* and *ullucu.* Here, within a few hours' journey, they could find days warm enough to dry and cure the *coca* leaves; nights cold enough to freeze potatoes in the approved aboriginal fashion.

Although the amount of arable land which could be made available with the most careful terracing was not large enough to support a very great population, Machu Picchu offered an impregnable citadel to the chiefs and priests and their handful of followers who were obliged to flee from the rich plains near Cuzco and the broad, pleasant valley of Yucay. Only dire necessity and terror could have forced a people which had reached such a stage in engineering, architecture, and agriculture, to leave hospitable valleys and tablelands for rugged canyons. Certainly there is no part of the Andes less fitted by nature to meet the requirements of an agricultural folk, unless their chief need was a safe refuge and retreat.

Here the wise remnant of the Amautas ultimately developed great ability. In the face of tremendous natural obstacles they utilized their ancient craft to wrest a living from the soil. Hemmed in between the savages of the Amazon jungles below and their enemies on the plateau above, they must have carried on border warfare for generations. Aided by the temperate climate in which they lived, and the ability to secure a wide variety of food within a few hours' climb up or down from their towns and cities, they became a hardy, vigorous tribe which in the course of time burst its boundaries, fought its way back to the rich Cuzco Valley, overthrew the descendants of the ancient invaders and established, with Cuzco as a capital, the Empire of the Incas.

After the first Inca, Manco Ccapac, had established himself in Cuzco, what more natural than that he should have built a fine temple in honor of his ancestors. Ancestor worship was common to the Incas, and nothing would have been more reasonable than the construction of the Temple of the Three Windows. As the Incas grew in power and extended their rule over the ancient empire of the Cuzco Amautas from whom they traced their descent, superstitious regard would have led them to establish their chief temples and palaces in the city of Cuzco itself. There was no longer any necessity to maintain the citadel of Tampu-tocco. It was probably deserted, while Cuzco grew and the Inca Empire flourished.

As the Incas increased in power they invented various myths to account for their origin. One of these traced their ancestry to the islands of Lake Titicaca. Finally the very location of Manco Ccapac's birthplace was forgotten by the common people—although undoubtedly known to the priests and those who preserved the most sacred secrets of the Incas.

Then came Pizarro and the bigoted *conquistadores*. The native chiefs faced the necessity of saving whatever was possible of the ancient religion. The Spaniards coveted gold and silver. The most precious possessions of the Incas, however, were not images and utensils, but the sacred Virgins of the Sun, who, like the Vestal Virgins of Rome, were from their earliest childhood trained to the service of the great Sun God. Looked at from the standpoint of an agricultural people who needed the sun to bring their food crops to fruition and keep them from hunger, it was of the utmost importance to placate him with sacrifices and secure the good effects of his smiling face. If he delayed his coming or kept himself hidden behind the clouds, the maize would mildew and the ears would not properly ripen. If he did not shine with his accustomed brightness after the harvest, the ears of corn could not be properly dried and kept over to the next year. In short, any unusual behavior on the part of the sun meant hunger and famine. Consequently their most beautiful daughters were consecrated to his service, as "Virgins" who lived in the temple and ministered to the wants of priests and rulers. Human sacrifice had long since been given up in Peru and its place taken by the consecration of these damsels. Some of the Virgins of the Sun in Cuzco were captured. Others escaped and accompanied Manco into the inaccessible canyons of Uilcapampa.

It will be remembered that Father Calancha relates the trials of the first two missionaries in this region, who at the peril of their lives urged the Inca to let them visit the "University of Idolatry," at "Vilcabamba Viejo," "the largest city" in the province. Machu Picchu admirably answers its requirements. Here it would have been very easy for the Inca Titu Cusi to have kept the monks in the vicinity of the Sacred City for three weeks without their catching a single glimpse of its unique temples and remarkable palaces. It would have been possible for Titu Cusi to bring Friar Marcos and Friar Diego to the village of Intihuatana near San Miguel, at the foot of the Machu Picchu cliffs. The sugar planters of the lower Urubamba Valley crossed the bridge of San Miguel annually for twenty years in blissful ignorance of what lay on top of the ridge above them. So the friars might easily have been lodged in huts at the foot of the mountain without their being aware of the extent and importance of the Inca "university." Apparently they returned to Puquiura with so little knowledge of the architectural character of "Vilcabamba Viejo" that no description of it could be given their friends, eventually to be reported by Calancha. Furthermore, the difficult journey across country from Puquiura might easily have taken "three days."

Finally, it appears from Dr. Eaton's studies that the last residents of Machu Picchu itself were mostly women. In the burial caves which we have found in the region roundabout Machu Picchu the proportion of skulls belonging to men is very large. There are many so-called "trepanned" skulls. Some of them seem to belong to soldiers injured in war by having their skulls crushed in, either with clubs or the favorite sling-stones of the Incas. In no case have we found more than twenty-five skulls without encountering some "trepanned" specimens among them. In striking contrast is the result of the excavations at Machu Picchu, where one hundred sixty-four skulls were found in the burial caves, yet not one had been "trepanned." Of the one hundred thirty-five skeletons whose sex could be accurately determined by Dr. Eaton, one hundred nine were females.

Furthermore, it was in the graves of the females that the finest artifacts were found, showing that they were persons of no little importance. Not a single representative of the robust male of the warrior type was found in the burial caves of Machu Picchu.

Another striking fact brought out by Dr. Eaton is that some of the female skeletons represent individuals from the seacoast. This fits in with Calancha's statement that Titu Cusi tempted the monks not only with beautiful women of the highlands, but also with those who came from the tribes of the Yungas, or "warm valleys." The "warm valleys" may be those of the rubber country, but Sir Clements Markham thought the oases of the coast were meant.

Furthermore, as Mr. Safford has pointed out, among the artifacts discovered at Machu Picchu was a "snuffing tube" intended for use with the narcotic snuff which was employed by the priests and necromancers to induce a hypnotic state. This powder was made from the seeds of the tree which the Incas called *huilca* or *uilca*, which, as has been pointed out in Chapter XI, grows near these ruins. This seems to me to furnish additional evidence of the identity of Machu Picchu with Calancha's "Vilcabamba."

It cannot be denied that the ruins of Machu Picchu satisfy the requirements of "the largest city, in which was the University of Idolatry." Until some one can find the ruins of another important place within three days' journey of Pucyura which was an important religious center and whose skeletal remains are chiefly those of women, I am inclined to believe that this was the "Vilcabamba Viejo" of Calancha, just as Espiritu Pampa was the "Vilcabamba Viejo" of Ocampo.

In the interesting account of the last Incas purporting to be by Titu Cusi, but actually written in excellent Spanish by Friar Marcos, he says that his father, Manco, fleeing from Cuzco went first "to Vilcabamba, the head of all that province."

In the "*Anales del Peru*" Montesinos says that Francisco Pizarro, thinking that the Inca Manco wished to make peace with him, tried to please the Inca by sending him a present of a very fine pony and a mulatto to take care of it. In place of rewarding the messenger, the Inca killed both man and beast. When Pizarro was informed of this, he took revenge on Manco by cruelly abusing the Inca's favorite wife, and putting her to death. She begged of her attendants that "when she should be dead they would put her remains in a basket and let it float down the Yucay [or Urubamba] River, that the current

LLACTAPATA, LOOKING TOWARD MACHU PICCHU
AND THE TORONTOY CANYON

might take it to her husband, the Inca." She must have believed that at that time Manco was near this river. Machu Picchu is on its banks. Espiritu Pampa is not.

We have already seen how Manco finally established himself at Uiticos, where he restored in some degree the fortunes of his house. Surrounded by fertile valleys, not too far removed from the great highway which the Spaniards were obliged to use in passing from Lima to Cuzco, he could readily attack them. At Machu Picchu he would not have been so conveniently located for robbing the Spanish caravans nor for supplying his followers with arable lands.

There is abundant archeological evidence that the citadel of Machu Picchu was at one time occupied by the Incas and partly built by them on the ruins of a far older city. Much of the pottery is unquestionably of the so-called Cuzco style, used by the last Incas. The more recent buildings resemble those structures on the island of Titicaca said to have been built by the later Incas. They also resemble the fortress of Uiticos, at Rosaspata, built by Manco about 1537. Furthermore, they are by far the largest and finest ruins in the mountains of the old province of Uilcapampa and represent the place which would naturally be spoken of by Titu Cusi as the "head of the province." Espiritu Pampa does not satisfy the demands of a place which was so important as to give its name to the entire province, to be referred to as "the largest city."

It seems quite possible that the inaccessible, forgotten citadel of Machu Picchu was the place chosen by Manco as the safest refuge for those Virgins of the Sun who had successfully escaped from Cuzco in the days of Pizarro. For them and their attendants Manco probably built many of the newer buildings and repaired some of the older ones. Here they lived out their days, secure in the knowledge that no Indians would ever breathe to the *conquistadores* the secret of their sacred refuge.

When the worship of the sun actually ceased on the heights of Machu Picchu no one can tell. That the secret of its existence was so well kept is one of the marvels of Andean history. Unless one accepts the theories of its identity with "Tampu-tocco" and "Vilcabamba Viejo," there is no clear reference to Machu Picchu until 1875, when Charles Wiener heard about it.

Some day we may be able to find a reference in one of the documents of the sixteenth or seventeenth centuries which will indicate that the energetic Viceroy Toledo, or a contemporary of his, knew of this marvelous citadel and visited it. Writers like Cieza de Leon and Polo de Ondegardo, who were assiduous in collecting information about all the holy places of the Incas, give the names of many places which as yet we have not been able to identify. Among them we may finally recognize the temples of Machu Picchu. On the other hand, it seems likely that if any of the Spanish soldiers, priests, or other chroniclers had seen this citadel, they would have described its chief edifices in unmistakable terms.

Until further light can be thrown on this fascinating problem it seems reasonable to conclude that at Machu Picchu we have the ruins of Tampu-tocco, the birthplace of the first Inca, Manco Ccapac, and also the ruins of a sacred city of the last Incas. Surely this granite citadel, which has made such a strong appeal to us on account of its striking beauty and the indescribable charm of its surroundings, appears to have had a most interesting history. Selected about 800 A.D. as the safest place of refuge for the last remnants of the old régime fleeing from southern invaders, it became the site of the capital of a new kingdom, and gave birth to the most remarkable family which South America has ever seen. Abandoned, about 1300, when Cuzco once more flashed into glory as the capital of Peruvian Empire, it seems to have been again sought out in time of trouble, when in 1534 another foreign invader arrived—this time from Europe—with a burning desire to extinguish all vestiges of the ancient religion. In its last state it became the home and refuge of the Virgins of the Sun, priestesses of the most humane cult of aboriginal America. Here, concealed in a canyon of remarkable grandeur, protected by art and nature, these consecrated women gradually passed away, leaving no known descendants, nor any records other than the masonry walls and artifacts to be described in another volume. Whoever they were, whatever name be finally assigned to this site by future historians, of this I feel sure—that few romances can ever surpass that of the granite citadel on top of the beetling precipices of Machu Picchu, the crown of Inca Land.

NATIONAL GEOGRAPHIC
ADVENTURE CLASSICS

✶

THE WORST JOURNEY IN THE WORLD
Apsley Cherry-Garrard

THE JOURNALS OF LEWIS AND CLARK
Meriwether Lewis and William Clark

THE CRUISE OF THE *Snark*
Jack London

THE TOMB OF TUTANKHAMUN
Howard Carter

20 HRS., 40 MIN.: OUR FLIGHT IN THE *Friendship*
Amelia Earhart

THE EXPLORATION OF THE COLORADO RIVER AND ITS CANYONS
John Wesley Powell

TRAVELS IN WEST AFRICA
Mary Kingsley

THE OREGON TRAIL
Francis Parkman

SCRAMBLES AMONGST THE ALPS
Edward Whymper

MY LIFE AS AN EXPLORER
Sven Anders Hedin

THE ADVENTURES OF CAPTAIN BONNEVILLE
Washington Irving